GOD'S BEST TO YOU ALWAYS!

JOURNEY
TO THE CENTER OF LIFE

Peter Lewis Whitebird

John 5:24

Copyright © 2011 Peter Lewis Whitebird

ISBN 978-1466284500

Journey To The Center Of Life
by Peter Lewis Whitebird

Printed in the United States of America

All rights reserved solely by the author. The author guarantees all contents are original and do not infringe upon the legal rights of any other person or work. No part of this book may be reproduced in any form without the permission of the author. The views in this book are not necessarily those of the publisher.

Except where otherwise indicated, scripture quotations are taken from the New King James Version.
Copyright © 1982 by Thomas Nelson, Inc.
Used by permission. All rights reserved.

Additional scripture references taken from the Amplified® Bible, Copyright © 1954, 1958, 1962, 1964, 1965, 1987 by The Lockman Foundation. Used by permission. All right reserved.
(www.Lockman.org)

Cover Design and interior graphics by Peter Lewis Whitebird

www.peterlewiswhitebird.com

Dedication

To my beloved Family, my wife, children and grandchildren, I love you.

ACKNOWLEDGMENTS

First, and foremost, I must thank God for the incredible journey He has designed for me. I may not have acquired great material wealth or possessions, but considering how my journey began, my life has been extremely blessed. I owe everything I know and everything I am to Him! I love You, Lord!

God has used many people to influence the direction and the quality of my life. I want to thank every member of my family who loved me unconditionally and had an impact on me for the Lord. Thanks to my mom, Joyce, who early on, instilled in me a belief that there is a God. I'll see you in heaven and hug you in person soon.

Thanks to all of my loved ones on mom's side of our family in Arkansas. Many of you had a faith in Jesus that, ultimately, played a role in my coming to faith in Him. My uncle, George Burks, was certainly a key figure in my coming to Christ. Thanks Uncle! I love you all. Thanks to my "step-family" who never treated me like a step-family member, especially, Grandpa and Grandma Kelly. I cherish your memory and your influence on my life.

Thanks to all of our sponsors who helped support this new ministry work with your prayer and finances. You have a part in every life that is changed by this book. Special thanks to my good friend, Michele Reese for adding your expertise to this project. You have always been an encouragement to me and my ministry. Thanks to my good friend, David Rusco, for your help with putting this manuscript into book form. You are a good and faithful buddy.

Last, but certainly not least, my wife, Judy, my children, Dana, Travis, Christa, Erin, and my wonderful grandchildren, I love you all more than I can adequately express. Second only to the Lord, you are my life. Thank you, Judy, for all that you do for Whitebird Ministries. Everyone (especially me) recognizes how hard you work. Our journey together has been quite the adventure.

CONTENTS

Introduction	Launching Out	9
Rest Area 1	Chasing the Wind	19
Rest Area 2	A Well Worn Path	33
Rest Area 3	Lord of the GPS	45
Rest Area 4	To Tell the Truth	65
Rest Area 5	Dead Man Walking	81
Rest Area 6	Radically Reconnected!	95
Rest Area 7	Too Good to be True	115
Rest Area 8	Nobody is Perfect	145
Rest Area 9	A Life to Die For	173
Rest Area 10	Together Again	191
Rest Area 11	God & Sons Inc.	205
Rest Area 12	Driving Under the Influence	225
Rest Area 13	Walking Tall	249
Conclusion	Vaja Con Dios! (Go with God)	279

LAUNCHING OUT

First Things First

It has been said that "Life is a journey and only you hold the map." Our natural birth is the beginning of our earthly journey. However, every human life journey began in the heart and mind of God long before He created time and space. And, because God is omniscient (knows all things—past, present, and future), He has always known what course each person's life would take, and ultimately, what their final destination would be. Though most of us are more interested in mapping out our own life journey, only God can guarantee us a route that leads to His abundant life.

Some people travel along life's highway without a clue as to what the journey is about or how it will culminate. Most prefer to travel an Interstate Highway (the broad way) because it is the fastest way to travel from one point to the next. My wife and I have traveled the roadways of America for more than a decade, and I have come to realize that, although the four-lane roads may get us to our destination faster, our Interstate Highways are, actually, much more congested and dangerous than our two-lane state highways. It may be much slower paced, but the way to the center of life is found on the byway (the narrow way) not the broad way.

> Enter by the narrow gate; for wide is the gate and broad is the way that leads to destruction, and there are many who go in by it. Because narrow is the gate and difficult is the way which leads to life, and there are few who find it. (Matthew 7:13, 14)

Some of life's travelers stay focused on the road ahead, while others become too focused on the rearview mirror. Certainly, it is important for us to look back to see where we have been, but there is a reason why the windshield on a vehicle is much larger than the rear view mirrors. Though we can all learn from the past, we can allow the past to rob us of what God has for us further down life's road. We all must learn how to look to the future while letting the pain of the past go.

Whether we are sleek, self-motivated, high-performance sports models traveling at high-speed in the fast lane, or muddled, mundane minivans slowly plodding along, God has planned a route for us that is guaranteed to deliver us to His ultimate destination, LIFE...if we are willing to let Him hold the map, that is. This book is not the journey, but simply part of God's roadmap to life.

The first thing my wife and I do when we are about to embark on a long road tour is pray for God's guidance, provision and protection. So, the best advice I could offer you as you begin your journey through the pages of this book is to simply pray:

> "God, I humbly ask you to speak to me through your Holy Spirit as I read this book. I acknowledge the fact that mere human intellect is not capable of comprehending your truth. Help me to grasp what you want me to know in a way that will allow you to change me from the inside-out. I want to experience the life that you have designed and reserved for me. I pray this in Jesus' name, Amen."

Now that you have asked God for His guidance, He has many wonderful things to show you! Not everyone is willing to acknowledge God as the giver of all good things. Nevertheless, He is always the initiator of the things that bless our lives. His desire, of course, is that we would not only respond to Him with gratitude but be willing to make Him Lord of our lives.

Flying Faith

When we board an airliner, we are making a faith commitment. We are placing our complete trust and safety in the hands of the pilot, the crew, and the engineers of that aircraft. We trust that the control tower that monitors the progress of our journey is in constant contact with the pilot and co-pilot, and that their instructions and coordinates are correctly communicated to those who are at the controls of the plane. We may not understand how all of that technology works, yet we trust that it will all work together to deliver us safely to our destination. No doubt, if you are like me, you send a simple, silent little prayer to God's control tower before liftoff.

As it is with flying, not trusting God with our life really is not an option. If we want to soar with Him, we must trust Him completely and allow Him to have the controls of our life. He wants us to believe in (trust and rely upon) Him and place ourselves in His care the same way that we do the pilot and crew of the airplane.

Geeks & Greeks

> Every good gift and every perfect gift is from above, and comes down from the Father of lights, with whom there is no variation or shadow of turning. (James 1:17)

God equips each of us and places many gifts in our hands for our earthly journey. Whether we realize it or not, or acknowledge it or not, every good gift comes down to us from Him. Whether they ever acknowledge God for their blessings or not, every talented and gifted person who lives on this planet received what they have from God. Some of these gifts are given to us genetically while others are placed in our hands along the way.

Initially, we may not understand how what He gives to us works, or how to use it. However, as we rely upon God's instructions (His Word) and His guidance (His Holy Spirit), through trial and error, those gifts have unlimited potential in our lives. Maybe sharing the following example will better illustrate what I'm talking about.

When I was first exposed to computers in Vocational-Technical School in my early forties, Hard Drives, Software, Ram and Megabytes were terms that were utterly foreign to me. I had no idea when I enrolled in a Commercial Art course that the course would include computer graphics.

At first, the whole computing experience was very intimidating and confusing to me...plus, the drab, off-white little computing monster had a keypad! By the time I owned my first desktop computer, I had forgotten much of what I had learned in my very limited education, including how to type. Everything about computers was Greek to me. Nevertheless, I recognized the potential of this wonderful new tool God had placed in my hands. Although it was difficult, I was eager to learn. I may not have become a "Computer Geek," but now, I do know how to navigate around one.

Likewise, when I first came to the Lord in 1973, the Bible seemed as foreign and confusing to me as my first computer did in 1992. Thank God...it didn't have a keypad! However, it might as well have been written entirely in its original languages (Hebrew, Aramaic, and Greek), because I didn't know the first thing about it. If that wasn't bad enough, my first Bible was the King James Version, printed in 1611 English! Are you kidding me?! At the time, I barely had a grasp on 1973 English!

Nevertheless, by God's grace, I recognized the supernatural, life-changing potential the Bible held for my life. After giving my life to Jesus, I had this strange, new desire to know and understand Biblical truth. This new desire to learn was stronger than my laziness and my inability to read, comprehend, and retain information. Thankfully, after years of trial and error, though I'm not a "Bible Geek"...um, excuse me, "Bible Scholar," I do know how to navigate around the Scriptures.

I have discovered that God does not place things into our hands merely for our personal gain or pleasure, but for us to use according to His purposes for our lives and the lives of others. When we are willing to thankfully acknowledge the true source of our gifts, and to use them to bless others, amazingly, they are multiplied many times over, whether it is our money, knowledge, talents or the use of our time.

> For we are His workmanship, created in Christ Jesus unto good works, which God hath before ordained that we should walk in them. (Ephesians 2:10)

Whether we realize it or not, God knew before we were born, not only who we would be, but what we could become if we are willing to allow Him to teach us and change us! Then, as we learn to "pay it forward," we are the ones who receive the greater blessing...sooner or later...in one way or another.

This book is my humble attempt to "pay forward" all of the wonderful blessings that God has placed in my hands; first of all, to my beloved children and grandchildren and then, to my siblings and extended family. And, finally, to anyone else who will listen. I may not be able to leave a rich inheritance to my loved ones, but at least I can leave to them a rich legacy for Jesus Christ. I hope this book will change their lives as they learn what truly changed mine.

A Peek in the Rear View

It hasn't been an easy road for me, but the gain has certainly been worth the pain. I've learned from the past that, no matter how life has treated us, anything is possible in our lives if we are willing to accept Jesus and listen to God. Considering the way that my journey began, it was highly unlikely that I would have ever become a public communicator of any kind.

The words of our 16th president, Abraham Lincoln, were branded in my mind as a small boy in elementary school: "It is better to remain silent and be thought a fool than to speak out and remove all doubt." As a result of my bad experiences—sharing my thoughts and ideas in class and having them laughed at or rejected—I quickly learned to do my best not to reveal my ignorance by speaking out or offering my opinions on anything.

As a young boy, I was so self-conscious and insecure that I could never have stood in front of people to speak about anything, much less sing, teach, and preach as I do today! Yet, ever so graciously and patiently, God reshaped me from the inside-out. In His perfect timing, He gave me just enough confidence and courage to respond to Him with "Yes, Lord," even when the challenge He was giving me seemed well beyond my ability. It has been a slow process, but the Lord has been faithful to me, even though I have faltered and failed numerous times along the way to who I am today. Indeed, I still struggle and He is still faithful. (2 Timothy 2:13) Thankfully, God never changes.

I recall how unqualified and unworthy I felt the first time God's Spirit gently urged me to use my inherited, yet untrained, undeveloped music talents in our church choir. That eventually led to reluctantly, and with great timidity, singing my first solo in church...then, to my feeble attempts at songwriting. Years down the road, as I continued to allow God to stretch me beyond my comfort zone, I was asked to teach a Sunday school class, and occasionally, to fill in for my pastor as a lay preacher. That would ultimately lead to the singing, teaching and preaching ministry God has blessed me with today.

And now, finally...you are holding this book in your hands! This comes from someone who had never even read a book cover to cover until after I came to know the Lord. This comes from someone who had never completed a book report in English class! Whodathunkit? Fugitaboutit! English was always one of my worst subjects in school...along with Math, Geography, Science and Social Studies...uh, you get the point. God's grace truly is amazing!

I must admit, compared to the multitude of teachers, preachers, pastors and Christian authors who have impacted my life over the course of my Christian journey, I feel extremely unqualified as a communicator of the Gospel, and especially, as an author. Yet, I have learned that God's calling, and His empowering Spirit, are the ultimate qualifiers for what He wants to accomplish through us. I feel eternally indebted and grateful to everyone God has used in my life to equip and encourage me. No doubt, my lack of formal education may have slowed me down a bit, but God is able to educate and equip anyone who will simply follow Him with an open heart and mind.

Inspired to Courage!

After a service in a church where I had shared my ministry, the pastor asked if I could define the word, "encourage." Isn't it funny how we use words every day, knowing generally what they mean, yet when asked to, we're unable to actually define them? I told him I wasn't quite sure how to verbalize it but, generally speaking, I understood what it meant. He explained, "It means to *inspire to courage.*" He told me that he appreciated the honesty and transparency in my presentation of the Gospel, and that he felt encouraged by my music and testimony.

As I was driving to my next engagement, I realized that he was actually trying to inspire *me* to courage. He had recognized my tendency to feel inadequate in my communication skills, even though I've presented the Gospel through my ministry and music thousands of times. His subtle wisdom did inspire courage in me. I suppose I've always been a little too transparent for my own good, yet I hope my honest self-exposure serves to encourage those who might think too little of themselves. I pray that sharing my faith and life in this book will inspire you to the courage that will enable you, through your God-given abilities, to accomplish more than you ever dreamed was possible.

Why a Book?

When the Lord first began to speak to my heart about writing this book, I asked, "Why me? I wouldn't know what to write a book about." He gently responded, "Why not you?! Just write about what I have showed you since you have come to know me." Well…now you hold the result of yet another "Yes, Lord" in my life.

While I was in the process of writing this book, many who know me asked if it was going to be about my travels on the road. Though I could certainly write a rather lengthy book about all of my wonderful adventures on the road over the past decade, the subject matter of this project is infinitely more important. This book does contain some things about my personal struggles and victories, but it is not about me or my life; it is about the benefits of receiving Jesus into our lives as Savior and Lord.

Quite honestly, the impression this new venture leaves about me in the minds of people isn't all that important. However, the impression it leaves in their hearts and minds about Jesus is eternally important! It wouldn't matter how intellectual or educated anyone considered me to be if the result of what I shared did not translate into the ability to live life as God intended for us to live it.

None of the biblical truths I've shared in this book are new. In fact, they are ancient. I have not attempted to re-invent anything that I have learned through others over the years. I just want to share the things I've learned in a simple, down-to-earth manner that will allow each reader to come away from this book thinking: "Hey! Christianity is not as dry, religious, and complicated as I thought it was! It's real! I may not be important to anyone else, but now I know how really important I am to God. Anything is possible in my life! I never realized just how much He loves me."

I have no way of knowing where your journey began or how rough the road has been for you. Nevertheless, I hope that, through my life experiences, you will get to know Jesus as you get to know me. Along the way, we will make a rest stop with each chapter to examine God's amazing love and grace. My hope is that as you travel with me through this book, regardless of your religious background, or lack thereof, you will open your heart and mind to Jesus. Just rely upon Him and allow Him to shape your thinking. In doing so, you may find yourself on a few new roads that challenge your old religious or denominational traditions. Some of the routes we traverse may make you uncomfortable because they sound unfamiliar.

However, I ask you to stay the course with me. I promise that every word I share will point you to Jesus Christ. I have no religious or denominational agenda. What you will find in these pages is an honest, down-to-earth, expression of what Christianity means to me. I have not tried to hide my personality. What you see is what you get.

I also encourage you to have your Bible handy as you read through these pages. Highlight the passages of scripture that speak to you personally and make notes in the margins of your Bible. Don't take my word for what is true; take God's Word for it.

If you will hang with me, you will discover that God's liberating truth just gets better and better the further we travel on our journey to the center of His incredibly amazing life! Let's launch out with the lyrics to the title song of one of my albums:

"Journey to the Center of Life."

There's a road that we all travel in this life;
Driven hard to get it better than gettin' by;
Navigatin' through life's twists and turns,
Headlong, hopin' things don't crash and burn,
Driven onward 'til we finally learn where true life is

hey, it gets better than this.

We're on a journey...We're on a journey, to the center of life.
Created solely, wholly for the only one who satisfies
He's the center of life.

To all the restless souls controlled by complacency,
There's a course God sets us on to set us free,
Ever faithful to direct our path;
Like a compass from the place we're at,
'Til we arrive where true life is at, to where his heart is,
Can't get no better than this.

It's really not that far from a broken' mind to a brand new heart,
as the road unwinds

We're on a journey...We're on a journey, to the center of life.
Created solely, wholly for the only One who satisfies;
He's the center of life.

There's a longing in us, only Christ can fill,
He offers life to whosoever will...choose life.

Chasing the Wind

The Passionate Pursuit

Luke 12:15

"Take heed and beware of covetousness, for one's life does not consist in the abundance of the things he possesses."

The only thing extraordinary about Homer's life was the Jesus that he loved and lived his life for. His life was simple...honor the Lord each day by working hard and providing the best you can for your beloved family.

Having never finished high school forced him into a grueling line of work that had left his hands heavily calloused. It was mostly brawn and not much brain as he labored in his dirty, sweaty job. Every morning he would emerge from his modest cracker box house with his lunch pail in hand and head out to his driveway, jump into his rusty, dented pickup truck and disappear into another hard day. It was not an easy life, but Homer felt blessed.

One thing was certain; he could always count on a little excitement and frustration to begin his day from a ruffled, ragtag mutt—let's see, why don't we call him, Chase—who lived two doors down from his humble home. Chase was a pooch of undistinguished pedigree whose purpose in life, it seemed, was to chase Homer's pickup. His life was simple too...contribute as much stress and anxiety as possible to Homer's drive to work! He had honed himself into a skillful bumper-biter who practiced his perilous pursuits with absolute precision and passion. Time after time, at high velocity, Chase darted deftly around the tires of Homer's truck, always able to somehow avoid becoming a poochie pancake.

Each morning he crept into position and waited for his target to emerge from his house. The front door would slam, and the stealthy mutt would slink to his mark. Homer's truck would come whizzing by and, bang, the race was on! With lips and ears flapping wildly and dog slobber spraying in the wind, Chase came roaring into the street in hot pursuit of Homer's pickup. Both Homer and Chase took their jobs seriously and their daily routines had become painfully intertwined...at least for the perturbed pickup driver.

Finally, Homer thought to himself, "There must be some way to get this mischievous mutt off of my bumper and out of my life!" So, one day he decided it was time for a little payback. The door slammed shut as he exited his house with Chase taking his position, as usual. He fired the ignition, revved the engine loudly and then turned it off, got out of the truck and went back into the house. The look on Chase's face was priceless!

Have you ever noticed one of the major differences between dogs and cats? Cats are poker-faced! You can never quite know for sure what a feline is thinking, so you can never truly trust a cat...can you? But dogs? Almost human-like, they wear their feelings on their faces. I love that about dogs! Homer had to laugh out loud at the perplexed pooch's face! With his head tilted slightly to the side, like the dog in the old RCA ad, Chase was like, "What just happened?!"

One day, Homer decided that Chase finally gets to make the "catch." That's right, He was going to allow Chase to catch what he had been chasing, um...so doggedly, for so long. Homer got into his truck and Chase got into position. He backed out of the drive and flew down the street with Chase in hot pursuit. Suddenly, Homer planted both feet firmly on his brakes, screeching to an abrupt halt! When the thick, white cloud of tire smoke cleared, Chase had narrowly avoided making himself a hot-link hotdog by running up Homer's tail pipe. Homer was in stitches!

You see, Chase had never actually caught anything he had pursued...well, except for a squirrel, a newspaper...and a not-so-poker-faced cat or two. Having caught the object of his passionate pursuit, but not knowing what in the world to do with it, Chase's existence became meaningless. He began to roam the city streets aimlessly, expressionless, at times sitting on the curb, resting his head on his front paws, pondering the vanity of his "dog-eat-dog" existence...okay, I might be carrying this story a little too far. So, what's the point? Like the mutt in this story, most of us live for the chase, and after catching what we've pursued so passionately, we realize that there has to be more to life than chasing and catching!

Enough is never Enough!

During a 2005 CBS "60 Minutes" [1] television interview, Tom Brady, three-time world champion NFL quarterback, uttered these words, "A lot of times I think I get very frustrated and introverted, and there's times where I'm not the person that I want to be. Why do I have three Super Bowl rings, and still think there's something greater out there for me? I mean, maybe a lot of people would say, 'Hey man, this is what it is. I reached my goal, my dream, my life.' Me, I think: God, it's gotta be more than this. I mean this can't be what it's all cracked up to be. I mean I've done it. I'm 27. And what else is there for me?" Brady went on to say that there were a lot of other parts about himself he was trying to find. Apparently, his "GQ" [2] good looks, success, fame and wealth revealed a gaping hole in his soul. When the interviewer asked Brady what the answer was to his lack of contentment, he responded: "I wish I knew...I wish I knew." Most of us hear this and wonder..."How could he have what he has and not be satisfied?" Someone once said, "There is a God shaped void in the heart of every man that only He can fill." This story is just one of many that proves it.

In America, we are blessed to have the liberty to *pursue happiness*, but in the Bible we're instructed instead to *learn contentment*. What's the difference? First, *happiness* depends on what *happens*. The word "happy" comes from the same root word as the words: happen, happenstance, and perhaps. All of these words are linked to luck or chance. For instance, if you ask someone if they are happy, their answer will usually depend on what is happening in their life. If things are happening the way they want them to, then they are happy. If not, they are unhappy.

Contentment, on the other hand, does not depend on what is happening in our lives. The word "content" comes from the same root word that means to contain or complete. We do not necessarily have to be happy in order to be content. Contentment is rooted in good character and is learned through the trials of life. It begins with Godly thankfulness for what we have been given. The Apostle, Paul, shares his thoughts on this in his letter to the Philippians:

> "...Not that I am implying that I was in any personal want, for I have learned how to be content (satisfied to the point where I am not disturbed or disquieted) in whatever state I am. I know how to be abased and live humbly in straitened circumstances, and I know also how to enjoy plenty and live in abundance. I have learned in any and all circumstances the secret of facing every situation, whether well-fed or going hungry, having a sufficiency and enough to spare or going without and being in want. I have strength for

all things in Christ Who empowers me [I am ready for anything and equal to anything through Him Who infuses inner strength into me; I am self-sufficient in Christ's sufficiency]". (Philippians 4:11-13)
(Amplified Bible)

Over the course of my time on earth, I have learned that it is unrealistic to expect everything to happen in my life the way I want it to all the time. Life is filled with little, and not-so-little, disappointments but when our expectations are realistic, we find that we are disappointed much less frequently. Besides, if God is sovereign (supremely in control of everything in His creation), nothing in my life happens by chance, coincidence or luck.

Contentment cannot be found in anything the world has to offer us. If it could, then surely those who have caught the most would be the most content. But, have you noticed that those who have the most are some of the most discontented people on earth?

Just before the turn of the 20th century, American oil magnate, John D. Rockefeller,[3] was one of the wealthiest men in the world. When an interviewer asked him, "How much money is enough?" He replied simply, "Just a little bit more." When it comes to fallen human nature, enough is never enough! Evidently, "having it all" isn't what life is about. Jesus talks about this type of vain, errant pursuit:

> And He said to them, "Take heed and beware of covetousness, for one's life does not consist in the abundance of the things he possesses." (Luke 12:15)

> "For what profit is it to a man if he gains the whole world, and loses his own soul? Or what will a man give in exchange for his soul?" (Matthew 16:26)

Obviously, Jesus taught that one's soul-life holds much more value than possessions or anything else the world has to offer us. Let's take a closer look at some key words and phrases in these verses. *Covetousness* means to have an unbalanced desire for material wealth and possessions.

> "For the love of money is a root of all kinds of evil, for which some have strayed from the faith in their greediness, and pierced themselves through with many sorrows." (1 Timothy 6:10)

Notice, it is not money that is the root of all kinds of evil, it is *the love of money* (greed). There is no doubt that the love of money drives the material world we live in. With wealth come prestige, power, and control. The love and lust for money and the things it brings produces all sorts of selfish, sinful desires in the hearts of men. Consequently, the world is full of sin, sorrow, corruption and conflict.

Unfortunately, the spirit of greed has crept into, and corrupted, nearly every human institution on earth. But, the sad fact is that money comes and goes, doesn't it?

> "Will you set your eyes on that which is not? For riches certainly make themselves wings; They fly away like an eagle toward heaven." (Proverbs 23:5)

Jesus is right; life doesn't consist in the abundance of riches. Likewise, life doesn't consist in *possessions*. Although I believe God wants to bless us, there is nothing in the Bible that guarantees us a right to the "American Dream." God is far more concerned about the content of our character than He is about the content of our bank account or investment portfolio. In fact, though He offers to become our indwelling comforter, God is far more concerned about our character than He is our comfort. This is why He allows us to experience difficulty and discomfort in life. God wants to shape our character into that of His Son, Jesus.

I am thankful that I was born in America because, in this country, we have the liberty to think, dream and achieve anything for which we are willing to work hard and sacrifice. But, even those who achieve the "American Dream" discover that it is not where true life is found.

Truth is...true life is experienced in the *soul*. Our soul is the intellectual, emotional and volitional part of who we are. Our soul is the seat of our personality. This is the part of us that is going to live forever after our body dies. The condition of this inner-life is what determines the quality of our outer-life experience.

> "...that He would grant you, according to the riches of His glory, to be strengthened with might through His Spirit in the inner man..." (Ephesians 3:16)

> "Therefore we do not lose heart. Even though our outward man is perishing, yet the inward man is being renewed day by day." (2 Corinthians 4:16)

According to these verses, there is an outer part and an inner part of our being. When it comes to living life, it is important that we understand the order in which we are to live. God created us to live from the inside-out, not from the outside-in. Consequently, trying to fulfill our lives with material things is like trying to stuff a burlap bag with wild cats; it is an endless, frustrating endeavor that leaves its mark on us. We'll take a closer look at what our inner life involves in a subsequent chapter.

Certainly, the world measures and judges success by the things we achieve and acquire outwardly, but God judges success by what we become inwardly. Wealth and prominence do not guarantee good character. We could gain all the wealth in the world and never find contentment. In the Books of 1 Kings, 2 Chronicles, and Ecclesiastes, we find a man named, Solomon, the epitome of human success.

He was a man blessed with wealth and wisdom beyond measure. By God's grace, he attained astounding greatness. Like his father, David, this young prince would eventually become the King of Israel. His royalty and riches allowed him to indulge in whatever pleasure his heart desired.

> "And God gave Solomon wisdom and exceedingly great understanding, and largeness of heart like the sand on the seashore. Thus Solomon's wisdom excelled the wisdom of all the men of the East and all the wisdom of Egypt. For he was wiser than all men..." (1 Kings 4:29-31)

When Solomon became the King of Israel, instead of asking God for power and wealth, he humbly asked Him for an "understanding heart." The Lord was pleased with his humility and told Solomon in a dream:

> "Because you have asked this thing, and have not asked long life for yourself, nor have asked riches for yourself, nor have asked the life of your enemies, but have asked for yourself understanding to discern justice, behold, I have done according to your words; see, I have given you a wise and understanding heart, so that there has not been anyone like you before you, nor shall any like you arise after you. And I have also given you what you have not asked: both riches and honor, so that there shall not be anyone like you among the kings all your days. So if you walk in My ways, to keep My statutes and My commandments,

as your father David walked, then I will lengthen your days." (1 Kings 3:11-14)

The richest and most powerful individuals in the history of mankind pale in comparison to the greatness Solomon enjoyed. Yet, the only man who truly "had it all" summed up all that he had chased and caught with these sad words, "Vanity of vanities, all is vanity." (Ecclesiastes 1:2) He continues to describe his frustration with his catch...

> I have seen all the works that are done under the sun; and indeed, all is vanity and grasping for the wind. I made my works great; I built myself houses, and planted myself vineyards. I made myself gardens and orchards, and I planted all kinds of fruit trees in them. I made myself water pools from which to water the growing trees of the grove. I acquired male and female servants, and had servants born in my house. Yes, I had greater possessions of herds and flocks than all who were in Jerusalem before me. I also gathered for myself silver and gold and the special treasures of kings and of the provinces. I acquired male and female singers, the delights of the sons of men, and musical instruments of all kinds. So I became great and excelled more than all who were before me in Jerusalem. Also my wisdom remained with me. Whatever my eyes desired I did not keep from them. I did not withhold my heart from any pleasure, For my heart rejoiced in all my labor; And this was my reward from all my labor. Then I looked on all the works that my hands had done and on the labor in which I had toiled; and indeed all

was vanity and grasping for the wind. There was no profit under the sun. (Ecclesiastes 1:14; 2:4-11)

According to Solomon, reaching the pinnacle of success in our passionate pursuit of happiness leaves us feeling hopelessly empty. Apparently, owning multiple dwellings, vineyards and orchards is utterly meaningless. Having a multitude of servants to do everything that needs doing and who cater to our every whim is not enough. Owning vast herds of livestock is worthless. Being wealthy beyond measure leaves us emotionally destitute. Having anything we want and enjoying any pleasure we desire only leaves us wanting more. Are you depressed yet? Someone once said, "Yeah, but I'd rather be rich and miserable than poor and miserable." I suppose that might be true, but in either case, if you're still miserable what does it matter? Following are the lyrics to a song the Lord gave me, inspired by the book of Ecclesiastes.

"Chasin' The Wind"

I'm worn out from tryin' to find contentment and peace of mind
It's hard chasin' the wind.
I'm tired of not sleepin' anymore; awake all night walkin' the floor
with an empty heart from chasin' the wind.
It's so hard to learn that all we earn
Will all be burned when this life is done
With death we find, we leave it all behind. Like a vapor,
What we've labored for is gone.

I'm not chasin' the wind anymore, not livin' a lie like before.
I'm not chasin' the wind since God breathed
a new wind in my heart.
I'm not chasin' the wind anymore, not livin' life hard like before.
I'm not chasin' the wind since God breathed

a new wind in my heart.

I've given up tryin' to be what others expect me to be,
It's vanity, and chasin' the wind.
I'm goin' against the flow, 'cause I've finally come to know,
In Jesus I'm free from chasin' the wind.
I've finally learned in him we earn
What will never burn when this life is done.
I've finally found that solid ground, in Christ,
to build my life upon.

I'm not chasin' the wind anymore, not livin' a lie like before.
I'm not chasin' the wind since God breathed
a new wind in my heart.
I'm not chasin' the wind anymore, not livin' life hard like before.
I'm not chasin' the wind since God breathed
a new wind in my heart.

Is there anything as empty as a handful of air? There has not been a person in the history of mankind who could begin to hold a candle to the greatness of King Solomon. Yet, it all amounted to nothing in the end. He finally summed up the hard realities of life with this statement:

> All has been heard; the end of the matter is: Fear God [*revere and worship Him, knowing that He is*] and keep His commandments, for this is the whole of man [*the full, original purpose of his creation, the object of God's providence, the root of character, the foundation of all happiness, the adjustment to all inharmonious circumstances and conditions under the sun*] and the whole [*duty*] for every man. (Ecclesiastes 12:13) (Amplified Bible)

If to live our lives here is all about money, then to die is to lose everything. If to live here is about possessions, then to die is to leave everything behind. I have never seen a heavenly U-Haul trailer hitched to a hearse! If to live here is about ascending to the top, then death is a dreadful demotion. But according to the apostle Paul, if our life is about knowing and becoming like Jesus, then not only is our life better while we are on earth, it gets gloriously better after we die! "For to me to live is Christ, and <u>to die is gain</u>" (Philippians 1:21) We spend our time on earth living from the outside-in, when in reality, true life is lived from the inside-out.

> "Lord, make me to know my end and [to appreciate] the measure of my days – what it is; let me know and realize how frail I am [how transient is my stay here]. Behold, You have made my days as [short as] handbreadths, and my lifetime is as nothing in Your sight. Truly every man at his best is merely a breath! Selah [pause, and think calmly of that]! Surely every man walks to and fro – like a shadow in a pantomime; surely for futility and emptiness he is in turmoil; each one heaps up riches, not knowing who will gather them. And now, Lord, what do I wait for and expect? My hope and expectation are in You. (Psalms 39:4-7) (Amplified Bible)

By now you are probably asking yourself what I asked myself after discovering this truth, "What is life really about then? What in the world makes life worth living?" God's Word holds the answer.

Central to our basic human needs are: The need to feel loved, secure and safe; the need to feel accepted, approved and appreciated; the need to feel complete and content. It would be great if the people in our lives from birth could provide these things for us, but the fact is, not all of us are that fortunate. Even our parents and families can, and do, fail us and disappoint us. When those relationships that are closest to us fail us, no one can ever fill the void but God. This is exactly what He wants to do in our lives. He gives us a new identity, a new purpose, and a new direction in life. When we have those things in our life settled, life finally has real meaning…regardless of wealth or worldly success.

You see, life is more than living for Friday night, for our next paycheck, or for the next party we use to disassociate ourselves from reality. Life is more than climbing the corporate ladder to success. It is more than ascending to the pinnacle of power and prestige. When knowing and becoming more like Jesus becomes the goal of our life, we begin to discover and experience His true life within us.

No one knows and understands the complex needs of the human heart better than the One who created it. God is the final "just a little bit more" for which everyone is searching. Only He can complete and fill the insatiable void that gnaws away at our heart! Jesus wants to complete your life. He's the only catch worth chasing. He's waiting for each of us to turn down the road that leads to Him.

A Well Worn Path

We all struggle. Grow up and get over it!

Psalms 103:14

For He knows our frame; He remembers that we are dust.

At first glance, the statement, "Grow up and get over it!" might sound harsh and insensitive. The painful path to maturity is tough enough without having someone tell us to simply "Get over it!" Yet, sometimes that swift kick in the pants is exactly what we need to help us get over the hump of a broken life.

It is natural for us to become focused on our problems to the point that we begin to feel sorry for ourselves. Haven't we all been guilty of that? However, if we are not careful, our struggles and bad experiences can evolve into resentment, bitterness, disillusionment, and depression. Our inability to overcome the pain that life can deal us can cripple us emotionally and render what should be our dearest relationships dysfunctional. God doesn't want that for any of us. He wants to heal us, grow us, and bless us! God knows all of our complex human frailties. He knows that we are "made of dust." It may not seem like it at times, but He understands our struggles and difficulties in life, and our welfare matters to Him. (Hebrews 4:15) He is able to help us get over the most painful episodes in our lives, and through the pain make us stronger if, instead of harboring our hurts, we are willing to surrender them to Him.

Though we may not be aware of it, God sees in each of us the undeveloped strengths and undiscovered talents and abilities that He created in us. His desire is to bring those things to the surface so we can be the best we can possibly be. His best for our lives is beyond what we could ever imagine or achieve on our own. Once God begins a work in our lives, though we may feel like quitting on Him, He never quits on us.

> And I am convinced and sure of this very thing, that He Who began a good work in you will continue until the day of Jesus Christ [*right up to the time of His return*], developing [*that good work*] and perfecting and bringing it to full completion in you.
> (Philippians 1:6) (Amplified Bible)

God created us for Himself and desires a personal relationship with each of us. If we are willing to walk in that relationship with Him, listening with an open, honest heart, willingly teachable, and willing to obey Him, He is able to shape us into His design for us. I am so glad this is not about religion!

> For I know the thoughts that I think toward you, says the LORD, thoughts of peace and not of evil, to give you a future and a hope. Then you will call upon Me and go and pray to Me, and I will listen to you. And you will seek Me and find Me, when you search for Me with all your heart. (Jeremiah 29:11-13)

Tragically, far too many people are unwilling to even acknowledge Him, much less yield the control of their lives to Him. We would rather be the lord of our lives and live it our own way. As a result, many of us never discover what our lives could have been.

> Trust in the LORD with all your heart, and lean not on your own understanding; In all your ways acknowledge Him, And He shall direct your paths. (Proverbs 3:5, 6)

Tragedy & Triumph

In the Book of Genesis, we find one of the greatest stories in the entire Bible: The story of Joseph. I'm going to give you just the highlights, but I urge you to read the whole story in Genesis, Chapters 37-50. There are also a few well-made movies that tell the story, as well. I have always been inspired by this touching story of betrayal, forgiveness, reconciliation and God's unfailing faithfulness.

Jacob had twelve sons by four different women. His first wife was Leah, whom Jacob never truly loved but had unwittingly married through a trick played on him by her father, Laban. She bore six of Jacob's sons: Reuben, Simeon, Levi, Judah, Issachar and Zebulun. She also bore his only daughter, Dinah. Leah's Handmaiden, Zilpah, bore him two sons, Gad and Asher. Next, Rachel's handmaiden, Bilhah, bore Jacob two sons named Dan and Naphtali. Whew! What a complicated family! Dr. Phil, where are you ?

Finally, Joseph, the 11th-born son, immediately became "daddy's favorite" when he was born to him by Rachel, the true love of Jacob's life. Later she would die giving birth to Benjamin, a baby brother Joseph would not meet until years later. When Jacob made Joseph a coat of many colors to demonstrate his love for him, his older half-siblings, who were already envious of their favored little half-brother, resented and hated him even more.

Nevertheless, the Lord's hand was upon Joseph's life because he loved God and believed in His promises. Eventually, God would use Joseph to save and bless his family in their time of greatest need. Through two dreams, He gave the uncommonly wise, yet still immature 17-year-old a vision of the incredibly powerful man that he would become one day. However, Joseph was only shown the end of the story, not the long, difficult journey that would mold him into the man he had seen in his dreams.

When Joseph told his brothers how someday they, and even his father, would bow down to him, they became enraged. In their anger, his brothers threw him into a pit, then sold him into Egyptian slavery. Then, they returned to their father with Joseph's blood-stained coat and a story they concocted about how "Some wild beast" had devoured him. Jacob believed the lie about what had happened to his favorite son and was extremely grief stricken.

Years would pass, and by the time Joseph was thirty, he had risen out of slavery to prominence when he was sold to Potiphar, an officer of Pharaoh, who was captain of the guard. Later, although he was completely innocent, Joseph would be accused of attempting to rape Potiphar's wife and thrown into prison. Nevertheless, because of his wisdom and good character, God would once again promote him. Joseph became Pharaoh's Governor over all of Egypt!

When famine fell on all of Canaan, his brothers were sent by their father, Jacob, to Egypt to buy food. The vision Joseph saw in his dreams was fulfilled when they finally bowed in fear before their brother, who was second in authority only to Pharaoh. They did not recognize him, but he certainly knew who they were. After discovering that his father, Jacob, was still alive and that he had a little brother, Benjamin, Joseph sent them back to Canaan with food for his father and their families. However, he devised a plan to teach them all a lesson for what they had done to him. He accused them of being spies and told them that he was going to hold their brother, Simeon, until they returned with Benjamin.

Jacob was angered and distressed when his sons returned and told him that they had left Simeon in Egypt and that the Governor had demanded that they return to him with Benjamin. Their father told them he had already lost one son, and that it would kill him to lose his youngest. Nevertheless, Jacob relented and they returned to Egypt with their baby brother.

Amazingly, despite what they had done to him, Joseph still loved his brothers. After seeing his younger brother, Benjamin, for the first time, Joseph could stand it no longer. He revealed to them who he was.

> And Joseph said to his brothers, Come near to me, I pray you. And they did so. And he said, I am Joseph your brother, whom you sold into Egypt! But now, do not be distressed and disheartened or vexed and angry with yourselves because you sold me here, for <u>God sent me ahead of you to preserve life</u>. For these two years the famine has been in the land, and there are still five years more in which there will be neither plowing nor harvest. God sent me before you to preserve for you a posterity and to continue a remnant on the earth, to save your lives by a great escape and save for you many survivors. So now <u>it was not you who sent me here, but God</u>; and He has made me a father to Pharaoh and lord of all his house and ruler over all the land of Egypt. (Genesis 45:4-8)

Joseph's brothers were astonished! He instructed them to go back to Jacob and tell him to bring all of his family and all that they owned to Egypt so they could survive the famine. On top of that, because Joseph held such favor with Pharaoh, he was instructed to give them everything they needed, along with allowing them to live in the best part of Egypt!

When Jacob and his sons returned to Egypt from Canaan with their families and all their possessions, Joseph and his father were finally reunited. They embraced and wept for a long time. A huge banquet was prepared and they enjoyed one another's company. Jacob lived in Egypt 17 years then died. His descendants multiplied and prospered with Joseph in Egypt.

In the end, when his brothers asked for Joseph's forgiveness, Joseph had already forgiven them in his heart. After Jacob died, Joseph's brothers said, "Perhaps Joseph will hate us, and may actually repay us for all the evil which we did to him." (Genesis 50:15) So they sent messengers to Joseph, saying,

> "Before your father died he commanded, saying, 'Thus you shall say to Joseph: "I beg you, please forgive the trespass of your brothers and their sin; for they did evil to you." Now, please, forgive the trespass of the servants of the God of your father." And Joseph wept when they spoke to him. Then his brothers also went and fell down before his face, and they said, "Behold, we are your servants." Joseph said to them, "Do not be afraid, for am I in the place of God? But as for you, <u>you meant evil against me; but God meant it for good</u>, in order to bring it about as it is this day, to save many people alive."
> (Genesis 50:15-20)

God has an incredible way of taking the hurts and hardships in our lives and turning them around for our good. In the New Testament, the Apostle, Paul, said as much in his letter to the believers in Rome:

> And we know that all things work together for good to those who love God, to those who are the called according to His purpose. (Romans 8:28)

Ultimately, God intends for us to use what happens to us in life to bless others who experience the same difficulties in their lives. A wise brother in the Lord once told me: "Peter, when you go through tough times in your life, through those circumstances, God is placing 'ministry tools' into your 'ministry tool box'. Someday you will be able to utilize those tools to help repair someone else who may be broken down along life's pathway."

Some people are unwilling to do what they are asked to do, while others merely do what they are asked to do. But, God blesses those who are willing to do more than they are asked to do. Joseph was blessed because he was this type of individual. He had every right to be bitter and feel sorry for himself because of the horrible things he had experienced. Nevertheless, he loved God, and though he may not have always understood his circumstances, he focused on God's plan for him and trusted that God would be faithful to bring to fruition everything that he saw in his dreams. Have those who are closest to you forsaken you? Like Joseph, can you believe that God has a plan for your life, in spite of your hardships? Can you forgive and love unconditionally? Your willingness to do so will make a huge difference in the quality of your life experience.

Potholes & Pitfalls

In the following testimony, you'll probably discover some all too familiar, painful landmarks. It's not always easy to re-visit the difficult territory we have traversed in the past. However, I do not believe God allows us to go through trials and trouble unless it is going to work for our good in the long run. We can be confident that He always has a purpose for whatever He allows us to experience. He will always use adversity to build our character and make us stronger. Someone once said, "What doesn't kill us only makes us stronger." I would say that this is true, *only* if we learn correctly from it and allow God to use it to strengthen our character.

Each of us is traveling a path unique to us and yet quite common. Unique in the sense that no one else can travel our course (live our life) for us and common in that we all experience many of the same difficulties in life. Though we all hope for a bright and fulfilling future, we can look back on the times in our lives that have either inspired *or* impaired us.

Some life journeys begin well but finish badly. Others begin badly and finish the same way. A good start is certainly an advantage, but regardless of how our life journey begins, God has a plan for us to finish extremely well if we will continue to trust Him.

My journey in life has not been without its bumps, potholes and detours. I've had my share of disappointments, and there have certainly been breakdowns along the way that required major repair by the "Master Mechanic," Jesus.

My first real pothole in life was when my dad and mom divorced. My younger sister and I were very young when dad took the off ramp and exited our family. Sadly, we never knew him, or heard much from him, while we were growing up. That left a void in our lives that our step-dad could never quite fill. I never developed much of a "Father-Son" relationship with my step-dad either.

Nevertheless, he, and especially my step-grandparents, instilled within me many of the things that shaped the basic values I hold to today. My step-dad worked hard and provided a modest life for our family. Yet, I'm sure he struggled with what many step-dads go through—learning to accept another man's son as his own. I remember my mom constantly reminding him, especially when I was small, that he needed to love me and involve me more. I know she only wanted what every divorced mom wants from a second husband...the love and acceptance of her kids.

In retrospect, I'm sure her efforts only made it more difficult for him to do the very thing she wanted him to do...love me. I certainly loved and needed him. He was the only dad I had ever known, and I wanted him to love me too. I'm not sure he ever truly did. At least I don't recall ever hearing him say so.

He and mom were married for about 11 years, had three children together, and then divorced. My biological sister and I loved our two little sisters and brother, and though our last names were different, as far as we were concerned, we were not half-siblings. We still feel that way today.

The circumstances surrounding our parents' split were very difficult for all of us to accept. My mom, now a twice divorced mother of five, went through a great deal of emotional pain and anxiety as she tried her very best to provide for her kids with welfare assistance. I remember her long bouts with depression and various physical illnesses. It was a tough time for all of us. We had nothing but each other, and to be quite honest, the future did not seem to hold much promise for any of us.

It became painfully clear after my mom's second divorce that whatever relationship I had with my step-dad was over. That stark reality left a boy just entering his teens confused and insecure. Consequently, after entering high school, I began to "fall in with the wrong crowd." This only compounded my lack of self-esteem.

It was the mid-sixties and America was still reeling from the assassination of President John Kennedy. The Vietnam War was boiling, and our country was in social turmoil. War protests and race riots dominated television news. The "Hippie" love and peace movement was in full-swing with its rock and roll music, psychedelic drugs, and free love (sex). I was a scrawny, pimple-faced kid searching for acceptance. Insecurity, inferiority, and inadequacy had shaped my personality, and the subsequent lack of self-confidence had conditioned me to expect failure in anything I attempted. Therefore, I didn't put much effort into anything.

I was not academically gifted, so I wasn't accepted by my classmates who were good students. I wasn't athletic, so I was not involved with sports. Far from being socially affluent or influential, we were a broken family trying to survive on welfare. There wasn't anything about me that would make me popular in school...so I was not and had very few friends. No doubt, I would have been nominated for, and won, the "Most Likely Not to Succeed Award," had such a thing existed. There certainly wasn't much about school that appealed to me, so I dropped out four months into my junior year. Not knowing Jesus yet, I had no clue where my life was going.

Like so many of the kids in every generation who grow up in dysfunctional families (they didn't call it that back then), I was more than willing to do whatever would allow me to fit in somewhere. Fitting in with the Hippies didn't require good looks, athleticism or intellectualism, so I followed the path of least resistance: Hendrix, Dylan and Led Zeppelin, drugs and Pot...Far out! Heavy, man! I suppose it was fortunate that I wasn't quite old enough to become a full-fledged Hippie, or no telling where that path would have led me to...San Francisco...Haight-Ashbury... groovy! Boy, talk about teen-aged delusion!

By the time I was 21, I was married with a daughter, learning a trade in construction work and had pretty much given up on the deception of "Flower Power." However, I was beginning to develop a dependency on alcohol and had narrowly missed on a suicide attempt shortly before Jesus entered into my life and set me on a new course...new to me, not to Him. That new start didn't necessarily make my road any smoother, but at least since then, I have been touring with a wonderfully compassionate guide who has become my best friend.

Like Joseph, God gave me a vision early in my Christianity about what my life would be someday. Though I didn't understand it at the time, I knew in my heart that He wanted me to serve Him full-time. I loved my new relationship with Jesus, and I was eager to follow God's call on my life. However, shortly after that vision, my first marriage ended. Suddenly, I found myself "disqualified" from the ministry that I knew God had called me to. I had no idea that it would take more than twenty years for God to develop me into someone that He could use effectively in His ministry. Everyone else may have given up on me, but God never did.

Unfortunately, broken families, abuse, neglect, and failure in life is a far too well-worn path for far too many of us. We all struggle with a multitude of personal issues in life, past and present. However, as I stated earlier, God understands our human weaknesses and doesn't just tell us to "grow up and get over it." Although our life path may be worn with disappointment, heartache, and failure, God loves us and is determined to help us get rid of our excess baggage by allowing us to check it at the cross of Christ.

Like the faithful Spiritual Parent that He is, He lovingly and patiently grows us up in the grace of His Son, Jesus, and helps us to get over the pain of our past. Hopefully, sharing my struggles and "wrong turns" with you will help you to see that, no matter how badly our life journey begins, God has a marvelous plan for each of us to finish well! Whatever your struggles are, ask God to help you overcome them so you can get over what may be detouring you from the planned route He has for you. Jesus is where your wonderful, new adventure begins.

Lord of the GPS

Not all roads lead to Rome.

John 14:6

"I am the way, the truth, and the life. No one comes to the Father except through Me."

I have discovered an amazing little gizmo called a GPS (Global Positioning System). It's pretty cool! You simply punch in the address of where you want to go, and turn by turn, it directs you to your destination, visually...and even audibly! That little black box mounted on my windshield is actually a small computer with a wireless receiver built into it. It receives a signal from a satellite orbiting just outside of our atmosphere, computes the coordinates and directs my route through a little map on a five-inch color screen. Amazing! What a great travel tool! I love it! I have discovered, however, that this nifty little invention isn't always completely accurate.

At times, I've had to ignore "Gabby" (the name I've given to my female GPS voice) because she once was instructing me to go down a gravel road that was actually the long way to my destination! There have been times when she instructed me to turn right when I needed to turn left. One time, she even sent me to the wrong town! On numerous occasions, I've had to resort to an old-fashion road map because I couldn't trust my confused little female navigator...uh, Gabby...not my wife. I suppose the fact is nothing conceived or designed by man can be expected to perform perfectly. That's not the case with (God's Positioning System).

Like an all-knowing satellite beyond time and space, God sends out a spiritual signal to our receiver (spirit), then our spirit relays it to our little computer (brain), and we are able to move along on the path that will position us where God wants us to be. It's comforting to know that He has known the spiritual coordinates of our entire journey to the center of His life since before we were born. You can absolutely rest assured that God is going to be 100 percent accurate, and that when we are following His directions, we are going to arrive at the right destination, right on time—every time! If only Gabby's directions were so precise and trustworthy!

Every Which Way but Free

For more than a decade, I have been traveling across America with my singing and teaching ministry. I have been willing to go into any church, large or small, regardless of denomination, to share the ministry that God has called me to and equipped me for. To say the least, it has been quite an eye-opening experience. I've sung and preached to crowds of thousands, and I've stood before crowds of...3 or 4 individuals (including the pastor and his wife). It's been quite an adventure that has certainly broadened my perspective on the Christian church in America.

I knew from the beginning that my understanding of biblical truth was not always going to line up with the doctrinal views of all the other denominations I would encounter. Funny thing is, even those who claim the same denominational names often differ among themselves in their doctrinal views. Nevertheless, I have kept an open mind and tried to simply focus on Jesus in my singing and teaching. There have been times when I've been confronted or challenged on my beliefs, but so far, I have been able to avoid being stoned and able to leave town with all of my body parts intact. That may sound humorous, but I have discovered that some folks are extremely adamant when it comes to their particular denominational persuasion.

After sharing my ministry in a Baptist church in California, an elderly couple from the church treated my wife and me to lunch at a local restaurant. They were very kind, and we enjoyed our time of fellowship together. However, during our conversation, it became quite apparent that they were extremely "dyed in the wool" Baptists. I had made the comment that if I were to start a church, it would simply be a "Jesus Church," and the sign in front of the building probably would not include the name, Baptist. The elderly wife replied sternly, "Well, if you don't put Baptist on the sign, then how will the Baptists know how to find you?" I kindly informed her that God had not called me into the ministry to win Baptists but to win the lost to Him. She was not impressed...

In another instance, I was preaching and singing in a revival meeting at a Baptist church in New Mexico. During one of my messages, I made the comment that if Jesus moved into town and started His own church across the street from this one that I would probably move my membership from this Baptist church to His church. After the service, a very well-dressed, distinguished-looking elderly lady approached me and stated, "Young man, (young to her) I am a born and bred Baptist. I have been a member of this Baptist Church all of my life. I intend to be a Baptist for the rest of my life, and I would not join another church, even if Jesus Himself started it and He was the new Pastor!" I could not believe my ears! It kind of made me wonder if she was a born again Baptist!

These stories certainly illustrate just how deep denominational bias can run. Please, believe me; I'm not picking on the Baptists. These are simply two examples of many similar statements members of various denominations have made to me over the years. I love the Baptists! Jesus certainly does…even though He is not a Baptist…or a Methodist…well, you get the point. A Nazarene pastor in California reminded me once that Jesus *was* a Nazarene!

I was introduced to Jesus and received Him into my life in a Free Will Baptist church in 1973. However, I soon learned that you don't have to be in a church (of any denomination) to become a born again Christian. God is willing to meet us right where we are. I never did join the Free Will Baptist denomination. Although eventually, I would be ordained by the Southern Baptists, my ministry today is what I like to refer to as "Cross-denominational," (heavy emphasis on the CROSS, as in the Cross of Christ). I've always stated that God does not "dye us in the wool," denominationally; He dyes us in "the blood" indelibly! That really is, and always has been, my heart.

Those of us who believe in, and follow, Jesus have certainly complicated it for folks who simply want to find the life that God offers. There are thousands of religious denominations in existence that claim to be Christian, and if that isn't mind-boggling enough, there are numerous variations of some denominations that cannot come together because of their differing doctrinal stances. I can tell you with absolute confidence that God isn't the least bit interested in what denomination or religion we adhere to, that is, unless our denomination or religion is errant in its teaching. He simply wants us to come to Him through His Son so He can bless us and set us free from religion. Here's where the rub comes…we all think we have it right! I don't know, but I suspect that when all the religious and theological dust settles, we will discover that none of us were completely accurate on every issue of God's truth.

Many races and religions exist today, but as far as God is concerned, there are only two classes of people on earth: those who are "in Christ," His Son, and those who are not. I like to call them "Saints" and "Ain'ts." No offense intended. Saint is the new name given to those who have invited and received Jesus into their hearts and have been made new creations in Him. Ain'ts are those who ain't done it yet (sic)! In addition to all of the Christian denominations, there are thousands of religions that don't claim to be Christian, yet claim to be the way to God.

True North

It has been said that "all roads lead to Rome" and in fact, they once did. The road system of the Ancient Romans was one of the greatest engineering marvels of its time. More than 50,000 miles of paved road radiated from the center of the city of Rome so there really were many routes to Rome. Though God's ultimate destination for us is Him, not all religious and denominational roads lead to Him. There are many things where a certain amount of inaccuracy is tolerable, but GPS units and the way to God are not among them!

One of the things I like about my GPS is the compass feature. When I feel confused about which direction I am traveling, I can check my compass. A compass is calibrated to magnetic north on our globe, also referred to as "true north." Consequently, if I am traveling north, I know that east is to my right and west is to my left. If I am heading east, then I know that north is to my left and south is to my right and so on. Road maps are designed with the compass printed on the pages. North is up and South is down.

Just as a compass is based on "true north," so the truth in God's Word has to be our true north. If our sense of direction in life is not based on His true north, then spiritually there is no telling what direction is correct. If our sense of morality doesn't have a true north, then how can we know what is right or wrong. Those who reject absolute truth in regard to morality certainly have a problem when someone wants to violate their so-called moral rights.

If there are no absolutes when it comes to right and wrong, then who is to say that it is wrong for me to take what belongs to you without your consent (your hard-earned money, possessions, spouse, children, etc.)? The world in which we live is in constant turmoil because neither human intellect, nor human conscience is, or ever can be, the final authority on what is right or wrong.

Our prisons are full of heartless criminals who have violated their human conscience to the point that they, seemingly, no longer possess one. These are not the types of individuals we want to encounter on our journey unless it is a divine appointment from God. There has to be a higher true north to guide us…than us! The Bible must be accepted as the true north for truth if we are ever going to truly know God and His will for our lives. No one alive today has any information about Him that they did not get from the Bible.

As I was gathering up my music equipment one Monday morning where I had shared my ministry the night before, the pastor and I were sharing our views on life and ministry. He graciously thanked me for my ministry, but knowing that we didn't exactly agree theologically, commented, "I believe that all religions ultimately lead to the same God."

I was stunned! I know he meant well and was trying to be "tolerant," but he was dead wrong! For one thing, *no* religion is capable of leading anyone to God, not even Christian religion. Christianity doesn't save anyone, Christ does. True Christianity is the outworking of His saving life in us! We can never be tolerant when it comes to the true north of God. We must hold fast to the truths that are presented in the Scriptures. Truth isn't subject to the transitory whims or baseless conjecture of men.

I always ask someone who shares a personal life view, or particular biblical view, with me to share what they base their view on. Is it based accurately on the Scriptures? Or, is it simply based on their personal opinion or experience. Again, it must be based on the true north for truth, the Bible.

You see, Christianity is not just a *religious practice*; it is a *resurrected person*, Jesus Christ, indwelling those He has saved through His death and resurrection. He said this about Himself:

"I am the way, the truth, and the life. NO ONE COMES TO THE FATHER EXCEPT THROUGH ME." (John 14:6)

Let me paraphrase this verse: "Jesus is the only route to God, the true north of truth, and the essence of eternal life. No one comes to God except through Him. There is not an alternative route to God—Jesus is the only way." There is no alternative accurate truth about God. Jesus revealed Him perfectly. (John 1:14, 18) There is no eternal life apart from Him; Jesus is the resurrection and the life. (John 11:25) I realize that this may sound extremely narrow and intolerant, even insensitive, to some, but it is the truth. The way to God is as narrow as one man, Jesus Christ! He wasn't apologetic about it, so why should I be?

Political Corruptness

No doubt about it, the notion that Jesus Christ is the only way to God is certainly politically and religiously incorrect these days, but God isn't any more interested in political or religious correctness than He is in Christian denominationalism. He really doesn't care if our feelings get hurt or if we feel insulted by the truth. Have you noticed that—in a country that was founded on the basic principles found in the Bible—it is "politically *correct*" to believe in, practice and publicly espouse, almost any religion or faith *except* Christianity?

We have the religious freedom to wear traditional religious clothing, walk around with a red dot in the middle of our forehead, or carry the Koran and any other religious book or symbol into public schools, public workplaces, the courthouse and the military. Yet, it is considered extremely insensitive and "politically *incorrect*" for Christians to wear clothing with Christian messages, designs or symbols, or to carry a Bible into public places because it might offend someone who doesn't believe in Jesus. Pardon me...let me say it again, this country was founded on the basic moral principles taught in the Bible! The message of the Bible is Christ-centered! It is called Christianity, and the truths found in the Bible are what made this the greatest country that has ever existed in the history of mankind!

Ask yourself these questions: What kind of world would our world be without the beacon of the Gospel that America has always been? What other country offers the level of freedom and opportunity that America offers? Who else in the world is more committed to fighting tyranny and terrorism than America? Who else defends human dignity and unalienable, God-given human rights more than America does? We are not perfect, but apart from Jesus, we are the world's greatest hope.

Regrettably, in our country today, it is almost politically incorrect to proudly wave our American flag because someone who is living here from another country, legally or illegally, might be offended. Ironically, the very ones who demand tolerance seem to be the most intolerant when it comes to Christianity and American patriotism. I am willing to concede that America is a racially and religiously pluralistic nation, but it is becoming quite apparent to me that the spirit of anti-Christ that exists around the globe is becoming more and more prevalent in our nation today. We are suffering from an acute case of "Political Corruptness!"

> Who is a liar but he who denies that Jesus is the Christ? He is antichrist who denies the Father and the Son. (1 John 2:22)

I know that when people who don't acknowledge the Bible hear this, they are offended. However, like a sword, the truth always divides. Unless you want to seriously injure yourself, you cannot sit on the edge of a sword. You have to stand on one side or the other. Jesus taught this principle to His disciples:

> "Therefore whoever confesses Me before men, him I will also confess before My Father who is in heaven. But whoever denies Me before men, him I will also deny before My Father who is in heaven. Do not think that I came to bring peace on earth. I did not come to bring peace but a sword. For I have come to 'SET A MAN AGAINST HIS FATHER, A DAUGHTER AGAINST HER MOTHER, AND A DAUGHTER-IN-LAW AGAINST HER MOTHER-IN-LAW'; and 'A MAN'S ENEMIES WILL BE THOSE OF HIS OWN HOUSEHOLD.' He who loves father or mother more than Me is not worthy of Me. And he who loves son or daughter more than Me is not worthy of Me. And he who does not take his cross and follow after Me is not worthy of Me. He who finds his life will lose it, and he who loses his life for My sake will find it. "He who receives you receives Me, and he who receives Me receives Him who sent Me..." (Matthew 10:32-40)

Interestingly, though Jesus is referred to as the "Prince of Peace," (Isaiah 9:6) His truth is a sword that divides. He made it very clear that we can't be neutral when it comes to what we believe about Him:

> He who is not with Me is against Me, and he who does not gather with Me scatters. (Luke 11:23)

Those who deny Jesus, He will deny before His Father who is in heaven. Those who receive Him also receive the God who sent

Him. In other words, you have to believe in Jesus in order to come to God, the Father. We cannot reject Jesus and know God. Paul spoke these words to Timothy:

> "For there is one God and one Mediator between God and men, the Man Christ Jesus" (1 Timothy 2:5)

Faith or Fiction?

Here is the bottom line: either we believe everything Jesus said or we can believe nothing that He said. We cannot pick and choose. Either His words are true or they are false. If they are false, then take your pick, Christianity is no better than any other religion in the world.

Someone might say, "Well, that's what you believe; that's just your opinion." An opinion is a personal belief or judgment that is not necessarily founded on proof or certainty. The only thing that makes an opinion valid is the truth that it is based on. In my case, my views are not just my opinion; they are based on what Jesus said in His own words..."NO ONE COMES TO THE FATHER EXCEPT THROUGH ME." Could these words be any clearer?

An Amazing Book!

One might counter, "Well, you believe what the Bible teaches, but how do you know it is the only truth about God?" Without going into an extended apologetic explanation of the authenticity of the Bible (which I am academically unqualified to do), let me say this: at some point in every person's life, we make a choice concerning what we are going to believe. Our beliefs form our philosophy on life and our world view. These dictate how we live out our lives.

Personally, I have chosen to believe in Jesus and the truths taught in the Bible. I know that, ultimately, God inspired even that choice, so I could never take credit for it. I can't explain it, but I know that I owe even my choice to believe in Jesus to God's grace.

Consider these facts about the book we call the Bible. What we refer to as *a book* is, in reality, a collection of 66 books, which is called the Canon of scriptures. It is a compilation of the writings of 40 different authors who lived, in some cases, centuries apart from one another, and in most cases, did not know each other and had never met. They came from a variety of backgrounds: shepherds, fishermen, doctors, kings, prophets, and a tax-collector. Their writings included a variety of genres: history, poetry, prophecy (foretelling future events), wisdom, literature, letters, and apocalyptic (prophetic, end-time destruction and judgment) just to name a few.

These writings were written in three different languages: Hebrew, Aramaic and Greek, by 40 authors from different historical, national and cultural backgrounds over a span of approximately 1,500 years on three different continents: Asia, Africa and Europe. The majority of them never had the opportunity to collaborate with one another in their writings. Nevertheless, amazingly, they all share the same timeline; the same storyline and theme—the creation and the fall of man into sin; God's love for fallen mankind and His redemptive plan in Christ; and a common promise: Whosoever will believe in Jesus and call upon His name shall be saved. The Bible shares all of these amazing commonalities and yet, there are no historical errors or contradictions! Peter wrote:

> ...knowing this first, that no prophecy of Scripture is of any private interpretation, for prophecy never came by the will of man, but holy men of God spoke as they were moved by the Holy Spirit.
> (2 Peter 1:20, 21)

I challenge anyone to go to any library and find 66 books written by 40 different authors from all different walks of life and diverse cultures, who spoke three different languages, from three different continents, who lived over a span of 1,500 years, who never knew or collaborated with each other, yet their writings all had the same storyline, theme and message without any historical errors or contradictions. There is only one collection of writings that can make that claim. We call it "The Bible." It is, without a doubt, the most purchased…yet, sadly, the most unread and misinterpreted book in human history.

How many of us own one or more copies of this amazing, one-of-a-kind book only to have it collecting dust in our home. Can you imagine what kind of world our world would be without the Bible? I hate to think about it. It is bad enough with the Bible!

Of course, God is the ultimate author of the Bible. He inspired and used human writers to record His truth, and it has been miraculously preserved through the centuries. Ask yourself this: "Why do I believe what I currently believe? How did I come to the conclusions that shaped my belief system? How accurate, valid and reliable is the information that has shaped what I believe?"

Faith always involves a choice—an act of the will. When we are presented with what someone tells us is true, we are faced with the choice to accept it, reject it or to do nothing with it. Everybody chooses to believe in something, but Biblical faith is a gift from God. Not everyone can simply believe, or understand, what the Bible says. In fact, to those who have not accepted Jesus by faith, everything in the Bible is foolishness. The Bible refers to those who have not accepted Jesus as "natural men." (1 Corinthians 2:14) Only His Spirit gives us the ability to comprehend and respond to His truth. Dead men can't see. One thing is for sure, if we don't discover it now, when our physical life is over, we will all find out what (and who) the eternal truth and life is. There will be no arguments and no excuses when that time comes.

After healing a man who had been lame from birth in Jerusalem, the apostle, Peter, "filled with the Holy Spirit" declared to the unbelieving Jewish leaders and priests in Jerusalem who had rejected and crucified Jesus:

"Rulers of the people and elders of Israel: If we this day are judged for a good deed done to a helpless man, by what means he has been made well, let it be known to you all, and to all the people of Israel, that by the name of Jesus Christ of Nazareth, whom you crucified, whom God raised from the dead, by Him this man stands here before you whole. This is the 'STONE WHICH WAS REJECTED BY YOU BUILDERS, WHICH HAS BECOME THE CHIEF CORNERSTONE.' Nor is there salvation in any other, for there is no other name under heaven given among men by which we must be saved."
(Acts 4:8-12)

Nothing much has changed in the world we live in today. Much of mankind still rejects Jesus as the only way to God and salvation.

Religion & Regeneration

The vast majority of religions in the world teach that, in one way or another, by some sacrifice or religious deed we offer, we can make ourselves acceptable to God. Yet, according to the scripture above, salvation comes only through Jesus. *Religion* is defined as man's attempt to satisfy God through something that we can do—making a way on our own for us to come to Him.

Christianity, on the other hand, is the Creator, Jesus, who satisfied forever God's righteousness on our behalf and comes to indwell and empower us forever because He paid for our sins and opened the way for us Himself. *Regeneration* is the re-introduction of God's life into our spirit through the new birth. Unlike religion, our only hope for salvation, and the opportunity to know God personally, rests in what Jesus has done, not in what we can do.

> For by grace you have been <u>saved through faith</u>, and <u>that not of yourselves; it is the gift of God, not of works</u>, lest anyone should boast.
> (Ephesians 2:8, 9)

Once again, the verse above points out that even faith to believe in Jesus is not of us; it is a gift from God. The apostle Paul declared this truth to the Greeks in Athens:

> Then Paul stood in the midst of the Areopagus and said, "Men of Athens, I perceive that in all things you are very religious (superstitious); for as I was passing through and considering the objects of your worship, I even found an altar with this inscription: TO THE UNKNOWN GOD. Therefore, the One whom you worship without knowing, Him I proclaim to you: God, who made the world and everything in it, since He is Lord of heaven and earth, does not dwell in temples made with hands. Nor is He worshiped with men's hands, as though He needed anything, since He gives to all life, breath, and all things. And He has made from one blood every nation of men to dwell on all the face of the earth, and has determined their pre-appointed times and the boundaries of their dwellings, so that they should seek the Lord, in the hope that they might grope for Him and find Him, though He is not far from each one of us; for in Him we live and move and have our being, as also some of your own poets have said, 'For we are also His offspring.' Therefore, since we are the offspring of God, we ought not to think that the Divine Nature is like gold or silver or stone, something shaped by art and man's devising. Truly, these times of ignorance God overlooked, but now commands all men

everywhere to repent, because He has appointed a day on which He (GOD) will judge the world in righteousness by the Man (JESUS) whom He has ordained. He has given assurance of this to all by raising Him from the dead." And when they heard of the resurrection of the dead, some mocked, while others said, "We will hear you again on this matter." (Acts 17:15-32)

God will, by Jesus whom He has raised from the dead, judge the world in righteousness someday. His bodily resurrection is the proof of that reality. In the end, the world will not be judged by Mohammed, Buddha or any other "god" or religious figure the world has ever concocted.

Sincere, but severely wrong.

Like the pastor I referred to earlier, someone might ask, "As long as you are sincere in your beliefs, does it really matter what religion a person believes in? Are they not all basically pointing us to the same God?" The truth is, not even all of those who espouse the teachings of Jesus are necessarily accurate in their beliefs.

In November, 1978, 909 sincere members of the People's Temple, 276 of them children, committed suicide and/or were murdered in "Jonestown" Guyana. Their charismatic leader, Jim Jones, who as a child studied Joseph Stalin, Karl Marx, Mahatma Gandhi and Adolf Hitler, led them to a mass suicide by poisoning: Kool-Aid® loaded with Cyanide, Phenergan, Valium and Chloral Hydrate. Tragically, their sincere beliefs led to their deaths.

Then, there are those who look to the heavens for their salvation. In March, 1997, 39 Heaven's Gate religious cult members, wanting to ascend to a "higher level of life," committed mass suicide by ingesting a lethal pudding concoction, believing their souls would board a space craft that was supposedly trailing the Hale-

Bopp comet. Their lifeless bodies were discovered in an upscale gated community residence. They were all intelligent, highly-educated and sincerely, fatally wrong.

The Muslim extremists who killed more than 3,000 people in New York, Washington D.C., and Pennsylvania in 2001 certainly were sincere in their beliefs. They actually believed that their disastrous, misguided deeds would earn them a revered place in heaven. The moment those airliners impacted their targets; I'm sure those sincere Muslim pilots discovered that they were sincerely wrong in their beliefs. No doubt, they know the truth today! As you can see, our beliefs cannot be based on feelings, sincerity or baseless opinions; they must be based on truth.

There are more religious ways to God in the minds of men than I can address in this book, but they couldn't possibly all lead to the same God. Among them are the: Muslim way, Hindu way, Buddhist way, Jehovah's Witness way, Mormon way, Native American way, even the "Good Ol' Boy" way! Some suggest that we can tune in to the "nature god" through the new age movement. The truth is that all of these religions are steering people in the wrong direction. They all lead to what God calls a "dead end."

> There is a way that seems right to a man and appears straight before him, but at the end of it is the way of death. (Proverbs 16:25) (Amplified Bible)
>
> Every way of a man is right in his own eyes, but the Lord weighs and tries the hearts. [Proverbs 24:12; Luke 16:15] (Proverbs 21:2) (Amplified Bible)

I find it ironic that what divides even those of us who believe in Jesus is our interpretation of biblical truth, especially after He promised this:

> However, when He, the Spirit of truth, has come,
> He will guide you into all truth; for He will not
> speak on His own authority, but whatever He hears
> He will speak; and He will tell you things to come.
> (John 16:13)

Some would counter: "Hey, I believe there is a God." Believing that there is a God is not enough to gain His acceptance. If it was, then even Satan and his demons would be in heaven. Thank God, they won't be! There is only one way to come to God; you must believe in Jesus. Biblical faith does not mean mere mental assent, it means to trust in, rely upon and to follow Him.

> You believe that there is one God. You do well.
> Even the demons believe—and tremble!
> (James 2:19)

Let me ask you a simple, but profound, question: If there is any other way to come to God than through the sacrifice of Jesus Christ and His cross, then what in the world was the cross about? If there is any other way to come to God than by Jesus Christ, then God judged, tortured, and killed His only begotten Son needlessly and unjustly. If there is any other way to God, then Jesus was a liar and a fraud. The whole framework of Biblical truth collapses! Nothing in the Bible is trustworthy if there is any other way to God! That is why the Devil hates the Word of God. He has been on a campaign to wipe it out since the beginning of time and his quest continues in the world today.

All religions could not possibly lead to the same God because many of them deny Jesus Christ and His deity. Many of them totally contradict each other. If this is true, how could they all point in the same direction? The fact is...only Jesus, through His death, burial and resurrection can truly deliver us from the penalty and power of our sin and bring us into a personal relationship with a holy God!

Man's Last Stand

I suppose it is true, regardless of the religious road that each human being travels; their route will someday put them before God's "Great White Throne" judgment. However, not all who stand before Him will enter into His kingdom.

> And I saw the dead, small and great, standing before God, and books were opened. And another book was opened, which is the Book of Life. And the dead were judged according to their works, by the things which were written in the books. The sea gave up the dead who were in it, and Death and Hades delivered up the dead who were in them. And they were judged, each one according to his works. Then Death and Hades were cast into the lake of fire. This is the second death. And anyone not found written in the Book of Life was cast into the lake of fire. (Revelation 20:12-15)

Every person from every generation in human history will be there! Standing side by side will be: Buddha, Muhammad, Joseph Smith, Jim Jones, our high school teachers and college professors, all of our family members, Oprah, Donald Trump and every other individual who ever lived on planet Earth. It will be quite a sight to behold! Regardless of their stature or status on earth, they will all be standing before God on level ground. All men will be judged on what they believed about Jesus. (Hebrews 9:27)

The Bible promises that someday every knee will bow and every tongue will confess that Jesus Christ is Lord. Paul quoted what God the Father said about Himself in the Book of Isaiah:

> For it is written: "AS I LIVE, SAYS THE LORD, EVERY KNEE SHALL BOW TO ME, AND EVERY TONGUE SHALL CONFESS TO GOD." (Romans 14:11)

> Look to Me and be saved, all the ends of the earth! For I am God, and there is no other. I have sworn by Myself, the word is gone out of My mouth in righteousness and shall not return, that unto Me every knee shall bow, every tongue shall swear [allegiance]. (Isaiah 45:22, 23) (Amplified Bible)

Then Paul attributes this same authority to Jesus:

> Therefore God also has highly exalted Him and given Him the name which is above every name, that at the name of Jesus every knee should bow, of those in heaven, and of those on earth, and of those under the earth, and that every tongue should confess that Jesus Christ is Lord, to the glory of God the Father. (Philippians 2:9-11)

> He is the image of the invisible God, the firstborn over all creation. For by Him all things were created that are in heaven and that are on earth, visible and invisible, whether thrones or dominions or principalities or powers. All things were created through Him and for Him. And He is before all things, and in Him all things consist. And He is the head of the body, the church, who is the beginning, the firstborn from the

dead, that in all things He may have the preeminence. (Colossians 1:15-18)

Maybe you have seen the bumper sticker that spells out "Co-exist" with the various religious and political symbols of the world. I do believe, despite our differences, that we should try to co-exist peacefully on earth. However, God is glorified only as a result of every knee bowing and every tongue confessing that Jesus Christ is Lord of the universe. The Bible doesn't attribute this authority to any other religious, political, or philosophical figure...not even Bob Dylan...dang! Any religion or faith that denies the deity of Jesus Christ, His exclusive payment for, and pardon of our sin, His virgin birth, sinless life or His literal resurrection is a *false religion*! Those who teach contrary to these truths are *false teachers*!

There have been false religions and religious "idols" since the fall of Adam and they continue today. We may be able to tolerate people and their errant religious beliefs, but when it comes to the true way to God, we can never compromise the truth. The thought that popped into your head as you read that last statement, popped into mine when I typed it: "That sure sounds judgmental and a little arrogant on your part." Look at what Paul told Timothy:

> "...there is only one God and one Mediator who can reconcile God and people. He is the man Christ Jesus." (1 Timothy 2:5)

Based on this verse, and the other scriptural evidence I have presented from the Bible, the only conclusion that we can come to is that Jesus is the true north to God, and only the Bible is the true north for the truth about God. When it comes to arriving at our final destination, GOD, alone is the Lord of the GPS!

To Tell the Truth

Will the real GOD please stand up?

Colossians 1:15

He is the image of the invisible God, the firstborn over all creation. For by Him all things were created that are in heaven and that are on earth, visible and invisible, whether thrones or dominions or principalities or powers. All things were created through Him and for Him. And He is before all things, and in Him all things consist.

You may be thinking, "Okay, so what makes Jesus any different than any of the other religious philosophers, gurus or religious founders in the world? Why should I live my life for Him? Why should I accept the teachings of Christianity? How can you have a relationship with a God you can't see?" These are all fair questions. God isn't offended when we ask honest questions about who Jesus is because He wants us to know Him. He is certainly not intimidated by our human reasoning. Why would He be? He created it! Colossians 1:15 pretty much spells it out for us, doesn't it?

When I was growing up, Bud Collyer hosted a very interesting television game show called: "To Tell The Truth." The show debuted on CBS in 1956 and ran in various forms on prime time and syndicated television for more than twenty years. On the show, a panel of four celebrities attempt to identify a described character that has a unique or unusual vocation or experience in life. The true character is accompanied by two impostors. Each panel member is given a set amount of time to question each of the contestants. The impostors are allowed to lie in their answers while the real character is sworn "to tell the truth."

After questioning, each panel member tries to identify who they believe is telling the truth. The true character wins prize money for each panel member who guesses wrong, while each impostor wins prize money for each panel member who is fooled by their misleading answers. Once the votes are cast, the host asks, "Will the real [person's name] please stand up?" As viewers at home, we would play along; trying to guess who we thought the real character was. No one knew for sure, however, until he or she stood up. Sometimes the truth was a big surprise!

When it comes to the issue of who the real God of the universe is, the stakes are much, much higher. Who we correctly identify as the true God of the universe will determine where each of us spends eternity! There are a multitude of impostors and impersonators out there who claim to be telling the truth. Most point to a special revelation or book of teachings to make their cases.

> But there were also false prophets among the people, even as there will be false teachers among you, who will secretly bring in destructive heresies, even denying the Lord who bought them, *and* bring on themselves swift destruction. And many will follow their

destructive ways, because of whom the way of truth will be blasphemed. By covetousness they will exploit you with deceptive words; for a long time their judgment has not been idle, and their destruction does not slumber. (2 Peter 2:1-3)

So, how do we identify the real character? I can only present to you the case the Bible makes for who Jesus is. You'll have to ask God to reveal to you whether or not what I present is true. Believe me; Jesus wants you to know the truth about who He is!

Making the Case

According to the Bible, Jesus was actually God coming down to earth to become like us in every way, except, of course, for committing sin.

> For we do not have a High Priest who cannot sympathize with our weaknesses, but was in all points tempted as we are, yet <u>without sin</u>. (Hebrews 4:15)

Amazing! It is hard to imagine that God has literally walked in our shoes as a human being and knows, first hand, what our struggles are, but it is true! He was willing to identify with us, so ultimately, we could identify with Him! Thankfully, Christianity is not a philosophy or religious practice; it is the Spirit of God taking up residence in those who have placed their faith in Him!

> And I will pray the Father, and He will give you <u>another Helper</u>, that He may abide <u>with you forever</u>—the <u>Spirit of truth</u>, whom the world cannot receive, because it neither sees Him nor knows Him; but you know Him, for <u>He dwells with you</u> and <u>will be in you</u>.

> I will not leave you orphans; <u>I will come to you.</u> "A little while longer and the world will see Me no more, but you will see Me. Because I live, you will live also. At that day you will know that <u>I *am* in My Father</u> and <u>you in Me</u>, and <u>I in you.</u> (John 14:16-20)

It is obvious within the context of the passage above that when Jesus is speaking to His disciples about the "Comforter," He is speaking of Himself. In the near future, He is going to abide within them forever. He is the Spirit of truth. He dwells *with* them physically, but He is going to be *in* them spiritually. He will come to them after His resurrection. He is *in* His Father; they are *in* Him and He is going to be *in* them. Like He did for His disciples then, when we believe in and accept Jesus, He does the same for us today! He is in the Father, we are in Him and He is in us forever as the Spirit of truth. I know, it is just too good to be true, but you can believe it because it is true!

While Jesus was in His earthly body, He asked his disciples this critical question: "...Who do men say that I, the Son of Man, am?" (Matthew 16:13) So they said, "Some say John the Baptist, some Elijah, and others Jeremiah or one of the prophets." In other words, they believed that He was just another man—just another prophet. Many are willing today to give Him at least that much credit, but Jesus was much more than just another human teacher or prophet. Then, He asked them, "But who do you say that I am?" Peter answered correctly:

> "You are the Christ, the Son of the living God." Jesus answered and said to him, "Blessed are you, Simon Bar-Jonah, for flesh and blood has not revealed this to you, but My Father who is in heaven. (Matthew 16:14-17)

Has He revealed this truth to you? What we think and believe about Jesus determines, not only the quality of the life we live here on earth, but where we will spend eternity. If He is everything the Bible says that He is, we cannot afford to be wrong about His true identity. Peter correctly stated that Jesus was the Christ. John also recognized Jesus as the Christ, and then gives us a clue as to what the word, "Christ" means.

> "...We have found the Messiah, which is, being interpreted, the Christ." (John 1:41)

What does the word, Christ, mean? Apparently, from this verse, it is equivalent to "Messiah." Messiah is a word that comes from the Hebrew word Moshiach, which means The Anointed. It can also mean The Chosen One. It is more than just part of His name; it is His title *and* His nature.

At this point, you are probably wondering, "Okay, what does anointed mean?" Good question! In Old Testament times, those who were approved and appointed to a position of authority, such as King, were anointed with oil. No, not motor oil or WD-40... Traditionally, it was a mixture of various spices mixed with Olive Oil. The term, "anoint," comes from the Hebrew word, Mashach. It means to pour, smear or rub. It was symbolic of an empowering to do what the individual was appointed to do. In the case of Jesus, all three terms, Christ, Messiah, and Anointed all mean the same thing. He is God's chosen deliverer, approved and appointed by the Father to be the ultimate King of Israel, the world, and the universe, through whom God created all things. Wow! Move the pups aside and let the Big Dog eat! I wanna be His homie (sic)!

Jesus often referred to Himself as, the "Son of Man" because, like us, He was born of a woman.

"But when the fullness of the time had come, God sent forth His Son, born of a woman, born under the law..." (Galatians 4:4)

Jesus was born in the flesh like you and me, but, as Peter also rightly observed, he was the "Son of the living God." That meant that He was no ordinary man. Both terms accurately describe Him. While He was on earth, He was both God and man. He was like us in His humanity, and He had to depend upon the Holy Spirit to live life perfectly. Thankfully, though we can't, He did! We get another huge clue to His identity in the Gospel of John, chapter one:

> In the beginning was the Word, and the Word was with God, and <u>the Word was God</u>. He was in the beginning with God. <u>All things were made through Him</u>, and without Him nothing was made that was made. <u>In Him was life</u>, and the life was the light of men. And <u>the Word became flesh and dwelt among us</u>, and we beheld His glory, the glory as of the only begotten of the Father, full of grace and truth. No one has seen God at any time. <u>The only begotten Son</u>, who is in the bosom of the Father, <u>He has declared Him</u>. (John 1:1-4, 14, 18)

Obviously, the "Word" referred to in these verses is Jesus. He was the Word who became flesh and dwelt among us. He's also referred to as, "the only begotten of the Father." Then, verse 18 says the only begotten of the Father (Jesus) has declared Him (God).

Two Adams?

God created Adam from the dust of the earth, and Jesus was miraculously conceived in Mary's womb by the Holy Spirit, so neither of them had an earthly father. This is why Jesus is referred to in scripture as the second Adam.

> And so it is written, "THE FIRST MAN ADAM BECAME A LIVING BEING." The last Adam (Jesus) BECAME A LIFE-GIVING SPIRIT. However, the spiritual is not first, but the natural, and afterward the spiritual. The first man was of the earth, made of dust; the second Man is the Lord from heaven. (1 Corinthians 15:45-47)

One Adam puts mankind in our current sin predicament but the other delivers us from it! Because of his sin, the first Adam brought death on all men. The second and last Adam, Jesus, is a "life-giving spirit" who causes us to reign in life!

> For if by the one man's offense death reigned through the one, much more those who receive abundance of grace and of the gift of righteousness will reign in life through the One, Jesus Christ. (Romans 5:17)

Though tempted in every way such as we are, He never sinned. He went to the cross innocent and became sin for us so that we who were guilty might become God's righteousness in Him. (2 Corinthians 5:21). No other human being who has ever lived can claim to be sinless. We all have a sin debt of our own that needs to be paid for! Therefore, no other human being is qualified to pay for our sins as Jesus was.

On another occasion, Jesus revealed who He was to Philip, one of His disciples:

> Philip said to Him, "Lord, show us the Father, and it is sufficient for us." Jesus said to him, "Have I been with you so long, and yet you have not known Me,

> Philip? He who has seen Me has seen the Father; so how can you say, 'Show us the Father'? (John 14:9)

The Jews certainly understood who Jesus claimed to be. Jesus said:

> "I and My Father are one." Then the Jews took up stones again to stone Him. Jesus answered them, "Many good works I have shown you from My Father. For which of those works do you stone Me?" The Jews answered Him, saying, "For a good work we do not stone You, but <u>for blasphemy</u>, and because <u>You, being a Man, make Yourself God</u>."
> (John 10:30-33)

They were enraged because Jesus was claiming to be...God! Ultimately, they would crucify Him for blasphemy. In reality, they hated Him because His presence was exposing who they really were and how they were taking advantage of their followers through religion. Those who are like Him still have that effect on religious frauds today.

The fact that Jesus did not correct His disciples when they worshiped Him is evidence that Jesus, Himself, knew who He was. (Matthew 14:33) He also forgave sin and claimed that He had the authority to do so.

> When Jesus saw their faith, He said to the paralytic, "Son, your sins are forgiven you." And some of the scribes were sitting there and reasoning in their hearts, "Why does this Man speak blasphemies like this? Who can forgive sins but God alone?" But immediately, when Jesus perceived in His spirit that they reasoned thus within themselves, He said to them, "Why do you reason about these things in your

hearts? Which is easier, to say to the paralytic, 'Your sins are forgiven you,' or to say, 'Arise, take up your bed and walk'? But that you may know that <u>the Son of Man has power on earth to forgive sins</u>"—He said to the paralytic, "I say to you, arise, take up your bed, and go to your house." Immediately he arose, took up the bed, and went out in the presence of them all, so that all were amazed and glorified God, saying, "We never saw anything like this!" (Mark 2:5-12)

Was Jesus a lunatic, or was He indeed who He claimed to be—God in the flesh? If we are willing to base the answer to that question solely on the basis of these verses in the Bible, it becomes clearer who He was and still is. Almost 750 years before Jesus' birth, the prophet, Isaiah, foretold it in the Old Testament:

> Therefore the Lord Himself will give you a sign: Behold, the virgin (Mary) shall conceive and bear a Son, and shall call His name Immanuel. (Isaiah 7:14)

Again, the prophet, Isaiah, revealed who this unique baby would be. This holy infant would become a man who would save the world from their sins.

> For unto us a Child is born, Unto us a Son is given; And the government will be upon His shoulder. And His name will be called Wonderful, Counselor, <u>Mighty God</u>, <u>Everlasting Father</u>, Prince of Peace. Of the increase of His government and peace there will be no end, Upon the throne of David and over His kingdom, to order it and establish it with judgment and justice from that time forward, even forever. (Isaiah 9:6, 7)

Do these ancient prophecies describe just another religious man? This brings us to yet another question. What does the name, Immanuel mean? We find the answer in the Gospel of Matthew:

> Now the birth of Jesus Christ was as follows: After His mother Mary was betrothed to Joseph, before they came together, <u>she was found with child of the Holy Spirit</u>. Then Joseph her husband, being a just man, and not wanting to make her a public example, was minded to put her away secretly. But while he thought about these things, behold, an angel of the Lord appeared to him in a dream, saying, "Joseph, son of David, do not be afraid to take to Mary as your wife, for that which is conceived in her is of the Holy Spirit. And she will bring forth a Son, and you shall call His name JESUS, for <u>He will save His people from their sins</u>." So all this was done that it might be fulfilled which was spoken by the Lord through the prophet, saying: "BEHOLD, THE VIRGIN SHALL BE WITH CHILD, AND BEAR A SON, AND THEY SHALL CALL HIS NAME IMMANUEL," which is translated, "<u>God with us</u>."
> (Matthew 1:18-23)

Joseph knew that Jesus was not conceived of his seed. These verses make it clear that God came to be with us in the person of His Son, Jesus. According to our main scripture text in this chapter, He was the literal physical manifestation of God on earth. The Amplified Bible makes it even clearer.

> [*Now*] He is the exact likeness of the unseen God [*the visible representation of the invisible*]; He is the Firstborn of all creation. For it was in Him that all

things were created, in heaven and on earth, things seen and things unseen, whether thrones, dominions, rulers, or authorities; all things were created and exist through Him [*by His service, intervention*] and in and for Him. And He Himself existed before all things, and in Him all things consist (cohere, are held together). [*Prov. 8:22-31.*] (Colossians 1:15-17)

Notice, He created everything in heaven and earth and beyond. They were all created by Him and for Him. Based on this information, Jesus is the Creator, right? In addition, He is before all things and all things consist in Him. Sounds like the sovereign (supreme authority or power) God of the Universe to me! These statements about Jesus are incredibly powerful. Either they are true or the apostle Paul was delusional, and Jesus was the greatest imposter in the history of mankind. The Apostle Paul warns us:

> See to it that no one carries you off as spoil or makes you yourselves captive by his so-called philosophy and intellectualism and vain deceit (idle fancies and plain nonsense), following human tradition (men's ideas of the material rather than the spiritual world), just crude notions following the rudimentary and elemental teachings of the universe and disregarding [*the teachings of*] Christ (the Messiah).
> (Colossians 2:8) (Amplified Bible)

According to Paul, we can be cheated in life by the philosophies and false traditional teachings of men who base their opinions and beliefs on the basic principles of the world. Each of us must ask ourselves, "Is the human intellect really the final authority on truth? Is the human conscience really all that trustworthy?" Look at human history and decide for yourself.

It doesn't take a genius to figure out that, in spite of our advances in knowledge and technology, our world has become an even more perilous place to live. Man's knowledge has not produced peace and harmony on earth. Why is this? It is because man never has been, and never will be, the final authority on anything. The problem with the world is that human nature is corrupt. I realize it is hard to go against the flow when the majority of the world's population gives overwhelming credence to human scientific and intellectual opinion. But, our opinions must be based on reliable data. That information is found in the Bible, not in our educational institutions. God is definitely not impressed with human intellectualism.

> For it is written, I will baffle and render useless and destroy the learning of the learned and the philosophy of the philosophers and the cleverness of the clever and the discernment of the discerning; I will frustrate and nullify [them] and bring [them] to nothing. [*Isa. 29:14.*] Where is the wise man (the philosopher)? Where is the scribe (the scholar)? Where is the investigator (the logician, the debater) of this present time and age? Has not God shown up the nonsense and the folly of this world's wisdom?
> (1 Corinthians 1:19-20) (Amplified Bible)

Look at what Paul has to say in the book of Philippians concerning Jesus:

> Who, although being essentially one with God and in the form of God [*possessing the fullness of the attributes which make God God*], did not think this equality with God was a thing to be eagerly grasped or retained, But stripped Himself [*of all privileges and rightful dignity*], so as to assume the guise of a servant (slave), in that He became like men and was

> born a human being. And after He had appeared in human form, He abased and humbled Himself [*still further*] and carried His obedience to the extreme of death, even the death of the cross! Therefore [*because He stooped so low*] God has highly exalted Him and has freely bestowed on Him the name that is above every name, That in (at) the name of Jesus every knee should (must) bow, in heaven and on earth and under the earth, And every tongue [*frankly and openly*] confess and acknowledge that Jesus Christ is Lord, to the glory of God the Father.
> (Philippians 2:6-11) (Amplified Bible)

Jesus, as a man, was not merely "God-like" but GOD, Himself, incarnate (in the flesh). The following verse is obviously talking about Jesus:

> And without controversy great is the mystery of godliness: God was manifested in the flesh, Justified in the Spirit, Seen by angels, Preached among the Gentiles, Believed on in the world, Received up in glory. (1 Timothy 3:16)

No man had ever seen God; He is Spirit. (John 4:24) God was invisible until He manifested Himself in His Son, Jesus, the Christ.

Tri-Unity

God is triune (three) in His makeup. The word "trinity" is not found in the Bible but the concept is unmistakable. Yet, He is one God. "Hear, O Israel! The LORD our God, the LORD is one!" (Deuteronomy 6:4) I suppose the term, "Tri-unity," would be a more accurate description of the Godhead. In his divine essence, God exists in three eternal "Persons": the Father, the Son and the Holy Spirit. They are all described as having identical attributes, making them all the same, not just in mind and purpose, but one in substance. All three are equally God, with each manifested differently to mankind. So in that sense, Jesus was exactly who He claimed to be...God. He is part of the tri-unity of the Godhead. In fact, while He was on the earth in the flesh, the scripture says that all of the Godhead indwelled Him bodily.

> For in Him the whole fullness of Deity (the Godhead) continues to dwell in bodily form [*giving complete expression of the divine nature*].
> (Colossians 2:9) (Amplified Bible)

The Bible says that man is created in His image. What does "created in His image" mean? Like God, man is triune in his makeup, fearfully and wonderfully made.

> I will praise You, for I am fearfully and wonderfully made; Marvelous are Your works, And that my soul knows very well. (Psalms 139:14)

When Jesus comes into our human spirit, He brings all of the attributes of a holy Godhead with Him. That triune presence within us makes us eternally complete in Him.

> And you are in Him, made full and having come to fullness of life [*in Christ you too are filled with the Godhead--Father, Son and Holy Spirit--and reach full spiritual stature*]. And He is the Head of all rule and authority [*of every angelic principality and power*].
> (Colossians 2:10) (Amplified Bible)

Human beings are a complex mixture of spirit, soul and body (1 Thessalonians 5:23). Like God, all three aspects of our triune makeup are distinct, yet together they make us who and what we are. We'll take a closer look at this later. Finally, we see these words in the book of Hebrews:

> God, who at various times and in various ways spoke in time past to the fathers by the prophets, has in these last days spoken to us by His Son, whom He has appointed heir of all things, through whom also He made the worlds; who being the brightness of His glory and the express image of His person, and upholding all things by the word of His power, when He had by Himself purged our sins, sat down at the right hand of the Majesty on high, having become so much better than the angels, as He has by inheritance obtained a more excellent name than they. (Hebrews 1:1-4)

Final Arguments

Based on these words, since the time of Jesus' birth, God has been speaking to the world through Him. He is the heir of all things because He made the worlds Himself! He is the brightness of God's glory and the exact earthly expression of who God is! He upholds all things by the power of His word. He Himself purges (takes away) our sins. He is currently seated in the most exalted seat in existence, the seat at the right hand of the Majesty on high. He is so much better than the angels because He created them. His rightful inheritance gives Him the name above every name...Jesus Christ, the Creator and God of the universe!

What astounds me is that there are denominations within the Christian church who do not agree on His deity! The argument rages on: was Jesus a man, or was He God? The answer is, yes! He was both God and man *simultaneously* while He was walking on earth. Let me just say this: If Jesus is not God, then how do we explain the overwhelming scriptural evidence presented from the bible in this chapter? I fail to see how any Bible Scholar could come to any other conclusion. Forget semantics…Jesus is who He claimed to be…God! The Word is clear and irrefutable!

The Defense Rests

We should give our lives to Jesus, not because He was an insightful master teacher, or one of many religious prophets who have tread upon the earth, or even because He gave His life for us on the cross. We should not believe in Him because we get something in return, but solely because He was and still is…the creator and God of all things—seen and unseen! He is the "Un-known God" the Greeks had never come to know. He alone completes our human experience.

There are many powers in existence that are higher than man. He is eternally more than merely a "higher power." He is the highest power—God, almighty! He alone is authorized to offer us eternal, abundant life! The real God of the universe and beyond has just stood up! Surprised?

Dead Man Walking

Our Real Problem

Ephesians 2:1

And you He made alive, who were dead in trespasses and sins...

In the beginning, God created everything in the universe, including the earth and every form of life on the earth. Next, He created a lifeless form that He named, Adam, from the dust of the earth. Then, God breathed His *breath of eternal Life* into Adam's nostrils, and the first man became a *living soul*. (Genesis 2:7) I believe the term, "created in God's image," means that Adam was created, like his Creator, a triune being; SPIRIT (breath), SOUL (personality) and BODY (dust). (See Triune Man diagram on page 85) We find a reference to this description of our human makeup in one of Paul's letters to the Thessalonian church:

> Now may the God of peace Himself sanctify you completely; and may your whole spirit, soul, and

<u>body</u> be preserved blameless at the coming of our Lord Jesus Christ. (1 Thessalonians 5:23)

Adam's newly created body—we'll call it his "EUV" (Earth Utility Vehicle)—was lifeless until God's breath (Eternal Spirit of life) was breathed into him. Once that supernatural life was introduced, Adam became a living soul, with a free mind, emotions, and will. Like his Creator, Adam could think, feel, choose and create. From the beginning of God's creation, man was designed to live a God-quality of life (Greek. "Zoe" God's life, the true source of Godliness) and placed into a perfect environment, the Garden of Eden.

Everything that he could possibly need for life was his, but he was created *co-dependent*. In other words, God never intended for Adam and Eve to live their lives independent of His life. They co-existed in a *life-union* with their maker. In the beginning, there was no such thing as death in God's new creation, or in Adam's human consciousness. He could never have imagined a condition as horrible as death, or that an act that God would call Sin could wreak such havoc on his perfect existence. How could he know that his act of disobedience would not only impact his life, but countless generations after him? But, at least for the moment, Adam was perfect and everything was hunky-dory! Well, almost...

It didn't take long for Adam to realize what God already knew...his life was missing something. He observed all of his Creator's creatures and probably said to himself, "Where's mine?" You see, God created all of the other creatures in the Garden of Eden with a mate! So...God created Eve from Adam, and together, they enjoyed a perfect existence in Eden. They experienced a unique relationship in perfect union with their Creator and with each other.

God gave them free reign and full dominion over all His earthly creation, with only one restriction...they could not eat the fruit of the "Tree of the Knowledge of Good and Evil." (Genesis 2:16, 17) Everything was within the boundaries that God gave them, including the "Tree of Life," but not this one particular tree. Why? They already possessed that information. Whether they realized it or not, they were living in perfect innocence and goodness. Is there anything better than the goodness of God? Of course not! Why look for something more? Enter the serpent, the fallen one, Satan...

Ironically, if you look at the description of all the trees in the Garden, there was virtually no difference in their appearance. They were all *"pleasant to the sight and good for food."* (Genesis 2:9, 10) The deception, and attraction, was that they could somehow know good and evil on their own if they ate of the forbidden tree. The temptation was to doubt God and be self-controlled. Man still makes the same mistake today. That is the progression of sin. First, there is deception (rejection of truth), then temptation (an alternative suggestion), and then sin (willful rebellion).

> Let no one say when he is tempted, "I am tempted by God"; for God cannot be tempted by evil, nor does He Himself tempt anyone. But each one is tempted when he is drawn away by his own desires and enticed. Then, when desire has conceived, it gives birth to sin; and sin, when it is full-grown, brings forth death. (James 1:13-15)

A fallen angel named, Lucifer—that is, Satan—lied and convinced the original "first couple" that God was holding out on them. (Genesis 3:1-6) They believed the lie: "Listen, you two, don't you realize that Mr. Big Shot is holding out on you? It is not going to kill you to know the difference between good and evil. God just doesn't want you to know what He knows because He doesn't want you to be like Him. Go ahead and eat from the tree, you'll see. You will not surely die. For God knows that in the day you eat of it your eyes will be opened and you will be like God, knowing good and evil." (vs. 4, 5)

The truth is they were already like God. They were made in His image and the sky was the limit as long as they trusted and obeyed Him. Nevertheless, they acted on their own, contrary to God's instructions. God had a way of life designed for them that would gloriously meet every conceivable need they would ever have, but they chose to go their own way.

Actually, the Bible says that Eve was deceived, but Adam chose to *sin*. (1 Timothy 2:14) Yep, it wasn't long until Adam grew his hair long and Eve cut hers short. She started wearing pant suits made of leaves, makeup and jewelry to church. He got his ears pierced, got tatted and started wearing leaf shorts in public and flip flops to church. Next, they started to dance, smoke and drink, then they began to...well, you get the point. We all have our list of things that we consider to be sin, but in the Bible, sin is simply man going his own way instead of God's way.

> All we like sheep have gone astray; We have turned, every one, to his own way; And the LORD has laid on Him the iniquity of us all. (Isaiah 53:6)

You see, God has a way of life designed to protect and prosper us, but we think we can make our lives more complete by doing things our own way. Sin is an attitude that says: "I don't need God, or anyone else, to tell me how to live my life. I can do this myself." That may seem right to us, but the end result of this attitude is separation from His life (DEATH).

> There is a way *that seems* right to a man, But its end *is* the way of death. (Proverbs 16:25)

Adam sinned when he decided that he would do his own thing, even though God had warned him, "...in the day you eat of it, (The Tree of the Knowledge of Good and Evil) you shall surely die." (Genesis 2:17)

TRIUNE MAN
Spirit - Soul - Body

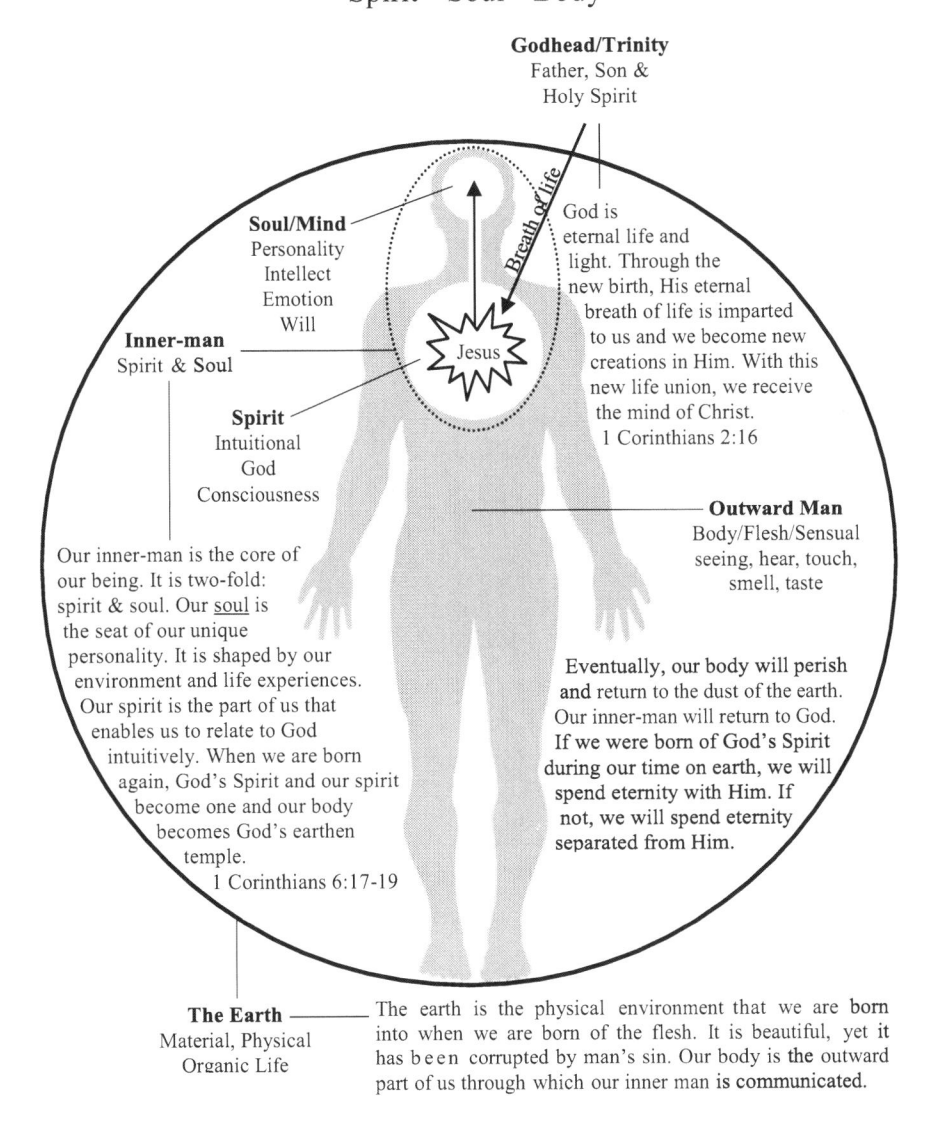

Godhead/Trinity
Father, Son &
Holy Spirit

Soul/Mind
Personality
Intellect
Emotion
Will

Inner-man
Spirit & Soul

Spirit
Intuitional
God
Consciousness

God is eternal life and light. Through the new birth, His eternal breath of life is imparted to us and we become new creations in Him. With this new life union, we receive the mind of Christ.
1 Corinthians 2:16

Outward Man
Body/Flesh/Sensual
seeing, hear, touch, smell, taste

Our inner-man is the core of our being. It is two-fold: spirit & soul. Our soul is the seat of our unique personality. It is shaped by our environment and life experiences. Our spirit is the part of us that enables us to relate to God intuitively. When we are born again, God's Spirit and our spirit become one and our body becomes God's earthen temple.
1 Corinthians 6:17-19

Eventually, our body will perish and return to the dust of the earth. Our inner-man will return to God. If we were born of God's Spirit during our time on earth, we will spend eternity with Him. If not, we will spend eternity separated from Him.

The Earth
Material, Physical
Organic Life

The earth is the physical environment that we are born into when we are born of the flesh. It is beautiful, yet it has been corrupted by man's sin. Our body is the outward part of us through which our inner man is communicated.

When they decided to go their own way, for the first time in their existence, Adam and Eve experienced separation from *true life*, *true Godliness*, and *true oneness with God*. They had never before seen or experienced death's effects in God's creation. They had never existed apart from God's empowering, enlightening presence, but now, everything would be tragically different. Of course, they did not die physically the day they disobeyed God, but a very real death (spiritual death) occurred with their disobedience, just as God had promised.

"Dead man walking!" This is what the prison guards would yell out, clearing the way as they escorted a condemned prisoner on their final walk from their cell on death row to the execution chamber. This prisoner had nothing more to lose. Though still walking, he was as good as dead already. He had been found guilty, condemned to death, and it was merely a matter of time until he would walk no more. His problem wasn't the prison food, the prison guards, or the judicial system...his problem was death. He had no hope of life. God has declared the whole world guilty of sin, and as with this condemned prisoner, *death* is mankind's greatest problem. I will illustrate later, in Rest Area 9, "A Life to Die For," how God has gloriously changed this condition.

Death = Separation

The Bible speaks of three different types of death: *Physical Death*, *Spiritual Death* and *Eternal Death*. All three involve separation. *Physical Death* occurs when a separation between our outer-man (Body) and our inner-man (spirit and soul) takes place. The spirit and soul are the part of us that is unseen but very real. For instance, you can't see the human mind by dissecting the physical brain because the brain is organic matter, and the mind is spiritual. Think of it this way; the brain is our hardware and the mind is our software. Both were designed and engineered by God—the hardware manufacturer and software programmer. The mind is intellectual, emotional and volitional (will, choice). It is the seat of the soul.

Our soul (personality) is unique to each of us, having been shaped by our genetics, our relationships and our life experiences.

Our inner-man is animated and expressed through our outer-man, our physical body. Though Adam and Eve did not die physically, they did experience a very real death the day they sinned, *spiritual death*. The union with God's Spirit of Life that they were created with was now severed and disconnected.

GLCN

When I was a kid growing up in the 1950s and '60s, there was no such thing as cable television. In fact, our family didn't own a color TV until about the time I was going into high school. We would use a TV antenna and "Rabbit Ears" (a small, portable, two-pronged antenna that sat on top of our television) with tin foil to pick up local stations, but at best, we could only pick up three or four snowy-screened stations. We used to have to hold one end of the Rabbit Ears, hold one leg out to the side, hold the other hand out in the opposite direction and stick our tongue out just to get a clearer picture…just kidding…but not much.

Today, modern technology has provided us with all sorts of high-tech choices: huge flat screen, HD (High Definition)…and now, even 3D (Three-Dimensional) TVs. We also have theater, stereo, surround sound to go with incredibly clear pictures.

Cable and satellite companies provide us with hundreds of channels to view. However, these high-tech inventions are worthless without a proper cable connection. Without the proper connection, the picture on the screen gets scrambled up pretty quickly. Most cable packages require a signal box that unscrambles the signal from cable networks so we can watch their programs. But, without the proper connection it's impossible to make out what we are trying to watch. This is exactly what happened to the first man and woman and to every person since who has chosen to go their own way in life.

By committing sin (going his own way), man has disconnected himself from GLCN—God's Life Communications Network. All we have to do is watch or read the daily news to see that man's picture of life has been severely scrambled. Sadly, we all see and experience the effects of spiritual death/separation in every aspect of human life every day.

Having sinned, Adam and Eve unplugged themselves from true spiritual life. (Genesis 5:3) They were alive physically, but dead spiritually. In fact, Adam would live physically for 930 years. He and Eve would have sons and daughters in their own image for centuries. My families in Wisconsin and Arkansas are big, but not that big!

Tragically, countless generations of their descendants would be born with their spiritually-unplugged condition. Because we are all born with the same nature as Adam, we all have the same tendency to pursue our own way.

> "Therefore, even as through one man sin entered into the world, and death by sin, and so death passed on to all men inasmuch as all sinned."
> (Romans 5:12)

We cannot blame Adam and Eve, however, for our spiritual separation from God. We may have inherited their sin nature, but the truth is we are accountable for *our own* sins.

> What then? Are we better than they? Not at all. For we have previously charged both Jews and Greeks that they are all under sin. As it is written: "THERE IS NONE RIGHTEOUS, NO, NOT ONE; THERE IS NONE WHO UNDERSTANDS; THERE IS NONE WHO SEEKS AFTER GOD. THEY HAVE ALL TURNED ASIDE; THEY HAVE TOGETHER BECOME UNPROFITABLE; THERE IS NONE WHO DOES GOOD, NO, NOT ONE." (Romans 3:9-12)

Our sins have separated us from God's life. If we die physically, in this dead (spiritually separated) condition, we pass into eternity *already separated* from God's life and our dead condition becomes our eternal state. The Bible describes this third type of death as *eternal death*. It is referred to as the "the second death" in the last book of the Bible. (Revelations 20:11-15) Someone once asked, "What does one have to do to go to hell?" The answer is, absolutely nothing; we're born bent in that direction.

We do, on the other hand, have to do something, to avoid eternal separation from God in hell. We must accept Jesus as our Savior and be regenerated. We must be born of His Holy Spirit. According to the verses in Revelation 20, if we are only born once, we will die twice. However, if we are born twice, then we will only die once! Uh…I'll take option number two…

You see, we are all guilty (Romans 3:23), to some degree, of living out our lives in our own way instead of God's way. We are all guilty of deciding for ourselves what is best for us, and of dealing with life's issues without considering or acknowledging the one who created us. For instance, God designed marriage and the family, but man wants to define it for himself. God wants to bless us, but we want to bless ourselves. Until Jesus reconnects us with His Spirit of life, we are what the Bible describes as, "sons of disobedience," and "children of wrath." (Ephesians 2:2, 3) It is our nature. We have rendered ourselves spiritually dead through sin.

This brings us to the all-important question: What does a person who is dead need? Do they need church? No, unfortunately, much of the church is dead too. How about better values or morals? A dead person can't express anything, good or bad. The obvious answer is, LIFE! That is exactly what God sent His Son, Jesus, to give us. Jesus gives us His eternal life as a gift.

> "The wages of sin is death, but the gift of God is eternal life in Christ, Jesus Christ our Lord."
> (Romans 6:23)

> "The thief comes only in order to steal and kill and destroy. I came that they may have and enjoy life, and have it in abundance (to the full, till it overflows)." (John 10:10) (Amplified Bible)

A spiritually dead person has no true sense or awareness of God's realm. The Bible refers to the spiritually dead as natural men.

> ...the natural man does not receive the things of the Spirit of God, for they are foolishness to him; nor can he know them, because they are spiritually discerned. (1 Corinthians 2:14)

According to this verse, the natural man (those who are not born of God's Spirit) cannot receive the things of the Spirit of God. Because the natural man's spiritual cable box has been unplugged, his picture of life is scrambled and confused. His fallen nature is blind to God's point of view. We are aliens to the life and nature of God until we receive Jesus (our Spiritual "Cable Guy") into our lives.

> ...having their understanding darkened, being alienated from the life of God, because of the ignorance that is in them, because of the blindness of their heart; (Ephesians 4:18)

Let's look at this condition a little closer. When the Bible states that as natural beings, we are, by nature, "sons of disobedience" (Ephesians 2:2); it is talking about what we are at the core of our being. Because, at our core, we have been unplugged, it is natural for us to want to do our own thing. Have you noticed that we don't have to teach our children to be disobedient or to do what is wrong? Rather, we must teach our kids to be obedient and to do what is good and right because selfishness and disobedience is part of their natural-born, separated nature. They are born knowing how to say, "No," to us. They are born wanting to do their own thing. This attitude begins to shift into warp speed as they reach their teens. Am I the only one who ever shrugged my shoulders and stated to my parents, "It's my life; I just want to live it my way!"?

Looks like a Duck…must be a Duck!

Our *birth determines our nature*. For instance, humans are born with a human nature, ducks have a duck nature, and eagles have an eagle nature. Our *nature determines our appetite*, and our *appetite determines our behavior*. Instinctively, we are driven by our nature, the essence of what we are. Let me give you an analogy that will make this a little clearer.

Let's take a duck egg and place it into an eagle's nest. The mother eagle sits on that egg, along with her other eagle eggs, and never notices the difference until they hatch. She loves all of her precious little hatchlings but notices that this "special" little eaglet—let's call him, Deagle—doesn't look, or behave, quite like her other precious new hatchlings. Nevertheless, mama loves him just the same.

She flies off each day to gather food for her hungry hatchlings, but Deagle just doesn't seem to be able to ingest, nor digest, the only thing on the menu…meat…Eeeuuw! In fact, he doesn't even seem to have an appetite for it. Gradually, Deagle grows weaker and weaker until the homely little eaglet eventually becomes eagle food for the others because it is their natural born nature to eat meat. Their eagle nature and their appetite dictate their behavior. Now, you can't blame an eagle for doing what is normal for eagles to do…can you? You've heard the old saying, "If it looks like a duck, walks like a duck and quacks like a duck, it must be…gulp, eagle food…Eeeuuw!"

Placing a duck egg into an Eagle's nest does not make a duck an Eagle. Or, as we would say it in Arkansas: "Sittin' in the Hen House don't make you no Chicken! Yuonta be a Chicken, ya gotta be hatched agin! (sic)" Likewise, sitting in the Church House does not make you a Christian. If you want to be a Christian, Jesus says: "You must be born again." (John 3:7)

If it looks like a sinner, lives like a sinner, talks like a sinner, it must be a sinner! It's true! Ultimately, as "Going-our-own-wayers, (sic)" we are basically self-centered, self-promoting, self-seekers. We are not sinners because we sin; we sin because, by nature, we are sinners. Our nature dictates our behavior. That is our natural tendency. As harmful and offensive as sin is, you really can't fault a sinner for doing what is normal for a sinner to do.

That is not to say that "Going-our-own-wayers" are incapable of extraordinary acts of kindness, generosity, or self-sacrifice. We see many times where people who are not plugged into God are willing to heroically pay the ultimate price for someone else, or some noble cause that they love and believe in. For example, we get to enjoy our American liberties today because of the supreme sacrifices of those who laid down their lives in the past for future generations of Americans. I thank God every day for their sacrifice. Certainly, we have all witnessed the love of parents sacrificing for their children and grandchildren. All of us who are parents and grandparents understand this quality of love, don't we? Well, we should if we don't.

You talkin' to me?

I believe everyone is born with a God-given conscience, and that His Holy Spirit speaks to every person through that conscience. However, over time, as we violate it again and again, we can become calloused and eventually grow dull of hearing God's still, small voice at all. The longer unplugged people go their own way, the less they hear God in their conscience. They are driven by their personal wants and desires. We can't really expect anything else from them and we certainly should not judge them because we who know the Lord were all guilty of the same behavior before we knew Him.

> And you He made alive, who were dead (spiritually separated from God) in trespasses and sins, in which you once walked (lived) according to the course of this world, according to the prince of the power of the air (Satan), the spirit who now works in the <u>sons of disobedience</u>, among whom also we all once conducted ourselves in the lusts of our flesh, fulfilling the desires of the flesh and of the mind, and were <u>by nature children of wrath</u>, just as the others. (Ephesians 2:1-3)

When God's Holy Spirit reconnects us to Him, our nature is miraculously changed forever. Because of His nature in us, it becomes our natural desire to please Him and to live for Him. His nature becomes our nature. Peter puts it this way in 2 Peter 1:4,

> ...by which have been given to us exceedingly great and precious promises, that through these you may be partakers of the divine nature, having escaped the corruption that is in the world through lust.

Our new birth has determined our new nature, and our new divine nature dictates our new appetite. Our new appetite drives our new behavior. We are no longer "Ducks" or "Deagles." We are God's spiritual Eagles, mounted up and soaring with His nature and life! (Isaiah 40:31) Therefore, as new creations in Christ, it is just as natural for us to live for God, as it was for us to live out the sinful desires of our old nature when we were disconnected from Him.

One of the many insightful Christian authors who impacted my understanding of Christianity was Watchman Nee. He called this new way of life, *"The Normal Christian Life."* [4] I highly recommend this book to those who are searching for the truth about what the Christian life is.

Our nature is the *"what"* of our human makeup, and our personality is the *"who"* of our being. What Ain'ts need is a miracle that changes their nature (the essence of *what*, and then *who*, they are). That is the only thing that can change their appetite, and ultimately their behavior and direction in life. They need a radical reconnection to God's Life Communications Network. That miracle comes through a new birth. It happens by placing our faith in Jesus Christ. We believe and God does the rest! We who have been plugged back in have the solution to their predicament. We should be living examples of what it means to be radically-alive men walking!

Radically Reconnected

Regenerated, not Resuscitated!

Ephesians 2:4-6

But God, who is rich in mercy, because of His great love with which He loved us, even when we were dead in trespasses, made us alive together with Christ (by grace you have been saved), and raised us up together, and made us sit together in the heavenly places in Christ Jesus...

The Glorious BUTS of the Bible

Thank God for the "BUTs" in the Bible! In Ephesians 2, we find one of the greatest "BUTs" in the scriptures. We were dead (spiritually separated) in our trespasses and sins, BUT God made us alive because of His great love and mercy. Here's another one:

> "For the wages of sin is death, BUT the gift of God
> is eternal life in Christ Jesus our Lord."
> (Romans 6:23)

The penalty for our sin is death, BUT God gives to us the gift of eternal life in His Son, Jesus! And, yet another one:

> BUT God demonstrates His own love toward us, in
> that while we were still sinners, Christ died for us.
> (Romans 5:8)

The greatness of these "BUTs" is that we were as bad off as anyone could possibly be (dead in our sins), BUT God loved us anyway and turned our hopeless situation completely around! We were dead and in need of life. Jesus was eternal life but died so we who were dead could live forever.

When I came to the Lord in November, 1973, I didn't realize that when you give your heart and life to Jesus, He actually gives His heart and life to you! I didn't realize that it is a miracle to become a Christian. Salvation is not only a radical removal of all that we were B.C. (Before Christ), but a radical reintroduction of His miraculous saving life into our spirit/heart. It is not a church choice; it isn't a denominational decision—it is a radical rebirth! We become radically reconnected to our original life source, Jesus!

Salvation is not just something that God *did for us* two thousand years ago when Jesus gave His life for us on the cross; it is something He *does to us* now when Christ gives His life to us through the new birth. We need to understand the difference between the two. Salvation is not just something God does for us; it is something He does to us. Salvation is a miraculous gift from God! Though I didn't understand it the night I was saved, the moment I believed in and received Him, God miraculously sent the Spirit of His Son into my heart and merged His spirit with mine.

> And because you [*really*] are [*His*] sons, God has sent the [*Holy*] Spirit of His Son into our hearts, crying, Abba (Father)! Father!
> (Galatians 4:6) (Amplified Bible)

Whew! I needed that more than I could ever have imagined! So does every other person who is going it alone in life.

When asked, "What does it mean to be a Christian?" a dear old Saint replied sincerely, "It means that Jesus died on the cross for my sins so I can go to heaven when I die." Let me tell you, if that is all you understand about your salvation, you are drastically short-changing yourself! You are missing the true Christian experience! Christianity is not salvation in the past tense; it is His radical saving life in the present tense! God doesn't save us merely to *get us into heaven*; He saves us to *get heaven into us*! He wants to radically change our life experience by allowing us to actually experience Him as our eternal life now.

What we all need is a life-giving transfusion of God's Holy Spirit into our lifeless spirit. That is what our salvation actually is! The true Christian experience is missed by those who view it as simply attempting to live a good religious life. Genuine Christianity is more than merely doing the best we can and expressing our gratefulness that our sins are removed by an historical Jesus so we can go to heaven when we die. To be sure, if that was all that our salvation involved, that would be far more than we deserve, but it is much better than that! Consider this, in God's *mercy*; He does not give us what we deserve, while in His *grace*, He gives us everything we could never deserve! Thankfully, it is really about a present, indwelling Jesus empowering us with His eternal, abundant life now!

Is your Jesus too small?

Far too many Christians have too small a concept of who Jesus actually is today. We visualize the Jesus who indwells us as the one who is depicted in the four Gospels: a meek carpenter/teacher who died on a cross as God's sacrificial Lamb to take away our sins. Thank God, He became that Jesus and He was willing to do that *for us*! However, we get a glimpse of the current Jesus in the Book of Revelation. The apostle, John, was in exile on the Isle of Patmos when he heard a thundering voice behind him:

> I was in the Spirit on the Lord's Day, and I heard behind me a loud voice, as of a trumpet, saying, "I am the Alpha and the Omega, the First and the Last," and, "What you see, write in a book and send *it* to the seven churches which are in Asia: to Ephesus, to Smyrna, to Pergamos, to Thyatira, to Sardis, to Philadelphia, and to Laodicea." Then I turned to see the voice that spoke with me. And having turned I saw seven golden lampstands, and in the midst of the seven lampstands *One* like the Son of Man, clothed with a garment down to the feet and girded about the chest with a golden band. His head and hair *were* white like wool, as white as snow, and His eyes like a flame of fire; His feet *were* like fine brass, as if refined in a furnace, and His voice as the sound of many waters; He had in His right hand seven stars, out of His mouth went a sharp two-edged sword, and His countenance *was* like the sun shining in its strength. And when I saw Him, I fell at His feet as dead. But He laid His right hand on me, saying to me, "Do not be afraid; I am the First and the Last. I *am* He who lives, and was dead, and behold, I am alive forevermore. Amen. And I have the keys of Hades and of Death. (Revelation 1:10-18)

The sight of the risen, ascended Christ was too much for John to behold! Looking at Jesus was more blinding than trying to look wide-eyed into the sun at high noon. He passed out cold! What encourages me is Jesus' response to John's apparent fear. He tenderly reaches out and touches John and reassures him, "Do not be afraid." This is the Jesus that will come again and judge the world. The second time the world beholds Him, he will not be a lamb for the slaughter; He will be a conquering lion! We receive this awesome, fearsome, yet compassionate Jesus the moment we *repent* (a change of mind that changes our way of living) of our sins and invite Him into our heart. Eternal Life is not just something that we get when we die and go to heaven someday. Jesus *is* our eternal life and salvation now and forever. If we have Him, we have eternal life. John points this out in the following verses:

> He who believes in the Son has everlasting life; and he who does not believe the Son shall not see life, but the wrath of God abides on him. (John 3:36)

> He who has the Son has life; he who does not have the Son of God does not have life. These things I have written to you who believe in the name of the Son of God, that you may know that you have eternal life, and that you may continue to believe in the name of the Son of God. (1 John 5:12, 13)

The only reason we will live forever with Jesus is because we live with Him now! He is our eternal life, not just in heaven someday, but in us on earth today!

As I began to learn more about the Bible, I began to realize what had actually transpired as a result of my simple "sinner's prayer" at the altar in that little church in Arkansas. I wasn't saved by the prayer; I was saved by grace, through faith. (Ephesians 2:8, 9) I recall thinking as I learned more about it, "This is radical, man! This is heavy! This is far out!" If you are a "Baby Boomer," you do remember expressing yourself like that back then...don't you?

The point is this: the Christian experience is RADICAL, not RELIGIOUS! It is a personal RELATIONSHIP, not RELIGION! Aren't you glad Christianity is far more than dead religious works and irrelevant, ineffective, impersonal religious ritual and tradition? It is more than merely going to church, week in and week out, trying hard to avoid sin and trying our hardest to imitate Jesus. Christianity is having this radical, resurrected, eternally alive Jesus, the creator and sovereign sustainer of all things, making Himself one spirit with our spirit! It is about becoming a miraculously born again, reconnected new creation in the saving life of Jesus Christ! Thank God! Remember the quote by Major Ian Thomas:

> "Godliness is not the consequence of your capacity to imitate God, but the consequence of His capacity to reproduce Himself in you; not self-righteousness, but Christ-righteousness; the righteousness which is by faith." [5]

We are not called by God to live the Christian life, we are called to be Godly. Godliness (the expression of His life) produces the true Christian experience and practice thereof. That can only happen when we are surrendered to Him. Listen to what Jesus told a very religious man named Nicodemus:

> "There was a man of the Pharisees named Nicodemus, a ruler of the Jews. This man came to Jesus by night and said to Him, "Rabbi, we know that You are a teacher come from God; for no one can do these signs that You do unless God is with him." Jesus answered and said to him, "Most assuredly, I say to you, unless one is born again (plugged back into God's Cable Service), he cannot see the kingdom of

God." (In other words, receive God's Learning Network.) Nicodemus said to Him, "How can a man be born when he is old? Can he enter a second time into his mother's womb and be born?" Jesus answered, "Most assuredly, I say to you, unless one is born of water and the Spirit, he cannot enter the kingdom of God (experience God's realm). That which is born of the flesh is flesh (natural), and that which is born of the Spirit is spirit (supernatural). Do not marvel that I said to you, 'You must be born (plugged in) again.' The wind blows where it wishes, and you hear the sound of it, but cannot tell where it comes from and where it goes. So is everyone who is born of (re-connected to) the Spirit." (John 3:1-8)

According to Jesus, there are two kinds of births: a birth by water and a birth of the Spirit. What does this mean? I believe the answer is found in the same passage. To be born of water is to be born of the flesh, *"That which is born of the flesh is flesh (natural),"* and, obviously, to be born of the Spirit is to be born of God's Spirit.

Sweet Tea & Sinners

Many Christians believe that Jesus forgives their sins and comes into their hearts to add just enough sweetener to them to get them into heaven someday. Until that day comes, they are merely "Sinners, saved by grace," doing the best they can until Jesus comes back. Genuine Christianity is infinitely better than that!

Half of my family members are full-blooded Chippewa Indians from Wisconsin. The rest are full-blooded Hillbillies from Arkansas. I guess you could say that makes me a "Redneck-Redskin!" I know from my redneck side of the family that, in most instances, if you dine in a restaurant in the southern United States, and you do not ask for unsweetened tea, the waitress will probably bring you "Sweet Tea." It's just a southern preference.

Conversely, if you ask for sweet tea in the northern part of the country the waitresses will tell you, "The sugar and artificial sweeteners are on the table." I always have to explain to them that simply adding sugar to iced tea does not make it "Sweet Tea."

Have you ever added sugar to iced tea? After pouring out a little packet of sugar into your glass and stirring it vigorously, you notice that not all of the sugar granules dissolve; you can still see stubborn, tiny sugar granules swirling around in your glass! After a quick sip, you realize that your iced tea still is not sweet enough. At this point, you proceed to pour in several more packets of sugar and stir your tea even more vigorously, but it soon becomes obvious that sugar just does not dissolve in cold water very well. After finishing your iced tea, you notice that there is still about a half-inch of sugar in the bottom of your glass. The three different elements: water, tea and sugar never do quite become one substance.

My redneck roots have taught me to know the difference. In order to make genuine "Sweet Tea," you have to add the sugar to the hot water while the tea is brewing. In that hot water, the sugar dissolves quickly and becomes one substance with both the water and the tea. In the same way, when Jesus comes into our hearts through the new birth, God pours His sweet Holy Spirit into our spirit. As a result, we become one substance with Him. We never refer to Sweet Tea as water with tea and sugar added. We simply call it what it has become—Sweet Tea!

Why then, would we refer to someone who has become "one spirit with Him," as a sinner, saved by grace? As a result of the new birth, we become eternally re-connected with God's Spirit. We do not have two natures; we have one eternally new nature. Of course, the flesh is still present with us, but that is not our nature. Placing our faith in Jesus makes us more than merely Sinners with a dose of sweetener added. We are one substance, "Sweet Tea" in the Lord and He enjoys our new flavor!

> "...he who is joined to the Lord is one spirit with Him." (1 Corinthians 6:17)

Isn't this what Jesus prayed for in the Garden of Gethsemane the night before His crucifixion?

> "I do not pray for these alone, but also for those who will believe in Me through their word; that they all may be one, as You, Father, *are* in Me, and I in You; that they also may be one in Us, that the world may believe that You sent Me. And the glory which You gave Me I have given them, that they may be one <u>just as We are one</u>: <u>I in them</u>, and <u>You in Me</u>; that they may be made perfect in one, and that the world may know that You have sent Me, and have loved them as You have loved Me.
> (John 17:20-23)

Only God can work this kind of glorious miracle! We can't receive it by joining a certain church or denomination. We don't receive it because we do something or sacrifice something for God. No pastor, priest, minister, or family member can do it for us. It doesn't matter what country we live in or what race or color we are. God is no respecter of persons. (Romans 2:12) He isn't impressed with our human accomplishments or our earthly status. The Bible says:

> "For WHOEVER CALLS ON THE NAME OF THE LORD SHALL BE SAVED." (Romans 10:13)

I may not be properly informed or educated, but to me, it seems clear that WHOSOEVER would include ANYONE who is willing to accept and follow Jesus as their Lord and Savior. What in the world did the disciples of Jesus do before Greek and Hebrew scholars in Theological Seminaries were present to explain to them just what Jesus meant??? The Apostle, Paul described the new birth like this:

> "...not by works of righteousness which we have done, but according to His mercy He saved us, through the washing of regeneration and renewing of the Holy Spirit, whom He poured out on us abundantly through Jesus Christ our Savior." (Titus 3:5, 6)

In order to be born again, we must come in humble, child-like faith to Jesus. Unfortunately, due to human pride, this is more difficult for some than it sounds.

Two reasons we struggle with this are: First, we all hate to admit that we are sinners, don't we? We all realize that we have committed sin, but we can think of a multitude of others who are worse sinners than we are. However, notice in the beginning of the verse above: we are not saved by our works; we are saved by God's mercy and by regeneration and renewing of the Holy Spirit. Thankfully, God doesn't judge us on the basis of how we compare to others. Secondly, before we are born again, our sinful, fallen nature causes us to make ourselves the little god of our lives. The truth is, there is only room for one lord in our lives and it is not us!

Those who have trusted in Jesus are saved by "the washing of regeneration." What does this mean, and how does it happen? It occurs by God's renewing of our spirit with His Spirit, whom He pours out on us abundantly through Jesus Christ. First, the entrance of God's Holy Spirit into our spirit makes us spiritually *one with His Holiness*. Can there be any form of cleansing that makes us any cleaner than this holy cleansing? Secondly, this reunion of spirit changes our nature and makes us completely new creations.

> "Therefore, if anyone is in Christ, he is a new creation; <u>old things have passed away</u>; behold, <u>all things have become new</u>. Now <u>all things are of God</u>, who has reconciled us to Himself through Jesus Christ..." (2 Corinthians 5:17-18a)

There is not another creature in all of God's creation like a new creation in Christ! Infused with His holy nature, God changes us and changes the direction of our lives forever. For the first time, we genuinely want to please Him, even if it means denying ourselves.

Like a caterpillar that has gone through metamorphosis and has been transformed into a butterfly, we enter into the tomb (cocoon) with Christ, and come out completely recreated (spiritually resurrected). That doesn't mean that we cannot revert back to living like a worm, but as new creations in Christ, we are equipped to live life above and beyond our old wormy ways. Why in the world would we want to crawl when we can fly?

Being the Jew that he was, Nicodemus believed that the way to God was through his own righteous works. He didn't realize this truth:

> But we are all like an unclean thing, And all our righteousnesses are like filthy rags; We all fade as a leaf, And our iniquities (sins), like the wind, Have taken us away. (Isaiah 64:6)

On his best day, Nicodemus' righteousness was a stench in God's nostrils (figuratively speaking). As devoted as he was, he could not comprehend being "born again." He was a teacher of the Jews, but he didn't understand this truth. Likewise, in God's estimation, our best Christian day falls far short of His glory!

There are many preachers, even today, who are like Nicodemus. Unfortunately, many of those who sit under their teaching and preaching hear that in order to become a "good Christian" they must imitate what they learn about Jesus; they must join that denomination and must be baptized in water for the remission of their sins. Many of these teachers seem reluctant to teach about the new birth, if they even teach it at all. To be sure, the born again experience was, and still is, a great mystery. Nevertheless, in order for our very nature to be changed; we must experience a second birth from God. Jesus said that without this new birth, we can neither see, nor enter into His Kingdom realm. (John 3:3, 5)

Before being "born from above," the apostle, Paul was a Pharisee and thought the same way that Nicodemus did. He hated this new group of Jesus followers called, "Christians," and was dedicated to wiping them from the face of the earth. In his religiosity, he actually thought he was serving God by putting these new believers in Jesus to death. He also believed that his works of righteousness were his ticket into the Kingdom of God. After meeting Jesus, face to face on the road to Damascus, Paul came to realize the truth that none of the Jews understood:

> For they being ignorant of God's righteousness, and seeking to establish their own righteousness, have not submitted to the righteousness of God.
> (Romans 10:3)

Apparently, there are two kinds of righteousness. There is *the righteousness of the Law*, based on religious works. Then, there is *the true righteousness of God*. Paul says that this second kind of righteousness is received by faith:

> For with the heart one believes unto righteousness, and with the mouth confession is made unto salvation. (Romans 10:10)

He was willing to turn his back on everything he believed about his Jewish religion in order to find this true righteousness/life:

> "...though I also might have confidence in the flesh. If anyone else thinks he may have confidence in the flesh, I more so: circumcised the eighth day, of the stock of Israel, of the tribe of Benjamin, a Hebrew of the Hebrews; concerning the law, a Pharisee; concerning zeal, persecuting the church; concerning the righteousness which is in the law, blameless. But what things were gain to me, these I have counted loss for Christ. Yet indeed I also count all things loss for the excellence of the knowledge of Christ Jesus my Lord, for whom I have suffered the loss of all things, and count them as rubbish, that I may gain Christ and be found in Him, not having my own righteousness, which is from the law, but that which is through faith in Christ, the righteousness which is from God by faith; that I may know Him and the power of His resurrection, and the fellowship of His sufferings, being..." (Philippians 3:4-10)

Let me ask those of us who consider ourselves to be: Baptists of the Baptists; Methodists of the Methodists; Lutherans of the Lutherans, even the Pentecostals of the Pentecostals, etc. etc. Would we be willing to completely abandon ourselves and our traditional religious persuasions in order to experience the power of His resurrection in our Christianity and find ourselves solely in Him? I have, and my hope is that my brothers in Christ would be willing to do the same. Simply dyed in the blood, not in the wool!

Don't get me wrong, I am proud to be ordained by the denomination that ordained me. Their recognition and acknowledgment of God's calling on my life is important to me. However, my first allegiance will always be to Christ and Christ alone. I understand that it is hard to be unbiased about the religious traditions that we might be accustomed to. For some, it is all they know. However, if those within my particular denomination were to change their stance on the essential doctrines of the faith concerning Jesus, adherence to the truth would force me to abandon it and follow Him!

Like Nicodemus, initially, I had a hard time understanding what it meant to be born again. In fact, I did not understand anything about Christianity the night I accepted Jesus into my heart. I did not know what the Bible taught about anything! I did not even know what doctrine was; but the truth is doctrine is not what saves us! Thank God, we don't have to understand all of the doctrines of the Bible in order to be saved. All it takes to be saved is child-like faith in Jesus. Doctrine is simply a framework of biblical truths and principles that enables us to understand what God wants us to know in order for us to live out the new life that He gives to us.

One of the sure signs that we have genuinely had this born again experience is that we begin to see personal, inward changes in our lives; sinful habits and personality traits, that we know we never before had the ability to change begin to peel away like the layers of an onion as we learn more about our saving life, Jesus. We begin to get brutally honest with ourselves and God about everything.

By the time I was saved at the age of 21, like so many others, I had picked up a few bad habits: smoking, chewing and drinking alcohol, and unfortunately, offensive language. To be quite candid, unlike a former President of ours, whose name I won't mention, I even inhaled a few times in the '60s! I loved my beer, but Jesus had entered into my life and I was learning to love Him too. No doubt about it, even as a new creation, I was raw material in

God's hands with no knowledge of truth except that I was forgiven for my sins. His forgiveness, at least what I knew about it at the time, had lifted a huge weight from my shoulders, but I was still ignorant about much of what the Bible was to teach me.

Like Homer, I worked in construction, and my life was much like his. The crew that I worked with back in the early 1970s was your typical construction crew. We worked hard, liked to cut up and clown around, and we all enjoyed our so-called "adult beverages." We had also developed an end-of-the-week tradition.

Each Friday, during our afternoon break, one of the guys would take orders for beer and each laborer's liquor of choice and head to the liquor store. When quitting-time came at 4:30 PM, we'd all sit around on the job site cutting up and sharing not-so-clean jokes and stories until the beer and liquor was gone, then most of us would go home to our families. I had this new relationship with Jesus, but I still had my old habits and, at least initially, was enjoying them both.

As we were enjoying one another's company one Friday evening, one of the three brothers who labored for us spoke up, "Hey Pete, I heard that you got Jesus in your life while you were on your deer hunting trip in Arkansas." With a dip in my lip, a smoke between my fingers, and a beer in my calloused hand, I proudly replied, "Yep, I sure did! I got borned (sic) again! I don't know too much about it yet, but my life is completely different now!" "Ha, Ha, Ha! Really?! Borned again, huh? You don't look or sound any different than us! Ha, Ha, Ha!" they bellowed at my response. I was speechless. Their raucous response caught me off guard, and I felt embarrassed. I knew in my heart that they were right.

I had joined a large church in Kansas City, Missouri and had been baptized after my salvation experience, but I guess it had never occurred to me that what I said and did on the outside needed to reflect what God had done to me on the inside. I became aware that those around me were paying close attention to my behavior and were waiting to see if my new life was real or not. I find it rather ironic that those who are "lost" are, many times, just as judgmental, if not more so, as some of those who are "found" when it comes to what is considered to be true holiness.

I was enjoying my new relationship with God and was learning more and more about Him each week, but there was much, much more that I needed to learn about living for Him. I sincerely wanted others, especially my family and friends, to know Him too. For the first time in my life, it mattered to me what would happen to these co-workers if they had to stand before God unsaved. Shouldn't a real friend care if their friends were going to spend eternity in heaven, or not? Wouldn't a family member want to do everything they could to assure that all of their family members could spend eternity together, with them and with God? Of course...yet, sadly, I soon discovered that not all of my friends and family members were willing to accept what I had to say about Jesus.

That night, on my drive home from work, God's Spirit spoke to my heart through a thought, "I was saved because Jesus loves me, but as long as I continue to live like those I want to see saved, they will never listen to what I have to say about God." Most of the time, God speaks to us in the first person...like we are thinking to ourselves. It makes sense that God would speak primarily to us through our own heart, especially when He indwells our heart. He is able, and does, speak to us in many ways, but if He is present within our hearts, he doesn't necessarily have to find an outside medium through which to communicate to us. Regardless, when I heard His inner voice, I had to decide at that moment what was more important to me, my right to enjoy my old habits or sharing my new salvation with others in a way that would influence them to come to Him.

It has been said, "Smoking and drinking won't send you to hell, but it will certainly make you smell and look like you just came from there!" True, but actually, it isn't the things we do that send us to hell. We are already condemned by unbelief. It is what we don't do that sends us there. God did not create Hell for human beings but for the devil and his angels.

> "Then He will also say to those on the left hand, 'Depart from Me, you cursed, into the everlasting fire <u>prepared for the devil and his angels</u>..."
> (Matthew 25:41)

God does not want anyone to spend eternity separated from Him in hell.

> The Lord is not slack concerning *His* promise, as some count slackness, but is longsuffering toward us, <u>not willing that any should perish</u> but that <u>all should come to repentance</u>. (2 Peter 3:9)

When we refuse to receive Jesus Christ, we forfeit our only hope for salvation and eternal life and condemn ourselves to an eternity separated from Him. Not only that, but we turn down God's offer of an abundant life here on earth! Why would anyone make this choice? It would be like a terminal cancer patient refusing a newly discovered cure for their disease. Why would anyone refuse a cure for suffering and death? The only reason I can think of is that they are spiritually blind to the truth. Only God can cure that blindness. What He told the nation of Israel in the Old Testament still applies to us today.

> I call heaven and earth as witnesses today against you, *that* I have set before you life and death, blessing and cursing; therefore choose life, that both you and your descendants may live; that you may love the LORD your God, that you may obey His voice,

> and that you may cling to Him, for He *is* your life
> and the length of your days; (Deuteronomy 30:19, 20)

I don't know about you, but I choose life! I began to ask God to do for me what I was unable to do for myself—change my heart and my desire for my old vices. I asked Him to make the outward changes in my life so people would take me more seriously. I can't take credit for the ability to quit any of those old habits. God alone inspired it and empowered it, but when we hear His voice, it is up to us to respond with a "Yes, Lord." God then begins to change the direction and quality of our life as He begins to change our character and what we value the most. He brings to us a new perspective, a new pursuit, and a new passion that changes what we chase, because he has changed us on the inside! When our goal is to *become like Jesus*, rather than simply *act like Jesus*, gradually being like Him becomes our undeniable witness that He is real.

Eventually, God did take away my desire for smoking and drinking and set me free from those old habits. That does not mean that I don't have to be on guard against the flesh or that I am perfect in my performance, but I am gaining ground. My old working buddies didn't necessarily believe in Jesus because of that, but they could never accuse me of living like them again. When we all stand before God someday, they won't be able to point a finger at me and blame me for their refusal to accept eternal life in Christ. It's ironic…when I quit living like them; they accused me of thinking that I was better than them! Man, you just can't win…can you?!

We are indwelled by a loving, guiding, empowering God who has become our new Father. We are never alone because He is *with us* and *within us*, now and for eternity in the person of His Holy Spirit.

> And I will pray the Father, and He will give you another Helper, that He may abide with you forever—

the Spirit of truth, whom the world cannot receive, because it neither sees Him nor knows Him; but you know Him, for He dwells with you and will be in you. (John 14:16, 17)

However, when He, the Spirit of truth, has come, He will guide you into all truth; for He will not speak on His own *authority,* but whatever He hears He will speak; and He will tell you things to come. (John 16:13)

Jesus made these promises to His disciples before His crucifixion. They would not grasp the significance of that reality until they were all filled with His Spirit on the day of Pentecost and the "Spirit of Truth" He promised was literally "in them". The lyrics of the following song came out of my realization of these truths...

"I Know You're Here."

When it feels like I'm losin' my grip,
The bottom's droppin' out of my life;
I feel myself startin' to slip,
I've barely got a hold on my mind.
When there's no one that I can run to
With my doubts and my fears,
That's when I look into my heart
For rest 'cause I know you're here.

I know you're here inside of me.
You're just as near as I want you to be.
When I need to hear you speakin' to me,
I know that you're here, inside my heart, and you'll always be.

When I've lost my spiritual sight, life puts me on my knees,

My spirit yearns for your light, the truth that will set me free.
I've learned I don't have far to run to, your Word makes it clear,
I know I can look in my heart for peace and I know you're here.

I know that I'm never alone; your Spirit abides in me.
You've made my heart your home,
And promised you'll never leave.

I know you're here inside of me.
You're just as near as I want you to be.
When I need to hear you speakin' to me,
I know that you're here, inside my heart, and you'll always be.

To be regenerated means to be re-infused with the Spirit of Christ. In Christ, we have been spiritually raised from the dead with His life in us (not resuscitated with our old life). Our old nature was put to death on the cross with Christ, and we were raised from the dead *in Him* to walk *with Him* in the newness of His life.

> Therefore we were buried with Him through baptism into death, that just as Christ was raised from the dead by the glory of the Father, even so we also should walk in newness of life. (Romans 6:4)

We will never be the same again, and we will never be alone again because we have been radically reconnected to our eternal life, Jesus Christ! That's heavenly, man!

Too Good to be True

But it is! Forgiven Forever!

Colossians 1:13, 14

He has delivered us from the power of darkness and conveyed us into the kingdom of the Son of His love, in whom we have redemption through His blood, the forgiveness of sins.

Have you ever had someone come up to you and say: "Boy, have I got good news for you! In fact, it is just too good to be true! You are not going to believe it!" I don't know about you, but I love it when that happens! At that point, they have my complete and undivided attention! I can't wait to hear about it because I know that I am about to have my socks blessed off! In the Bible, God has recorded and preserved for us a Gospel (Good News) message that is just too good to be true, but it is true! I have been sharing it with you already. But, wait! There's more! I can't wait to tell you about it, and I hope that by this point, you can't wait to hear it!

Expunged?

As a result of living out the "Prodigal Life," (Luke 15:11-32) as a backslidden Christian, I had been convicted of two DUIs (Driving Under the Influence). The word, "prodigal" means to be recklessly wasteful. After much heartache and struggle, I returned home to my Heavenly Father's house, (church) and like the wandering son in the Bible story, my Father cleaned me up and restored me to full family status like nothing had ever happened.

I had joined a church; married my current wife of more than 30 years, and we had become very active in church. Of course, I understand all too well that, although God is forgiving and gracious, sin leaves a mark on our lives. Most of the time, we still have to deal with the consequences of our sins. As a result of my wayward lifestyle, I still had to visit my probation officer once a month for about a year, even though I was forgiven, restored and serving the Lord in church. As far as the court was concerned, I was still a convicted law-breaker.

When my probation period was over, my probation officer informed me: "Peter, I have some very good news for you. Because of the remarkable turnaround in your life over the past year and the fact that you have been able to overcome your drinking problem, the Court is going to expunge your record." With a surprised, and puzzled, look on my face I replied, "That's great! Uh...what does expunge mean?" She smiled and said, "To expunge means to erase, to wipe the slate clean. Once your record is expunged, you will no longer have a record. It will be as if you had never broken the law!

That was too good to be true great news! Not only was the Court willing to forgive me for my offenses because my debt to the law had been paid, they were willing to wipe the slate clean! I didn't have to worry about my bad record anymore, it was gone! It would no longer be a factor with the cost of my car insurance or employment opportunities. That is exactly what God has done for us concerning our sin record! We have a clean slate! It is as if we had never sinned!

The only reason He can offer this amazing "too good to be true" clean start to us is because His only begotten son, Jesus Christ, has forever paid our sin debt through His blood sacrifice on the cross! It is finished! (John 19:30) He has "expunged" our sin record.

> And you, being dead in your trespasses and the uncircumcision of your flesh, He has made alive together with Him, having forgiven you all trespasses, having wiped out the handwriting of requirements that was against us, which was contrary to us. And He has taken it out of the way, having nailed it to the cross. (Colossians 2:13, 14)

Please notice, Paul is speaking in the past tense. This is already an accomplished fact. Our sin is no longer a barrier between us and a holy God. We are free to know Him and to have a relationship with Him. That's right, true Christianity is not about religion; it is a relationship with God. We no longer have to live meaningless, purposeless, directionless, hopeless, empty lives here on earth. We don't have to figure it out and work it all out on our own. We can know Him by entering into an eternal personal relationship with Him, a relationship where we don't have to walk on eggshells, constantly worrying about whether He is angry and fed up with us. God offers all of this to us freely! Well, it is free to us, but it cost Him dearly. It cost Him the life blood of His only begotten Son, Jesus.

> For when we were still without strength, in due time Christ died for the ungodly. For scarcely for a righteous man will one die; yet perhaps for a good man someone would even dare to die. But God demonstrates His own love toward us, in that while we were still sinners, Christ died for us. (Romans 5:6-8)

It takes a supreme quality of love to cause someone to offer the life of their offspring for someone else. Let me ask you a question. If God came to you as you were laying your head on your pillow in bed and said, "At 6:00 AM tomorrow morning, I am going to take your life so that someone in your church can live;" some of us might at least be willing to pray about it. No doubt, this level of sacrifice would move us well beyond the realm of percentages, such as ten percent! " Greater love has no one than this, than to lay down one's life for his friends." (John 15:13)

Suppose God said, "At 6:00 AM, I am going to take your life so that one of your children or grandchildren can live." Well, I don't know about you, but my love for my children and grandchildren has always cost me far more than ten percent. I would not even have to pray about this sacrifice. It would be an automatic, "Yes, Lord." When it comes to sacrificing for our family we certainly don't think in terms of percentages, do we?

However, let's suppose that God said, "First thing in the morning, I am going to take the life of your child or grandchild so that the worst of sinners can have life." What?! I could never make that sacrifice; not for the best of people, much less, for the worst of sinners. Incomprehensible! Yet, that is exactly what God did for you and me...and for the worst of sinners for all time! I really do not know how He did it. It boggles the mind!

This kind of brings the sacrifice of Jesus down to where we live, doesn't it? This is amazing love and grace! God's willingness to sacrifice that much for you and me is the only hope we had for complete forgiveness. He would not make so great a sacrifice unless it was going to be complete and last forever! The price tag for you and me was more than any man could pay, but it was not too high a price for God to pay and He did so completely.

Forgiven, but...

Until we understand God's complete forgiveness of our sins, we can never truly forgive ourselves. When this is the case, though we have been set free, we will walk around feeling guilty and the devil will certainly see to it that we are put back into emotional bondage. When we are unable to forgive ourselves, it is almost impossible to completely forgive those who have sinned against us. After all, why should we cut anyone else any slack when we can't cut ourselves any slack?

Whether we realize it or not, each of us carries a debt sheet in our hearts, both for our own transgressions and the transgressions of others against us. It is a personal set of ordinances (boundaries) that people have violated by hurting us or letting us down in one manner or another. As a result, we all have a "crimes against us" record upon which we keep track of their infractions. Like a "rap sheet," every time they violate us, we add the new offenses to their record. After a while, their offenses accrue to the point that we just quit associating with them.

We keep that sheet in our heart and mind, sometimes even after they have apologized and asked for forgiveness. We never quite forget it. Even when we are willing to forgive them for their past offenses, we are ever on guard and ready to take note of any offense that they might commit in the future. When they violate us again, we simply add their new offenses to their not-quite-forgiven rap sheet. Consequently, if they are fortunate enough to have actually been forgiven by us, our future forgiveness is subject to their continued behavior. Human forgiveness almost always has conditions attached to it. Are they willing to ask for forgiveness? Are they willing to cease offending us? That is how human forgiveness works.

Is this really the way that God's forgiveness works? Many Christians, and even many teachers and preachers of the Word of

God believe that it is! They believe that our past sins are forgiven but forgiveness for the sins that we commit after we are saved is based upon our willingness to ask for it. If Jesus has not paid for ALL of our sins, this would be true. What is the basis of our forgiveness from God? The blood of Jesus. How many times did He shed His precious blood to purchase our redemption? One time. Will it ever have to be repeated? Of course not, it is finished!

As forgiven, born again children of God, what if we forget to ask for forgiveness after we commit a sin or we die before we have the chance to ask for it? Can we go to heaven with unforgiven sin? Does God turn His back on us and have nothing to do with us until we ask for forgiveness? How could that be? I've actually had some preachers answer this question with: "Tough luck, buddy, you should have 'fessed up and repented while you had the chance. It's too late once you die with unforgiven sin on you record. You are going to split hell wide open!" Really?!

If God forgave only part of our sin on the cross, which part is left unforgiven? I believe that the blood of Jesus was powerful enough to pay for ALL of our sins: past, present, and yes, even future sins; even if we forget, or never get the chance, to ask for forgiveness for the sins we commit subsequent to our initial salvation experience.

God knows our heart and has always known everything about us. He knew every sin of every man for all time when He sent His Son, Jesus to the cross to pay for them. In His omniscience, (His ability to see and know all things at the same time) He saw ahead of time, all of our days and all of our sins. (Psalms 139:15, 16) Are we to believe that God's forgiveness is not big enough and that the blood of Jesus is not powerful enough and Jesus' sacrifice is not complete enough to pay for it all? Incredibly, some would say "No!"

Did His sacrifice pay for our past sins, but we can mark the black board up again with our sins after we're saved? Must we ask for forgiveness each time we sin in order to have it forgiven and erased again? Personally, I believe He not only erased ALL of our sins with the blood of His Son, but that He took the black board completely out of the way. There is no board to write our sins on. It is gone forever! Let's take another look at Colossians 2:13, 14.

> And you, being dead in your trespasses and the uncircumcision of your flesh, He has made alive together with Him, <u>having forgiven you *all* trespasses</u>, having wiped out the handwriting of requirements that was against us, which was contrary to us. And <u>He has taken it out of the way, having nailed it to the cross</u>. (Colossians 2:13, 14)

When we read these verses carefully, it becomes apparent that ALL of our sins have been forgiven (past tense) and God has torn up our debt sheet. If this is true, we are free! This is why He is able to empower us to forgive the way that He does. Is it really accurate for us to assume that only our past sins were recorded on this debt sheet that was against us, taken out of the way and nailed to His cross? Let me ask you a question. When Jesus died for our sins, at that time, how much of the sins that we would commit in our lifetime were future sins? The answer is obvious…ALL of them! I believe that Jesus died, not merely for our personal *individual sins,* but for our *collective sin.* That is the power and greatness of His love and mercy, not merely for us, but in us!

Understanding that God has torn our debt sheet up and removed it forever, helps us to do the same for those who have sinned against us. Until we are willing to tear up every debt sheet for those who have hurt and offended us, though God has completely forgiven us, we can never truly experience the peace that comes along with that forgiveness. However, when we do forgive others, we discover that setting them free actually helps to set us free from the bondage of guilt.

As this principle began to become a reality in my life, I was able to truly be set free from the hurts and disappointments of the past. Today, I can honestly say, "Nobody owes me anything, not even an apology. I hold no grudges or debt sheets against anyone. If they have hurt me or disappointed me, they are forgiven, whether they ever ask for it or not." Forgiveness is an attitude of Agape, (God's supernatural, grace/love) not a product of our own goodness. That is the only way I can explain it. I never had that ability or peace before Jesus was in my life.

Take a moment and look into your heart. Are there people in your life, a father, a mother, a sister or brother, a friend or co-worker, or someone else who has hurt you, failed you, or let you down? Do you still use their offenses as an excuse for how you or your life turned out? Do you still harbor resentment and bitterness in your heart for something they did to you or didn't do for you? Believe me, that attitude will eat away at your heart and you will never truly be free emotionally until you tear their debt sheet up and ask God to help you forgive even the offenses that they have not committed against you before they commit them.

This kind of forgiveness may be humanly impossible for us, but that is precisely why God's Holy Spirit indwells us—to do the humanly impossible in and through us, to manifest His loving holiness in us. If you are willing to ask Him to help you to forgive every offense, yes, even the ones that have not been committed against you yet, I guarantee you, He will set you free with a peace you have never known. That is the power of God's amazing grace and love *in us* and *through us*. It is one thing for us to experience God's love *for us*; it is entirely another to experience His love *in us*!

As I have traveled across the United States with my music ministry for more than a decade, I have asked this critical question in churches of just about every denomination: "When Jesus died on the cross for your sins and mine nearly two thousand years ago, how much of our sin did His blood pay for?" Amazingly, in every church, the congregations have always responded, "All of it!" Incredible! Every time, in every church, they get the answer right! Their systematic theology may not allow them to live it out, but intuitively, they know the correct answer to the question. If all of our sins were not paid for by His blood, can someone tell me which ones were and which ones were not? When Jesus uttered these three dying words from the cross, "It is finished," what did He mean? I believe He meant exactly what He said! It is over! He has completed what the Father gave Him to do. No more sacrifices for sin!

Déjà vu all over again!

Lawrence Peter "Yogi" Berra, Hall of fame Major League Baseball catcher, outfielder, and manager, best remembered for his 19-year career as a New York Yankee, was also famous for his "Yogi-isms." Commenting on baseball, he once said: "90 percent of the game is half mental." Priceless! Probably two quips he was best known for were: "It's Déjà vu all over again," and "It ain't over till it's over." We have all experienced our "Déjà vu" moments. The term literally means "already seen." It is that eerie feeling that we have already seen, heard or experienced a current situation sometime in the past, either in a dream or an actual experience.

While listening to a politician speak, one Texas cowboy leaned over to another cowboy and whispered, "I ain't sure, pardner, but I believe I just had a Déjà moo." When the other cowboy asked what he meant by his comment, the first cowboy removed the piece of straw that he had been chewing on from his lips, spit a brown stream of chew into the dust, squinted, and in his best Clint Eastwood impersonation, responded, "I don't know, but I think I've heard this bull before."

Is it really "Déjà vu" all over again," when it comes to God's forgiveness of our sins? I don't think so. I believe the sin issue is over when Jesus says "It is finished!" If it isn't, what do we have left to finish it with, another sacrifice of one sort or another, another cross, another Lamb, another confession? There isn't anything left to offer, and we don't have to repeatedly revisit the cross, but simply reckon it finished.

> For *the death* that He died, <u>He died to sin once for all</u>; but *the life* that He lives, He lives to God. Likewise you also, reckon yourselves to be <u>dead indeed to sin</u>, but <u>alive to God in Christ Jesus</u> our Lord. Therefore do not let sin reign in your mortal body, that you should obey it in its lusts. And do not present your members *as* instruments of unrighteousness to sin, but present yourselves to God as being <u>alive from the dead</u>, and your members *as* instruments of righteousness to God. For <u>sin shall not have dominion over you</u>, for <u>you are not under law but under grace</u>. (Romans 6:10-14)

We are to reckon (count as true) that, like Jesus, we have died indeed to sin and been made alive to live unto God. The reason sin no longer has dominion over us is because we are not under law but under the grace of God's complete and unconditional forgiveness! Not only was the Old Covenant (God's old agreement/promise of how He would deal with man's sin under the law) fulfilled by Jesus' sinless life and atoning death, but His blood sacrifice for all of the sins of all men, for all time is complete and final. Romans 6:23 says, *"For the wages of sin is death..."* Someone had to pay that penalty, either us or Jesus. We don't have to pay today because He did, completely, 2,000 years ago! It is over! Peter puts it this way:

> "For Christ also suffered <u>once</u> for sins, the just (Jesus) for the unjust, (you and me) that He might bring

us to God, being put to death in the flesh but made alive by the Spirit..." (1 Peter 3:18)

The refrain from the old hymn, "Jesus Paid It All," states it well:

> Jesus paid it all, All to Him I owe;
> Sin had left a crimson stain, He washed it white as snow.

His blood paid for, and took away, our sins so that we might be brought into a personal relationship with God!

> "And according to the law almost all things are purified with blood, and without shedding of blood there is no remission." (Hebrews 9:22)

Remission means to be paid for, taken away, and forgiven. The sacrifice of Jesus has accomplished this once, and for all! Let's look at these amazing statements in Hebrews, chapter 10:

> "By that (His sacrifice) will we have been sanctified (distinctively set apart) through the offering of the body of Jesus Christ <u>once for all</u>. And every priest stands ministering daily and offering repeatedly the same sacrifices, which can never take away sins. But this Man (Jesus), after He had offered <u>one sacrifice for sins forever</u>, sat down at the right hand of God, from that time waiting till His enemies are made His footstool. For <u>by one offering</u> He has perfected forever those who are being sanctified. But the Holy Spirit also witnesses to us; for after He had said before, "THIS IS THE COVENANT THAT I WILL MAKE WITH THEM AFTER THOSE DAYS, SAYS THE LORD: I WILL PUT MY LAWS INTO THEIR HEARTS, AND IN THEIR MINDS I WILL

WRITE THEM," then He adds, "THEIR SINS AND THEIR LAWLESS DEEDS I WILL REMEMBER NO MORE." Now where there is remission of these, <u>there is no longer</u> an offering for sin. Therefore, brethren, having boldness to enter the Holiest by the blood of Jesus, <u>by a new and living way</u> which He consecrated for us, through the veil, that is, His flesh, and having a High Priest over the house of God, let us draw near with a true heart in full assurance of faith, having our hearts sprinkled from an evil conscience and our bodies washed with pure water." (Hebrews 10:10-22)

Not only has our sin been forgiven and removed forever, but the blood of Christ has cleansed us forever! Paul shared this truth in the book of Ephesians:

"In Him we have redemption through His blood, the forgiveness of sins, according to the riches of His grace..." (Ephesians 1:7)

How rich is God's grace? Rich enough to pay for and forgive ALL of our sins forever! Like an old southern preacher stated with a southern drawl: "Awll means Awll, and that is Awll, Awll means!"

Notice in the Hebrew passage above, Jesus offered up His body for <u>all</u> of the sins of <u>all</u> men ONE TIME for ALL TIME. His sacrifice for sin is not going to be repeated again. God does not have a "reserve cross" in the back room of heaven that He must bring out each time we sin. There is not a "reserve lamb" in a pen somewhere for willful sin emergencies. There is never going to be another sacrifice offered for the sins of men. Jesus finished it!

This was not the case under the Old Covenant prior to the cross. Under that covenant, each sacrifice paid only for the past sins of the individual who brought their sacrifice in that particular instance. As soon as the offering was made, they would leave the altar and immediately they were back under guilt and condemnation for another year until they could bring another sacrifice to the priest. They would live in fear until that next sacrifice was offered up. According to the way some define God's forgiveness of sin, if they were unable to bring a sacrifice for each sin they committed, as they were committed, they would surely "split hell wide open." That is not the case with the sacrifice of "God's Lamb" offered up once, for all, under the new covenant. Look at what John the Baptist stated as Jesus approached him one day:

> "The next day John saw Jesus coming toward him, and said, "Behold! The Lamb of God who takes away the sin of the world!" (John 1:29)

What God wants us to understand is that Jesus Himself is our advocate because He Himself was, and eternally is, the means through which all of our sins were and are perpetually being remitted (taken away) forever.

That doesn't mean that we will never be tempted to sin or that, in our flesh, we are not capable of sinning after we are saved. It simply means that ALL of our sins have been paid for. You might be asking yourself, "Well, what if we do sin after we are forgiven...what then?" As we discussed before, that is a reasonable question. Let's take a look at what the Apostle, John says:

> "My little children, these things I write to you, so that you may not sin. And if anyone sins, we have an Advocate with the Father, Jesus Christ the righteous. And He Himself is the propitiation *(substitute/source of remittance, taking away of, satisfaction)* for our sins, and not for ours only but also for the whole world." (1 John 2:1, 2) (Italics mine)

Though God loves us infinitely, He cannot, and never would, violate His righteous justice. He can't just say, "Oh well, I will overlook your sin because I love you." His righteousness has to be satisfied. That is what "propitiation" means. The too good to be true good news is Christ's sacrificial death and shed blood has eternally satisfied God's righteousness in regard to our sin. God is not waiting day in and day out for us to add something to what Jesus has already accomplished on the cross. We could never add anything to it or take anything away from it by our actions, good or bad. But notice, Jesus Himself, is still the perpetual (on-going, uninterrupted by time) propitiation (satisfying substitute) for our sins today as our advocate (legal counsel) before the Holy Justice (God) in heaven.

His blood paid the entire sin debt we owed, (not only ours, but the whole world) which in turn, allowed God in His absolute justice, to completely forgive us! We are now totally debt free! When the infernal prosecuting attorney, Satan, stands before the holy judicial bench in heaven today, and every day, and accuses us before God, "Your Honor, it is clear that this so-called newly created Saint of yours has sinned again!" Jesus, our eternal defense attorney (advocate) steps up and replies, "Your Highest Honor, the defense objects! I have already paid for the accused in full, and I am the perpetual propitiation (substitutionary payment) for this one who has sinned yet again. The fine has already been paid for in advance." God responds: "I have acknowledged that payment, case closed! Mr. Prosecutor, you and your worthless accusations are dismissed back to your infernal chambers!"

I know, it's hard to resist the thought, "Yeah, but if you preach that, you are going to encourage forgiven Saints to go out and sin!" Really? Though I have been guilty of sin since I was saved, my life isn't driven by the desire to sin; it is driven by the nails and the love of Jesus! The following song lyrics came out of my understanding of this truth.

"Driven By The Nails"

Floatin' like a feather on the winds of time,
Flowin' in a river of the flesh and mind
Goin' crazy in this mixed up world of mine...existing.

Growin' disillusioned and devoid of truth,
Throwin' conscience to the wind, I've paid my dues
With nothin' much to show for all that I've pursued,
But, now I'm through resisting.

My heart is driven by the nails,
that pierced His hands, and held Him there
Forgiven by the nails, I'm driven by His sacrifice for me,
I'm driven by the nails.

Now, I'm floatin' like a feather on His holy wind,
Flowin' in the wellspring of my new best friend.
Knowin' He indwells me through life's thick and thin's a blessing.

Listenin' to His voice, now I can see the truth;
glistenin' like the morning sun upon the dew
Trustin' Him in every valley I walk through,
I'm in His truth and resting.

Forgiven for the sin that nailed Him to that rugged tree, I'm free
I'm driven by the nails and love that held Him there for me.

I'm driven by the nails that pierced His hands, and held Him there
Forgiven by the nails, I'm driven by His sacrifice for me;
I'm driven by the nails.

When I was saved and God imparted His nature to me and we became one in spirit (1 Corinthians 6:17), for the first time in my life, I noticed that I had a new conflict and discomfort with sin. My relationship with sin would never be the same. Sin was now an affront to me and bothered me intensely. In fact, I became aware of sins in my life that I had never before noticed or even considered to be sin. Like scattering cockroaches when a light is turned on, my daily sins became painfully more obvious and offensive to me. God's holy presence in my spirit had made me even more sensitive to sin...not merely outward offenses, but inward attitudes of the heart, as well.

I was sitting in my living room late one summer afternoon as the sun was setting low on the western horizon. The drapes were pulled closed except for a narrow gap through which a thin shaft of sunlight stretched across the semi-darkened room. To my utter amazement, I noticed something that was not visible until the lighting conditions in the room were just right. Looking into that golden ribbon of sunlight, I saw a multitude of tiny dust and fiber particles floating in the air. I had never noticed just how dirty the air in our living room was under normal electric lighting.

In the same way, when God's Son-light began to shine into my heart, I noticed sin in my inner living room that I had never before noticed. I felt convicted and I wanted Him to change my life in a way that would make Him proud of me. God hates sin because it always hurts us. It always robs, kills and destroys. (John 10:10) When I examine what sin has done in my life and the lives of those that I love, I hate it for the same reasons that God does.

Initially, I was confused about my new life. Even though I had a new love for God and the Bible and my new life in Jesus, and genuinely wanted to please my new Father; I realized that sin was still very active in my thoughts and actions. What I didn't understand at the time was that, although I was a new creation on the inside, my outside (flesh/body/old way of thinking), though paid for, is not going to be changed until Jesus comes back for me. When that time comes, in a moment, in the twinkling of an eye, my flesh is going to be changed forever. (1 Corinthians 15:52) Until then, I have to deal with it every day.

Let me explain. The flesh is more than just the body. When the Bible talks about the flesh, it also means our old frame of mind, the way we used to think, what it refers to as the "carnal mind." The carnal mind is never going to become obedient to God. It isn't even possible.

> Because the carnal mind is enmity against God; for it is not subject to the law of God, nor indeed can be. (Romans 8:7)

This verse really cleared up my understanding of why we, as believers, continue to struggle with sin. We may be new creations on the inside, but our outward man is, as of yet, unredeemed. That doesn't mean that Jesus hasn't paid for it yet; He has, but He hasn't come back yet to "pick us up." When He comes, instantly, our flesh will be changed and made incorruptible forever! Whew! What a relief that will be! No doubt about it; we are responsible for the actions of our flesh, even though God relates to us on the basis of our new identity in Jesus. We must be honest with ourselves, and with God, about our personal conduct.

Please, I hope you understand; Christianity is not about focusing on sin, it is about focusing on Jesus and our loving relationship with the Father. Nevertheless, when we truly begin to love Him and His word begins to illuminate our heart and mind, we will begin to recognize sin for what it really is and we will truly hate it, not love it.

I love the illustration in Bob George's book, *"Classic Christianity,"* [6] about a cafeteria owner who finds a homeless bum digging through the dumpster behind his business. Following is my version: The owner yanks the startled garbage pilferer out of the dumpster by the seat of his pants and asks, "What in the world are you doing in this dumpster? Get out of there! Don't eat that garbage!" Startled; the bum replies, "I'm sorry. I was just looking for something to eat. I figured that with a place this nice, you probably throw a lot of scraps in here that would be more than good enough for me to eat."

The buffet owner was touched and replied, "Listen, I own this buffet. It is the finest in town and from now on, whenever you feel hungry, you don't have to dig in this dumpster; you can come inside and eat all the food you want. It's all on me from now on."

He takes him into the restaurant and the starving man can hardly believe his eyes. He has never seen a spread like this in his life! The bum says, "You mean I can eat anything I want, anytime I want?" The owner replies: "Yes, anything, anytime!" After a moment, with a curious look on his face, the bum responds, "Does that mean that I can still eat out of the dumpster whenever I want to?" What?! Are you kidding me? That would be ridiculous, wouldn't it?

It is just as absurd to think that preaching God's amazing grace to folks who have received His absolute forgiveness would drive them away from the generosity of a loving heavenly Father, and make them want to take up a lifestyle of sin again. A truly born again, Holy Spirit indwelt Saint is not ever going to love sin again. Though I still commit sin, I hate it, and I'm drawn to Him by His amazing love and grace. This would not be true if we did not have a new, holy nature that is one with His holy nature. Though we can choose to walk (live according to) the flesh, instead of walking in the Spirit, our deepest desire is to live for God. Our goal is not to stop sinning, it is to become like the Jesus who saved us and has become our life.

Judge or Parent?

Think about this: As parents, what do we do when one of our children is disobedient? Do we disown them? God forbid! Do we ignore their disobedience? Of course not. Would we allow them to do whatever they want without correction and discipline? We wouldn't think of it! Why? Because we love them too much! God is no different in the way that He deals with His children. He doesn't disown us because of our disobedience; He loves us too much. He can't ignore it; He cares too much about our character. He has an agenda for our lives! Therefore, He deals with us as sons and disciplines us in love. Look at these words in Hebrews:

> And you have forgotten the exhortation which speaks to you as to sons: "MY SON, DO NOT DESPISE THE CHASTENING OF THE LORD, NOR BE DISCOURAGED WHEN YOU ARE REBUKED BY HIM; FOR WHOM THE LORD LOVES HE CHASTENS, AND SCOURGES EVERY SON WHOM HE RECEIVES." If you endure chastening, God deals with you as with sons; for what son is there whom a father does not chasten? But if you are without chastening, of which all have become partakers, then you are illegitimate and not sons. Furthermore, we have had human fathers who corrected *us,* and we paid *them* respect. Shall we not much more readily be in subjection to the Father of spirits and live? For they indeed for a few days chastened *us* as seemed *best* to them, but He for *our* profit, that *we* may be partakers of His holiness. Now no chastening seems to be joyful for the present, but painful; nevertheless, afterward it yields the peaceable fruit of righteousness to those who have been trained by it. (Hebrews 12:5-11)

You see, God isn't interested in merely changing our outward behavior, He is determined to shape our inward attitude into the "peaceable fruit of His righteousness." His goal is to train us up in the way that we should go. The "law" could not accomplish this before the new covenant and it still can't under the new covenant. But...His amazing parental love and grace can!

Think about this: as loving parents, when we discipline our children, we are not simply trying to change their bad behavior; we are trying to change the attitude that produces their bad behavior. Any discipline on our part that does not accomplish that objective is wasted effort. We must be aware of how our children are reacting to our discipline. If there is defiance in their crying or their voice after we have applied discipline, we are not finished with the discipline. Loving parental discipline always aims at the heart, not merely at the hind end. The goal in raising our kids should always be instruction and correction. That is the way that God disciplines His children. I promise you, God is always aware of our attitude and response to His discipline in our lives! He is not simply trying to change our bad behavior. He will always continue to apply the heat until our attitude changes.

Grace too amazing to be true!

As I see it, we have three choices as preachers and teachers of the Gospel: 1. Preach Grace (Love/Life) 2. Preach Law (Religion/Death) 3. Preach a deadly mixture of the two.

1. Grace (Life/Love) - Grace is God's gift to all who will respond to His Lordship and love. It is totally free and unmerited. The result is a quality of life like none found anywhere else in the universe.

> "There is therefore now no condemnation to those who are in Christ Jesus, who do not walk (who's life source is not) according to the flesh, but according to the Spirit. For the law of the Spirit of life in Christ Jesus has made me free from the law of sin and death. For what the law could not do, in that it

was weak through the flesh, (make us perfect and change us on the inside) God did (How?) by sending His own Son in the likeness of sinful flesh, on account of sin: He condemned sin in the flesh, (of His Son) that the righteous requirement of the law (perfect holiness) might be fulfilled in us who do not walk (who's life source is not) according to the flesh but according to the Spirit." (Romans 8:1-4)

Our life source is not the law, the flesh or religion, but the Spirit of life in Christ. His Spirit of life frees us up to live abundantly because He has fulfilled the righteous requirement of the law (perfection) through His sinless life and rendered us dead to sin through His death (Romans 6:3). Now, because He was perfectly and eternally successful in His sinless life and sacrifice for sin, He has fulfilled that righteous requirement of the Law in us! God's righteousness is no longer engraved on tablets of stone, but written in our hearts forever. The Spirit of the Law *is* our new heart and life! Remember what we looked at in Hebrews 10:16?

> "THIS IS THE COVENANT THAT I WILL MAKE WITH THEM AFTER THOSE DAYS, SAYS THE LORD: I WILL PUT MY LAWS INTO THEIR HEARTS, AND IN THEIR MINDS I WILL WRITE THEM."

We live under a new "life covenant" with God where He has actually made His righteousness our new nature. The Spirit gives life, but the letter of the law kills.

> "Not that we are sufficient of ourselves to think of anything as being from ourselves, but our sufficiency is from God, who also made us sufficient as ministers of the new covenant, not of the letter (law) but of the

Spirit (life); for the letter kills, but the Spirit gives life." (2 Corinthians 3:5, 6)

One of the surest ways to suck the life out of a church is to put them under some sort of performance-based theology and religion.

Gravity & Grace

Early in the fifteenth century, Sir Isaac Newton discovered the Laws of Gravity, Motion, and Aerodynamics. On November 17, 1903, two Bicycle Shop owners, Orville and Wilbur Wright, would implement those principles in order to fly the first motorized airplane. That twelve-second powered flight became known as "twelve seconds that changed the world." It sure did!

There is a law (principle) in place on God's created earth called *Gravity*. Whether we realize it or not, it is constantly doing its work. In one way, gravity is a good law because it keeps us and everything on earth from flying wildly into space. On the other hand, it has its negative effects. For instance, have you noticed the effects of gravity on our bodies as we grow older? Over time, its force causes our bodies to bag and sag, stoop and drupe and our bones and joints to arch and ache! We notice the pull on our bodies much more in our fifties than we do in our twenties, don't we? The law of gravity hasn't changed one bit over the years, but its effects certainly change us for the worse!

Fortunately, there is another law present in God's creation: The Law of *Aerodynamics*. At least temporarily, this law supersedes the Law of Gravity. Forward thrust and momentum, forcing air over a plane (or wing) causes lift that allows man-made vessels to soar into the air. It used to be said that, due to gravity, "what goes up, must come down," because, though we could temporarily defy gravity with aerodynamics, it only lasted as long as the fuel that powered the aircraft. Well, that remained true until the discovery and development of "Rocket Science" Now we can hurl ourselves into space and out of earth's gravitational pull. We have to re-enter it in order for it to do its dirty work on us again.

By His Spirit, through grace, God has launched His newly created vessels (believers) out of the spiritual Law of Gravity (sin). *For the law of the Spirit of life in Christ Jesus has made me free from the law of sin and death.* (Romans 8:2) However, we can certainly allow the gravity of sin to have its negative effects on our lives when we decide to re-enter it and walk in the flesh instead of the Spirit.

Dust in the Wind

I love flying! Cruising along at 30 to 40 thousand feet changes my whole perspective on this vast globe we live on. What amazes me is that even at that altitude, you still cannot see an arch on the horizon. It is still a straight horizontal line as far as the eye can see in both directions! This reality makes me feel large and yet small; large in the sense that, from that altitude, I can see so much more of the earth I live on, yet small in that it makes me realize just how miniscule earthlings are, compared to everything else that God has created.

> When I consider Your heavens, the work of Your fingers, The moon and the stars, which You have ordained, What is man that You are mindful of him, And the son of man that You visit him?
> (Psalms 8:3, 4)

Human beings are like microscopic particles of dust on the earth. Yet, compared to the universe, as enormous as the earth is, it too, is a microscopic particle of dust! What staggers me is that we are so important to the God who created it all. Could it be because we tiny dust specs in the wind are the only thing in all of God's incredible creation that the Bible says was created in His image?

Like gravity, the Law of Sin is constantly pulling on us, dragging and slowing us down, but the Law of the Spirit of Life (spiritual aerodynamics) in Christ sets us free to live free and soar!

> But those who wait on the LORD Shall renew their strength; They shall mount up with wings like eagles, They shall run and not be weary, They shall walk and not faint. (Isaiah 40:31)

Notice that those who wait on God: soar, run without burnout, and walk without giving up. The *Spirit of the Law* in Christ is love, grace and life. Now that is a law that we can live abundantly in!

2. Law (Religion/Death) - According to the Apostle Paul, in the Book of Romans, guilting and obligating people to live right, through religion or law-oriented theology has exactly the opposite effect on their lives.

> "But now we <u>have been delivered</u> from the law, <u>having died</u> to what we were held by, so that we should <u>serve in the newness of the Spirit</u> and not in <u>the oldness of the letter</u>. What shall we say then? Is the law sin? Certainly not! On the contrary, I would not have known sin except through the law. For I would not have known covetousness unless the law had said, "YOU SHALL NOT COVET." But sin, taking opportunity by the commandment, produced in me all manner of evil desire. For apart from the law sin was dead. I was alive once without the law, but when the commandment came, sin revived and I died. And the commandment, which was to bring life, I found to bring death. For sin, taking occasion by the com-

mandment, deceived me, and by it killed me." (Romans 7:6-11)

A Giant Sucking Sound

Because we still live in a fleshly body, in a fallen environment, to attempt to use the principle of law and rules to effect righteous behavior in the lives of Saints, or anyone else for that matter, actually produces the opposite effect. Anytime we are trying to motivate people to be obedient by some form of performance standard, we have fallen into the death trap of life-robbing, legalistic religion. Law produces a fear of failure, instead of loving reliance upon and compliant confidence in our indwelling life—Jesus Christ.

"A giant sucking sound" was a colorful quip United States Presidential candidate, Ross Perot, used during his campaign to describe what he believed would be the negative effects of the North American Free Trade Agreement (NAFTA – a trade agreement between America, Mexico and Canada), which he opposed. Perot believed it would suck what He coined as the "American Dream," from the grasp of average Americans. Sitting President, George H.W. Bush, believed in and promoted the agreement, even though many Americans believed that this trade arrangement would diminish our national sovereignty and adversely affect American jobs and our economy. Ultimately, both Bush and Perot would lose the presidential race to Bill Clinton in 1992. Clinton signed NAFTA into law on December 8, 1993; it went into effect on January 1, 1994. Americans are still waiting to see the positive benefits of the agreement today.

In the same way, I believe that preaching performance-based theology is a prescription for fear, condemnation and failure that will suck the "Christian Dream" right out of a thriving, loving church. Pass the Kool-Aid®, please!

Religion is best defined this way: man's attempt to come to God on his own merit through something that he offers for his justification. That would include religious works, gifts and sacrifices. Almost every religion in the world, including many so-called Christian religions, operates on some kind of man-made sacrificial system. Their doctrine may pay lip service to the cross, yet it still requires its followers to do something to make themselves acceptable to a Holy God on a daily basis.

3. A mixture of the two - Are you kidding me? Mixing law with grace would be like trying to mix oil and water! How can you mix life and death? Like an oil spill, this too is a toxic concoction promoted by those who could not possibly understand the power of God's grace or the completeness of God's forgiveness! How can we possibly live the Christ-life here with one foot in the grave of LAW, and one foot in the life of GRACE? We are not under two covenants with God, or under a mixture of the two, we are under only one covenant, the new one! Oh, man! ...Beam me up, Jesus!

When it comes to poison, we can administer one large dose that kills very quickly. However, the devil doesn't operate this way. He is shrewd enough to administer small, poisonous, religious doses over time, knowing that he can accomplish the same result: a slow death that produces a pathetic, lethargic, ineffective church. Satan can't do anything about our eternal destiny, but he can certainly hinder our spiritual growth and effectiveness while we're still here.

We are not saved by not sinning; we're saved by God's grace and Christ's shed blood. Many times I've had people tell me, "I'll come to God when I get my life a little more in order, but I'm not ready yet." That is like a person who has just been run over by a cement truck saying, "I don't need an ambulance or physician yet, I want to get better first, then I'll go to the hospital." If we could fix ourselves and make ourselves better, we wouldn't need a physician. We come to Jesus, our "Great Physician," just as we are, and then He cleanses our sin wounds and heals us from our sins and weaknesses. Neither are we kept saved by not sinning. Thank God!

Salvation Elements

Let's look at just what is accomplished by God on our behalf when He saves us.

1. We are completely redeemed, *forgiven for* and *cleansed from* our sins, past, present and future. (Colossians 2:13)
2. We are justified and declared righteous. (Romans 3:24; 1 Corinthians 6:11)
3. We are born again as a result of God sending the Spirit of His Son, Jesus into our heart. (Galatians 4:4-6; 1 Peter 1:23)
4. As a result, our body becomes the Temple of the living God. (1 Corinthians 6:19, 20)
5. We become one spirit with God's Holy Spirit. (1 Corinthians 6:17) (2 Peter 1:4)
6. We are sealed by God's Holy Spirit—our guarantee unto the day of redemption and heaven. (Ephesians 1:13)
7. God's Law is written in our heart and mind. (Hebrews 10:16)
8. We receive the adoption as God's sons. (Romans 8:15)
9. We also become His offspring—the children of God. (John 1:12; Acts 17:28; 1 John 3:1, 2)
10. We are reconciled to God. (Colossians 1:21)
11. We are made heirs and joint-heirs with Jesus Christ. (Romans 8:17; Galatians 3:29))

12. As a result of that, we are raised to walk in newness of life and are given a seat in the heavenly places with Christ. (Ephesians 2:6)
13. We are made acceptable to God in the beloved. (Ephesians 1:6)
14. We have passed from death into eternal life and shall not come into further judgment. (John 5:24)
15. We are delivered from the kingdom of darkness. (Colossians 1:13)
16. He has delivered us from the power of darkness. (Ephesians 5:8; 1 Thessalonians 5:5)

These are only a few aspects of our salvation in Christ. I could go on. All things considered, I cannot imagine God doing, undoing and then redoing all of these finished realities every time we sin, or for one reason or another, fail to ask for forgiveness. If all of these aspects of our salvation can be undone and lost…can they be restored over and over again? In light of all that our salvation in Christ involves, the idea that God could, or would, undo our salvation and redo it over and over again is absurd.

Knowing that we are forgiven forever sets us free to focus on the love relationship we have with a holy God who has become our loving, Father. I know that the Bible describes God as a fearsome, awesome, God of wrath. I understand that it's a fearful thing to fall into His hands as a sinner. (Hebrews 10:37) Jesus will return someday as the Judge of this world, and God will pour His wrath out on a sinful world that has rejected Him and his Son. I believe this. However, that same God, thanks to what He has accomplished through His Son, is now a loving, compassionate Abba, Father to those who have been born of His Spirit.

Signed, Sealed, Delivered, We're His!

Saints don't want to sin. (1 John 3:9) It is because of who we are. It cuts against the grain of our new nature in Christ. We are forgiven and debt free forever! God has poured His love into our hearts by the Holy Spirit. (Romans 5:5) We do not want to exploit His love and forgiveness. God's Son has signed the title of ownership with his indelible blood, sealed us and stamped His righteousness upon our hearts through His Holy Spirit, and delivered us from sin and death through His death and resurrection! In the words of the pop song of the late 1960s: We're signed (in the Lamb's Book of Life), sealed (by His Holy Spirit), and delivered (by His Life), we're His! Your ticket to eternal life has forever been punched by His blood and paid for! I know…some might say, "When something sounds too good to be true, it probably isn't." In this case, it is all true! Enjoy the free ride!

Nobody is Perfect

Except the Saints!

Hebrews 10:14

> For by a single offering He has forever completely cleansed and perfected those who are consecrated and made holy. (Amplified Bible)

We have all heard or even used this excuse: "Nobody is perfect, I'm only human." That may be true before we are born again, but it is not quite accurate as a description of born again believers in Christ. Though it may be true that none of us is perfect in our daily walk, we must be perfect in order to go to heaven. Yes, you read that right, 100 percent perfection! Why? Because heaven will be a perfect place. To allow anyone into heaven that is not perfect would make heaven an imperfect environment, and God could never allow that. Do we really want to spend eternity in a heaven that is not perfect? I don't think so. This is bad news for those of us who know that our behavior here on earth, even as Christians, is far from 100 percent perfect. Well, it is bad news, unless we understand how God has perfected us through the gift of His Son, Jesus. None of us has any hope of heaven without Christ in our lives. Notice what Paul has to say in the following passage:

> Do you not know that the unrighteous and the wrongdoers will not inherit or have any share in the kingdom of God? Do not be deceived (misled): neither the impure and immoral, nor idolaters, nor adulterers, nor those who participate in homosexuality, nor cheats (swindlers and thieves), nor greedy graspers, nor drunkards, nor foulmouthed revilers and slanderers, nor extortioners and robbers will inherit or have any share in the kingdom of God. And such some of you were [once]. BUT <u>you were washed clean</u> (purified by a complete atonement for sin and made free from the guilt of sin), and <u>you were consecrated</u> (set apart, hallowed), and <u>you were justified</u> [pronounced righteous, by trusting] in the name of the Lord Jesus Christ and in the [Holy] Spirit of our God. (1 Corinthians 6:9-11)
> (Amplified Bible)

It's looking pretty grim for all of us in the first half of this passage...then, God inserts another too good to be true, "BUT," right in the middle of the passage! According to this passage, we were all guilty of sin to some degree. You might be thinking, "Well, I'm not a murderer or an adulterer, or a homosexual, etc..." That may be true, but all of us were [once] guilty of sin in one form or another. In God's view, sin is sin. He doesn't grade us on a scale.

> These six things the LORD hates, Yes, seven are an abomination to Him: A proud look, A lying tongue, Hands that shed innocent blood, A heart that devises wicked plans, Feet that are swift in running to

evil, A false witness who speaks lies, And one who sows discord among brethren. (Proverbs 6:16-19)

A Proud Look?

When God declares something to be an abomination, it means that He abhors it and is thoroughly disgusted by it. It is repugnant to Him, and He rejects it totally. Interestingly, the first abomination that He mentions in this passage is a "proud look" and equates it with lying, manipulation, violence and trouble-making.

God absolutely detests arrogance and self-righteousness. I have personally observed this kind of behavior numerous times in the church by those who consider themselves to be "above-average Christians." Ironically, many such Christians are guilty of sowing discord among the brethren in one fashion or another.

The point in all of this is that we were all guilty of sin in one fashion or another, BUT God is merciful and cleanses us from our sins through the blood of His Son, Jesus.

> For it pleased the Father that in Him all the fullness should dwell, and by Him to reconcile all things to Himself, by Him, whether things on earth or things in heaven, having made peace through the blood of His cross. And you, who once were alienated and enemies in your mind by wicked works, yet now He has reconciled in the body of His flesh through death, to present you holy, and blameless, and above reproach in His sight—if indeed you continue in the faith, grounded and steadfast, and are not moved away from the hope of the gospel which you heard, which was preached to every creature under heaven, of which I, Paul, became a minister.
> (Colossians 1:19-23)

Through Jesus, we were "...washed clean." (Purified by a complete atonement for sin and made free from the guilt of sin) We were also "consecrated (Set apart, hallowed), and were justified and pronounced "righteous" in God's sight! Too good to be true, but it is the truth! Saints are clothed in the righteousness of Jesus Christ.

> For as many [of you] as were baptized (spiritually) into Christ [into a spiritual union and communion with Christ, the Anointed One, the Messiah] have put on (clothed yourselves with) Christ.
> (Galatians 3:27) (Amplified Bible)

If we are in Christ and have been clothed with Him, we have been clothed in His righteousness. Hebrews 10:10 says that we are sanctified though the body of Jesus Christ once for all.

Sanctify means: to make pure or free from sin or guilt. We are sanctified before a holy God by: 1. Faith in Jesus (Acts 26:18); 2. By the Holy Spirit (Romans 15:16); 3. By the Word of God (1 Timothy 4:5); 4. By the body of Jesus (Hebrews 10:10); 5. By God, the Father (Jude 1:1). Based on these scriptures, we must conclude that Saints are thoroughly SANCTIFIED!

What does it mean when Hebrews 10:14 says that He has "perfected forever" them that are sanctified? There are two kinds of perfection to consider. First: There is an outward perfection. Hebrews 6:1 says, "Let us go on to perfection." This means the working out of the sanctified perfection that God has, by the multiple means cited above, worked into us. (Philippians. 2:12) In other words, we are to go on to maturity. We are to learn, grow and mature until we come into the fullness and stature of Jesus. (Ephesians 4:13) This is a progressive growth process that some refer to as, *"progressive sanctification"* or maturation. Not that any believer will achieve absolute perfection in their lifetime on earth, as far as personal conduct is concerned, but our behavior should certainly begin to change for the better once we are filled with the Spirit of Jesus, which is His love—true holiness.

Secondly: There is an inner-perfection in regard to conscience. The writer of Hebrews wrote these words, concerning the Jewish Priest who ministered in the old Temple:

> Now when these things had been thus prepared, the priests always went into the first part of the tabernacle, performing the services. But into the second part the high priest went alone once a year, not without blood, which he offered for himself and for the people's sins committed in ignorance; the Holy Spirit indicating this, that the way into the Holiest of All was not yet made manifest while the first tabernacle was still standing. It was symbolic for the present time in which both gifts and sacrifices are offered <u>which cannot make him who performed the service perfect in regard to the conscience</u>... (Hebrews 9:6-9)

Perfect inner spiritual life was not available to the high priest or anyone else as long as the first tabernacle was standing or while they were still under the old covenant law (rules, regulations and religious rituals). Those sacrifices could not perfect the one who offered them (in regard to conscience). This is not the case with those of us who are under the New Covenant of Life and Love in Christ.

> There is now therefore, no condemnation to those who are in Christ Jesus. (Romans 8:1)

Why are we no longer condemned? Romans 5:1, tells us that we now have peace with God because we are justified by faith in Christ. There is a perfection of the conscience that frees us to follow Jesus with confidence because we have been declared "justified" by a holy God. Back to Hebrews 9:13, 14:

> ...For if the blood of bulls and goats and the ashes of a heifer, sprinkling the unclean, sanctifies for the purifying of the flesh, how much more shall <u>the blood of Christ</u>, who through the eternal Spirit offered Himself without spot to God, <u>cleanse your conscience from dead works to serve the living God?</u>

We can serve God with a clear conscience because we have been declared innocent/justified. Guilt and condemnation sucks the spiritual life out of our worship and our Christian service. However, the blood of Jesus has cleansed us so we can worship and serve the living God without constantly feeling guilty, even though we are guilty of sin, in one form or another, every day. The old covenant law was inadequate to perfect us in this manner.

> For the law, having a shadow of the good things to come, and not the very image of the things, can never with these same sacrifices, which they offer continually year by year, make those who approach perfect. Now, if these old sacrifices were able to accomplish this liberation of conscience, then they would not have had to have been offered again. For then would they not have ceased to be offered? For the worshipers, once purified, (sanctified) would have had no more consciousness of sins. (Hebrews 10:1, 2)

What does this verse mean? To be conscious of something means to be aware of it. Once purged by the blood of Jesus, we should be able to serve the living God without constantly being aware of our past sins. Because God has forgiven and forgotten our past sins, we too should let them go. Sounds simple, but many believers continue to struggle with this for years after they place their faith in Jesus.

If you are still carrying the guilt and weight of your past, even though you have received God's forgiveness in Christ, you are living under the burden of something that God doesn't even remember!

> "...FOR I WILL BE MERCIFUL TO THEIR UN-RIGHTEOUSNESS, AND THEIR SINS AND THEIR LAWLESS DEEDS I WILL REMEMBER NO MORE." (Hebrews 8:12)

Let it go, and move on…God has! This doesn't mean that we are incapable of sinning once we are declared "not guilty;" it simply means that we serve in the newness of the spirit, not the oldness of the letter of the law. In other words, we don't have to serve in constant fear of breaking the rules. We can now focus on why we serve Him—because we love Him. (Romans 7:6; 2 Corinthians 3:6)

Jesus, the second Adam, is a life-giving Spirit. (1 Corinthians 15:45) He came that we might live and serve God guilt-free for the rest of our time here on earth. That is how wonderful and complete our salvation is through the precious blood of Jesus! Yes, we have blessed assurance!

> Now where there is absolute remission (forgiveness and cancellation of the penalty) of these [sins and law breaking], there is no longer any offering made to atone for sin. Therefore, brethren, since we have full freedom and confidence to enter into the [Holy of] Holies [by the power and virtue] in the blood of Jesus, By this fresh (new) and living way which He initiated and dedicated and opened for us through the separating curtain (veil of the Holy of Holies), that is,

> through His flesh, And since we have [such] a great and wonderful and noble Priest [Who rules] over the house of God, Let us all come forward and draw near with true (honest and sincere) hearts in unqualified assurance and absolute conviction engendered by faith (by that leaning of the entire human personality on God in absolute trust and confidence in His power, wisdom, and goodness), having our hearts sprinkled and purified from a guilty (evil) conscience and our bodies cleansed with pure water. So let us seize and hold fast and retain without wavering the hope we cherish and confess and our acknowledgement of it, for He Who promised is reliable (sure) and faithful to His word. (Hebrews 10:18-23) (Amplified Bible)

Wow! None of this is based on our goodness, or our best Christian performance. It is an accomplished work of God through His son, Jesus. His blood has cleansed our hearts from an evil conscience. He has saved us to the uttermost, and Jesus lives forever to make intercession for us…here and for all eternity.

> Therefore He is also able to save to the uttermost those who come to God through Him, since He always lives to make intercession for them.
> (Hebrews 7:25) (Amplified Bible)

Don't Give Up!

Here is what the devil does when we slip up and sin: He comes to us and says: "You shouldn't go to church and worship God because you're nothing but a hypocrite! You shouldn't tell others about your so-called salvation because you, yourself, sin every day. You shouldn't serve God because you're unworthy!"

When the devil accuses me, I don't deny that all of this is true. We are certainly unworthy, in and of ourselves, to worship and serve God. However, we do not worship Him because we are worthy. We serve Him, because *He is worthy* of our worship and service, regardless of our failures. That is why we continue to worship Him and serve Him, even when we feel that we have failed Him.

For instance, there have been times when my wife and I would bicker all the way to church on Sunday morning. Right before we would walk into church, she would say: "I suppose you are going to put on your "happy church-face" and shake hands with everyone like nothing is wrong. I don't know how you can argue with me and then walk through that church door and smile at everyone like everything is great. Don't you think that makes you a hypocrite?!" I would always remind her, "It doesn't make us hypocrites when we smile and shake hands with folks in church like nothing is wrong, even though we have been bickering all the way to church. We're not mad at them; we're mad at each other! Why should we unload our frustration with each other on them?"

I knew that our bickering was wrong and it certainly did make me feel hypocritical, but the truth is I had commitments—I was a Sunday school teacher—and I had to show up and do what God had called me to do, regardless of my disagreements with my wife. That, of course, does not mean that our heavenly Father is going to allow us to continue to behave immaturely toward those we love. He wants me to love my wife as Christ loves the church. (Ephesians 5:25)

Nevertheless, if we were to quit every time we slip and fall, no one could continue to serve Him. Look at all the Saints who have served God in the Bible. Don't you think that they felt unworthy and unclean in their failures? Of course they did. Aren't you glad they didn't quit? I am! I don't intend to quit either.

God's righteousness and sanctification are not an accomplishment on our part; they are strictly the gift of God. How do we receive this gift?

> ...if you confess with your mouth the Lord Jesus and believe in your heart that God has raised Him from the dead, you will be saved. For with the heart one believes unto righteousness, and with the mouth confession is made unto salvation. For the Scripture says, "WHOEVER BELIEVES ON HIM <u>WILL NOT BE PUT TO SHAME</u>." (Romans 10:9-11)

We receive forgiveness, justification and sanctification through faith, just as Abraham did. (Romans 4:3) It is not accomplished by our works, it is a gift received by grace through faith. (Ephesians 2:8, 9)

Imputation & Impartation

How does God do this? Through both: <u>Imputation</u> and <u>Impartation</u>. *Imputation* means to put to one's account. For example: I had shared my ministry in a Cowboy Church in Orchard, Texas, one Sunday morning and my wife and I went to lunch near Houston after the service. We were seated in the crowded restaurant and enjoyed a nice meal together. When we were finished, instead of bringing our check for the meal, the waitress laid a business card on the table and told us that our meal had already been paid for. As you can imagine, we were both quite pleasantly surprised!

I looked at the card and this is, more or less, what it said: "We noticed that you gave thanks to the Lord for your meal in prayer before you ate, and we want to bless you by paying for your meal today." The card had the name of the church on the other side.

I was not acquainted with this group of believers. They were complete strangers to my wife and me. Quickly, I glanced around the restaurant to see if I could see who had paid our bill, but I could not see any sign of God's "Secret Blessers." Don't you just love it when God does things like that? I do. I was free from payment because it was already paid in full. That generous gesture on their part made our day!

That is precisely what Jesus' blood has done for you and me. He picked up our check for sin and paid for it in full! We are now free of any sin debt. By faith, God has imputed His righteousness to us. We didn't work for it. We didn't do anything in order to earn it. It was supplied to us as a gift. That is what the Bible says about the gift of our salvation.

> What then shall we say that Abraham our father has found according to the flesh? For if Abraham was justified by works, he has something to boast about, but not before God. For what does the Scripture say? "ABRAHAM BELIEVED GOD, AND IT WAS ACCOUNTED TO HIM FOR RIGHTEOUSNESS." Now to him who works, the wages are not counted as grace but as debt. But to him who does not work but believes on Him who justifies the ungodly, his faith is accounted for righteousness... (Romans 4:1-5)

Like Abraham, we are justified by faith, not works. The word, JUSTIFY, means to acquit or declare not guilty. This passage goes on to say in verses 6-8:

> ...just as David also describes the blessedness of the man to whom God imputes righteousness apart from works: "BLESSED ARE THOSE WHOSE LAWLESS DEEDS ARE FORGIVEN, AND WHOSE SINS ARE COVERED; BLESSED IS THE

MAN TO WHOM THE LORD SHALL NOT <u>IMPUTE</u> SIN."

On the one hand, God does not put our sin to our account. On the other hand, He puts to our account His very righteousness. His forgiveness and even His righteousness are imputed, (accounted to us) simply by faith. We believe what he offers us and receive it freely...no works, of any kind, necessary! Because we are Justified and Righteous in His sight, we can be reconciled to Him.

> ...that is, that God was in Christ reconciling the world to Himself, not imputing their trespasses to them, and has committed to us the word of reconciliation. (2 Corinthians 5:19)

We do not deserve this new status, it too is a gift. Thank God and praise Him! Righteousness is purely a gift, straight from the loving hand of God Almighty to you and me.

> For if by the one man's offense death reigned through the one, much more those who receive abundance of grace and of the gift of righteousness will reign in life through the One, Jesus Christ. (Romans 5:17)

Remember? Salvation is more than what God did FOR US through the sacrifice of His Son, Jesus...it is something that He does TO US when His resurrected Son comes into our heart. This is where the second aspect of our righteousness comes into play: *Impartation*. Imputation is something put to our account, a declaration of innocence. On the other hand, impartation is something that is put into us through His Spirit! It is one thing for God to say, "I declare you righteous!" It is an even more incredible thing for Him to put His righteousness into us! And just how does He accomplish this? Through the new birth! As we have already established in earlier chapters; He sends the Spirit of His Son, Jesus, into our spirit and our spirit becomes one with His HOLY Spirit! (Galatians 4:6; 1 Corinthians 6:17).

Imputation is *a declaration* from God. Impartation is *a miracle* from God that changes our spiritual DNA! Our nature becomes one with His nature. It is through the precious promises of scripture that these facts become a reality in us. (2 Peter 1:4) Don't take my word for it; take God's Word for it! Please, I encourage you to look up and highlight all of these verses in your Bible.

Both *Imputation* and *Impartation* are required for us to be saved and made new creations in Christ, and both have been accomplished on our behalf by Jesus forever! Too good to be true, but it is eternally true!

Righteousness & Holiness

There is also a difference between righteousness and holiness: *Righteousness* is the right standing that God has imputed and imparted to us as a free gift through faith. *Holiness* is the outworking of the imparted gift of His life through His indwelling Spirit. Holiness is the outworking of righteousness, not the means to it. Just as good character produces good behavior, so the indwelling, empowering character of God, through His Holy Spirit, changes our heart and character from the inside-out. The result is our maturation in holiness. God has declared us Righteous, but we must be perfected (matured) in holiness.

> Therefore, having these promises, beloved, let us cleanse ourselves from all filthiness of the flesh and spirit, perfecting holiness in the fear (respect/reverence) of God. (2 Corinthians 7:1)

Once again, Paul is talking about this principle in this verse:

Therefore, my beloved, as you have always obeyed, not as in my presence only, but now much more in my absence, work out your own salvation with fear and trembling (reverent respect and utter humility) (Philippians 2:12)

Is it hard to praise and worship God when we are able to live a guilt-free life? Of course not! We are guilt-free because we are not condemned by Him. We are not condemned because God has laid on Him the iniquity of us all.

All we like sheep have gone astray; We have turned, every one, to his own way; And the LORD has laid on Him the iniquity of us all. (Isaiah 53:6)

Jesus-colored Glasses

For our sake He (God) made Christ [*virtually*] to be sin Who knew no sin, so that in and through Him we might become [*endued with, viewed as being in, and examples of*] the righteousness of God [*what we ought to be, approved and acceptable and in right relationship with Him, by His goodness*].
(2 Corinthians 5:21) (Amplified Bible)

Christians are as righteous (spiritually) as Jesus Christ right now. If this was not true, we could not possibly have a relationship with Him. No one is going to heaven without God's perfect righteousness! Remember what we looked at in First Corinthians:

BUT you were washed clean (purified by a complete atonement for sin and made free from the guilt of sin), and you were consecrated (set apart, hallowed),

> and you were justified [pronounced righteous, by trusting] in the name of the Lord Jesus Christ and in the [Holy] Spirit of our God. (1 Corinthians 6:11) (Amplified Bible)

We were unclean, but the blood of Jesus has washed us clean and purified us. He has set us free from guilt, set us apart for His unique purpose, and justified us forever. Amazingly, God sees us through Jesus-colored glasses! Cool, dude! I want a pair of those! Oh, wait...I do have a pair...the Word of God! Thank you, Jesus! You do too; put 'em on!

We must be constantly reminded from the scriptures that, not only has God forgiven our sins, He has forgotten them.

> ...then He adds, "THEIR SINS AND THEIR LAWLESS DEEDS I WILL REMEMBER NO MORE." (Hebrews 10:17)

He casts our sins into the depths of the sea. (Micah 7:19) Romans 4:15 says: *"...for where there is no law there is no transgression."* Since we are dead to the law, sin has no power over us. In Romans 5:13 it says: *"For until the law sin was in the world, but sin is not imputed (put to our account) when there is no law."*

Driving under the Grace Limit

Those who are born again are not under law, but under grace. Where there is no law, there is no transgression of the law. For instance, if there are no speed limit signs, there is no speed limit. If there is no sign posted saying that the limit is 70 miles per hour (MPH), then you have not broken the law if you drive 90 MPH. But, if that 70 MPH limit/law is posted, you become a law breaker if you drive faster than 70 MPH. Isn't it amazing how that, no matter what the speed limit is, we still drive as much over that posted limit as the law will tolerate. As I've traveled around the country, I've discovered that the tolerance level varies state by state. However, with God's law, there is no tolerance...if you break the law, you pay! (James 2:10) The purpose of God's Old Testament law was to make the nation of Israel aware of their sin and their inability to make themselves right by their works in order that they might come to Christ as their only hope for salvation. (Galatians 3:23-25) Are Saints under the law today? No, we are under grace.

> For sin shall not have dominion over you, for you are not under law but under grace. (Romans 6:14)

Sin loses its power when the law is not a factor. For example, the surest way to get finger prints on your freshly painted wall is to put up a sign that says: WET PAINT, DO NOT TOUCH! Fallen human nature is bent towards breaking rules. It's natural! If you do not put up a "DO NOT TOUCH" sign, someone may brush up against it or touch it by accident, but they would not be tempted to do so intentionally because they would not have any awareness that the paint was wet, or that it was wrong to touch it. Get the point? Where there is no law/sign, there is no offense...or temptation. We are not under the law in the new covenant because Jesus died for us (we died with Him), rose from death for us (we were raised in new life with Him), and entered into us (His presence in us is our righteousness). In doing so, He ended the power of sin over us. (Colossians 2:14) Remember 1 Corinthians 15:56? The strength of sin is the law! If there is no religious law sign hanging over our head, then sin loses its power over us. Paul even goes so far as to say that since we are under grace, all things are lawful for us:

> Everything is permissible (allowable and lawful) for me; but not all things are helpful (good for me to

do, expedient and profitable when considered with other things). Everything is lawful for me, but I will not become the slave of anything or be brought under its power. (1 Corinthians 6:12) (Amplified Bible)

What does this mean exactly? Well, in Christ, we are not under an outward law; we are indwelt by the *Spirit of God's law.* We drive according to the "grace limit." Any judge worth his salt knows and understands the difference between the letter of the law and the spirit of the law. The letter of the law is written in the law books, while the spirit of the law is the *intent of the law*. The intent of the law is what the law is put in place to accomplish. Lawyers make their living manipulating the letter of the law in order to win their cases. Judges who understand the intent of the law, however, make their judgments based on what the laws were put into the books to accomplish. Hopefully, they render their decisions based on the intent of the law, not some slick attorney's manipulation of the letter of the law. God does that with us.

God writes His law on our hearts under the new covenant. (Romans 8:10) Think about this...if the outward speed limit was written on the hearts of all drivers, it wouldn't have to be written in law books or on speed limit signs. We would all know inwardly and want to do outwardly what is right by nature. Unfortunately, that isn't possible in the natural world of laws and limits. No doubt, you have heard people say: "You can't legislate righteousness." They are absolutely right. If making laws against wrong-doing could keep people from doing wrong, our prisons would be empty! However, as believers, in the spiritual realm, we have the law of God written in our new nature. Not that we are never tempted to sin, but because of the grace (the essence and power of God's holy nature) that is written in our hearts, He is free to abound toward us and to empower us to say "NO" to the devil! As Saints, we no longer have to knuckle under to the world, the flesh and the devil! (Romans 6:14)

Temptation & Sin

Something else that is important for us to understand is the difference between *temptation* and *sin*. This is another area where the devil confuses and defeats believers. First of all, it is not a sin to be tempted. Jesus was tempted by the devil, yet He never sinned. If being tempted is a sin, then certainly Jesus committed sin because He was tempted. Temptation is when the devil offers to us an alternative to what God says is right. Sin is accepting that suggestion, and acting on it…just as Adam and Eve did.

I once heard Pastor, and Christian author, Charles Stanley, explain it like this: "Temptation is like a bird flying over our head. We can't prevent that. Sin, on the other hand, is like allowing that bird to build its nest in our hair. We can prevent that!" We can't always prevent a sinful thought from entering our mind, but we don't have to dwell on it. It only becomes sin when we do. See the difference? The devil offered Jesus alternatives to the will of God, but Jesus never accepted Satan's suggestions…not once! (Matthew 4:1-11) That is the only reason He was qualified to die in our place on the cross. He wasn't there for His own sin; He was there for yours and mine.

Power and Life in the Blood

What is the purpose of physical blood? Life is supplied by the blood. Life-giving nutrients from the food we digest are delivered to the multitude of cells in our body through the blood; therefore, life is in the blood. (Leviticus 17:11) Our blood also purifies us and protects us from disease and infection through antibodies. Antibodies are protein on the surface of B-cells that are released into our bloodstream to attack and neutralize bacteria, viruses and parasites. Likewise, the spiritual blood of Jesus is life giving nutrition and a sin detergent to us. When we sin, the blood isn't like spot remover that we apply to our sin in each occurrence. Rather, I believe it is our constant, perpetual inner-life sin immune system that purifies us on the journey.

Believers are the containers of the royal spiritual blood of Jesus! Like a self-cleaning oven, His life blood is flowing through our spiritual veins every moment of our life as His new creations! Praise God! We can walk free from the power of sin, the law, condemnation, guilt and shame by the blood of Jesus! This is why the Apostle, Peter says that we have been made a "Royal Priesthood." Of course we have! In Jesus, we are a chosen race who comes from a royal bloodline!

> But you are a chosen race, a royal priesthood, a dedicated nation, [*God's*] own purchased, special people, that you may set forth the wonderful deeds and display the virtues and perfections of Him Who called you out of darkness into His marvelous light. [*Exod. 19:5, 6.*] (1 Peter 2:9) (Amplified Bible)

In 1899, Lewis E. Jones, obviously aware of this scriptural truth, penned the lyrics to this, now famous, hymn:

"There Is Power In The Blood"
(Public Domain)

Would you be free from the burden of sin?
There's pow'r in the blood, pow'r in the blood;
Would you o'er evil a victory win?
There's wonderful pow'r in the blood.

Refrain:

There is pow'r, pow'r, wonder-working pow'r
in the blood of the Lamb;

There is pow'r, pow'r, wonder-working pow'r
in the precious blood of the Lamb.

Would you be free from your passion and pride?
There's pow'r in the blood, pow'r in the blood;
Come for a cleansing to Calvary's tide,
There's wonderful pow'r in the blood.

Would you be whiter, much whiter than snow?
There's pow'r in the blood, pow'r in the blood;
Sin-stains are lost in its life-giving flow;
There's wonderful pow'r in the blood.

Would you do service for Jesus your King?
There's pow'r in the blood, pow'r in the blood;
Would you live daily His praises to sing?
There's wonderful pow'r in the blood.

Forgiveness – Conditional Act or Continuous Attitude?

Are we forgiven ONCE FOR ALL only for our past sins when we accept Jesus as Savior? Then, from that point forward, God must forgive us a multitude of times, each time we sin after we accept Him? I believe it is not a matter of how many times He forgives us for the sins we commit on a daily basis. Rather, it is the fact that they are ALL forgiven, past, present and future that allows us to live confidently in regard to conscience for the Lord.

As we have established already, since God exists outside of created time and space, He sees our past, present and future at the same time! There is no past, present and future with Him. When He sent His Son to the cross, He dealt with all sin according to His time, (GST – God's Standard Time). I believe His forgiveness is based on

His time, which is not subject to created time and space. In Matthew 18:21-35, Peter asked Jesus about how he should extend forgiveness:

> "Lord, how often shall my brother sin against me, and I forgive him? Up to seven times?" Jesus answered: "I do not say to you, up to seven times, but up to seventy times seven."

We can all relate to Peter's frustration with people who repeatedly hurt or offend us. It can be difficult to forgive one time, much less seven times...but four hundred and ninety times?! Give me a break! What was Jesus' point? Was it the number of times that forgiveness should be extended? I don't believe so. What Jesus was trying to get across to Peter was that we should have a heart that is so filled with Jesus' love and grace for others that we do not even keep an account of their sins against us. Look at what Paul had to say about this:

> Love endures long and is patient and kind; love never is envious nor boils over with jealousy, is not boastful or vainglorious, does not display itself haughtily. It is not conceited (arrogant and inflated with pride); it is not rude (unmannerly) and does not act unbecomingly. Love (God's love in us) <u>does not insist on its own rights or its own way,</u> for <u>it is not self-seeking; it is not touchy or fretful or resentful; it takes no account of the evil done to it</u> [it pays no attention to a suffered wrong]. (1 Corinthians 13:4, 5) (Amplified Bible)

This attitude of Love is the product of God's character! "He who does not love does not know God, for God is love." (1 John 4:8) If we don't have the capacity to love like this, John says that we don't truly know God. But, we who do know God do have His ability to love in this manner because we have God, and therefore, we have His love in our hearts. Love is our new nature.

I believe that Jesus was trying to help Peter realize that forgiveness is an attitude of the heart, not merely a series of acts. Who has a perfect heart like this? Who forgives perfectly like this? God Does! His forgiveness is not simply extended to us on an "as needed" basis for every occurrence of sin we commit each day. His forgiveness is His ongoing amazing grace; made possible because of the blood of His Son, Jesus, who lives forever to intercede for us as our perpetual propitiation (substitutionary satisfaction of God's righteousness)!

I know that what I am saying may be considered extremely controversial in some, if not most, theological circles. Nevertheless, I believe it is something that we should, at least, be willing to chew on before we spit it out. How could we ever sing, "Blessed assurance, Jesus is mine; Oh, what a foretaste of glory divine..." if we continually had to worry about our standing and acceptance, based on how much we sin or don't sin on a daily basis. Or, for that matter, whether or not we are "'fessed up and prayed up" in order to be forgiven for every sin we commit as Christians? We would be walking on egg shells every step of our journey instead of walking in confidence by the blood of Jesus. Would this brand of grace really be all that amazing? Is God's forgiveness conditional or a free gift?

God's forgiveness is a continual attitude, not merely a conditional act that He must repeat over and over again when we confess our sins. Jesus is our confession and His heart is our righteousness. We are not forgiven because we confess our sins. We confess our sins because we are forgiven and have God's imparted righteousness as our new nature. We do not confess our sins to get forgiveness; we confess our sins in order to experience our forgiveness. Our sins are forgiven, once and for all, through faith in the shed blood of Jesus. Confession allows us to get the condemnation off of our shoulders.

To confess literally means to, "say after God," what He says about our sins. We do not make or offer excuses for our sin. We take full responsibility without placing blame on anyone or anything else. Because we are one spirit with Him, we agree in our heart with Him on just what our sin is. Then, by faith, we rest in Him and His finished work in the cross of Christ. This sets us free from guilt to walk with God and to serve Him.

What does being free from sin mean? It means that, not only are we free from sin's *penalty*, we are free from its *power*. What power does sin have over us if we fail to understand what I believe God is saying about our forgiveness? First, it has the power to induce us to habitual sinful behavior. Secondly, it has the power of shame and guilt to discourage and defeat us in our walk as Christians.

Honestly, I understand that I sin every day to one degree or another. Some sins are sins of *commission*. These are sins where I willfully do or say something that is offensive to God or offend someone else. Then, there are sins of *omission*. These are sins where I refuse, or neglect, to do what God tells or leads me to do. What about sins in our hearts and attitudes that we are not even aware of? How do we confess them in order to receive forgiveness?

It doesn't matter how long we have been walking with Jesus, this is true for all of us every day. Our sin can be something as simple as arrogance, bitterness, jealousy, favoritism, prejudice, revenge, etc. All are *willful sins of the heart* that we all struggle with every day. If we had to confess every sin, every time we commit one, in order to get forgiveness, we would need to be on our faces in prostrate confession constantly. Our prayers would be constantly focused on asking for forgiveness, and we would not have time to do anything for God.

I believe forgiveness, repentance (a God-inspired change of heart and mind) and confession (owning our failures and taking personal responsibility for them) should be an attitude of the heart, not merely a repetitious, mechanical ritual. Part of the Holy Spirit's ministry in us is to convict us of sin when it occurs in our life. We know immediately when we sin in attitude or action because the Holy Spirit in us convicts (not condemns) us. That should produce an immediate acknowledgment on our part.

When a believer is walking around under a constant fear or feeling of condemnation, I can guarantee you, the power of sin is defeating that individual and making him ineffective for the Kingdom of God. That believer is losing more than winning day-to-day. When we understand and believe that we are not on a cyclical routine of—sin, confess, get forgiven—basis with God, but that the sacrifice of Jesus on the cross has already accomplished our forgiveness, then we can truly serve Him freely. Now, that is amazing Grace! We serve God from a spirit of love, not a spirit of fear:

> ...God has not given us a spirit of fear, but of power and of love and of a sound mind. (2 Timothy 1:7)

> For [*the Spirit which*] you have now received [*is*] not a spirit of slavery to put you once more in bondage to fear, but you have received the Spirit of adoption [*the Spirit producing sonship*] in [*the bliss of*] which we cry, Abba (Father)! Father! (Romans 8:15)
> (Amplified Bible)

God is a just and holy God, but He is more than that to us; He's our Abba, Father! We'll look a little closer at this "Abba" thing later. Consequently, our focus should not be on sin, it should be on serving Him because we love Him and we know that He loves us as His children. When sin rears its ugly head, we own it, agree with God about it, and thank God for the blood of Jesus, through which we have received eternal forgiveness for it and move on in victory!

Isn't it amazing how when we are focused on, and busy, serving Him (not because it's right—of course it's right—or because we are supposed to do what's right, but because we love Him), it becomes more difficult for the devil to get our attention. Like the old hymn says: "Turn your eyes upon Jesus; look full in His wonderful face, and the things of earth will grow strangely dim, in the light of His glory and grace."

Chastisement & Judgment

Again, let me make this clear: I am not saying that, as Christians, we never sin. I am not saying that The Holy Spirit in us does not convict us when we sin willfully. I am not saying that we should not confess, own up to, and take responsibility for our sins and repent of them. I am not saying that, as Christians, we can just live our lives any way we want to. If you think God, who deals with us as sons (Hebrews 12:7), is going to put up with that, you are in for a rude awakening. He is far too good a parent to allow His children to run wild. I can guarantee that you will experience God's chastisement (not judgment). *Chastisement* is God's loving (not necessarily painless) correction that changes the character and direction of His beloved children.

Judgment, on the other hand, is God's wrath, poured out upon unrepentant, rebellious, non-believers, condemning them to an everlasting hell. There is a huge difference. According to John 5:24; we who believe in Him will not come into judgment:

> "Most assuredly, I say to you, he who hears My word and believes in Him who sent Me has everlasting life, and shall not come into judgment, but has passed from death into life.

Why will we *not come into judgment*? Because those of us who have placed our faith in the death of Jesus for our sins, have been judged once and for all in Him. We have been crucified with Him!

What I am saying is that we are free from the law and condemnation because we are forgiven and perfected forever by the blood of the perfect Lamb of God. It is finished! For the born again, the law is not an outward righteous requirement, it is an inward, life-changing, holy reality! We have a new, holy nature in Christ. It is more than our duty to obey Him; it is our hearts desire to obey Him! When we fail in our obedience, Jesus is a faithful, eternal intercessor for us before a holy God, who happens to be our Father, not just our Judge.

Satan deploys his little WMDs, "Weapons of Mass Distraction," (demons) to distract us with anything that gets us off the track of truth. Believe me, the devil knows, and hates, the truth in the Bible. He also knows that as long as he can keep us focused on trying not to sin, he can keep us on the defense so we cannot mount a good offense for God. If he can keep us on our emotional heels, trying to "not sin," instead of on our spiritual toes, in love with, living for and confidently serving the Lord, he can keep us in bondage and render us ineffective for the Kingdom.

> But we belong to the day; therefore, let us be sober and put on the breastplate (corselet) of faith and love and for a helmet the hope of salvation. For God has not appointed us to [incur His] wrath [He did not select us to condemn us], but [that we might] obtain [His] salvation through our Lord Jesus Christ (the Messiah) Who died for us so that whether we are still alive or dead [at Christ's appearing], we might live together with Him and share His life. Therefore encourage (admonish, exhort) one another and edify (strengthen and build up) one another, just as you are doing. (1Thessalonians 5:8-11)
> (Amplified Bible)

Thank the Lord! His forgiveness, through the life-blood of Jesus, is more powerful than all of Satan's WMDs! Our perfection in Him has set us free to know Him, love Him and serve Him with a clear conscience! At this time, only if you want to, you have my permission to put the book down so you can raise your hands toward heaven, jump up and down and "go Pentecostal!" It's okay! If you can free yourself to do it, your loving Heavenly Father will love it and…guess what…you will, too!

9

A Life to Die For

From Death into Life

John 5:24

"Most assuredly, I say to you, he who hears My word and believes in Him who sent Me has everlasting life, and shall not come into judgment, but has passed from death into life."

Throughout this chapter, I encourage you to keep referring back to the following verses because I believe that they will become clearer each time you read them.

"Or do you not know that as many of us as were baptized into Christ Jesus were baptized into His death? Therefore we were buried with Him through baptism into death, that just as Christ was raised from the dead by the glory of the Father, even so we also should walk in newness of life. For if we have been united together in the likeness of His death, certainly we also shall be in the likeness of His resurrection, knowing this, that our old man was crucified with Him, that the body of sin might be done away with, that we should no longer be slaves of sin. For he who has died has been freed from sin. (That's us!) Now if we died with Christ, we believe that we shall also live with Him, knowing that Christ, having been raised from the dead, dies no more. Death no longer has dominion over Him. (or us!) For the death that He died, He died to sin once for all; but the life that He lives, He lives to God. Likewise you also, reckon yourselves to be dead indeed to sin, but alive to God in Christ Jesus our Lord." (Romans 6:3-11)

According to these words, what happened when Jesus died for us on the cross? Who did the Apostle Paul say died? He makes it clear in Galatians 2:20:

"I <u>have been crucified</u> with Christ; it is no longer I who live, but <u>Christ lives in me</u>; and the *life* which I now live in the flesh I live by faith in the Son of God, who loved me and gave Himself for me."

When Jesus died, we died. That is the only way we can be freed from the law that condemns us and separates us from a loving God. Jesus, "who knew no sin," suffered condemnation and judgment (spiritual separation from God) in our place. He "became sin for us." Think about this...because God accepted His Son's sacrifice ONCE for ALL, those who accept His sacrificial death will never experience a "second death." (Revelation 20) In His death, Jesus suffered that separation for us. (Mark 15:34) Death and the grave, however, could not hold Him because He was sinless.

When did we who accepted Him die our second death? Two thousand years ago when we were put to death with Him! I believe the Bible teaches that when Jesus died for us on the cross, He became our "second death," and we died that death along with Him. (Read Romans 6:3-11 again.) Therefore, God is free to do more than just forgive us. Our co-death with Jesus, and God's subsequent forgiveness through His shed blood, is just the prerequisite for our spiritual restoration/regeneration.

We are redeemed (purchased) and reconciled (reunited) to God by His death, but we are saved (regenerated-born again), by His life! (Romans 5:10) If we have already been put to death for our sins in Him, and raised in Him to walk in newness of life through the new birth, will we ever have to be crucified again? Will we have to face another death for our sins in eternity? If we do, then His crucifixion and death were for nothing.

What validated Jesus' sacrificial death on the cross, and our justification through that sacrifice, was His resurrection. (Romans 4:25) Without His resurrection, the cross was for nothing. (1 Corinthians 15:17) If we have to die for *any* of our sins again, now or in the future, you can ignore the Bible and live your life your way. This is all that we get, so live it up! Thank God, the Bible is true! We, who are in Him, will never have to die a second death. Hopefully, the following illustration will help you to grasp this truth.

One Death, One Time

Let's suppose you were brought before a court for a crime that demanded the death penalty. You are tried, convicted, and sentenced to death. The authorities put you on "death row" until the day of your execution. On that final hopeless morning after your "last breakfast," the Chaplain comes in and gives you your last rites. The prison guard yells out, "Dead man walking!" as you are escorted to the death chamber. They seat you in a cold, hard, steel chair, strap your arms and legs down, and pull a hood over your head. After a short, silent pause, the Prison Warden nods his head and the executioner pulls the lever, sending a death-rendering electrical current through your body. After you stiffen and then slump lifelessly in "The Chair," expressionless, the coroner enters the room. He examines your lifeless body and pronounces you DEAD. Justice has been served and your debt has been paid.

Alrighty (sic), then! You're free to go. Oh! But, wait! You're dead! That's the inconvenient thing about death...you can't go anywhere or do anything! So it is with all who pay for their own sins. The problem with paying for our own sins is that there is never going to be a point in eternity where God will say, "Okay, I guess you have paid enough. You are free to go." The second death (eternal separation from God) is ETERNAL DEATH! Why would anyone want to pay eternally for something that has already been eternally paid for by Jesus? I don't know about you, but I'll take His payment for my sins! Anyway, back to our analogy.

The executioner's attendants come in and take your lifeless body to the morgue. The mortician comes to do his handiwork only to discover you sitting up, more alive than you've ever been! Startled, he asks, "Aren't you the guy they just executed in the electric chair?" Scratching your head, you reply, "Uh...yeah. I don't quite understand what just happened, but I am him!" Wondering if he is living out an episode of the "Twilight Zone,"[7] he rushes out of the room and gathers all of the prison officials, including the Executioner, the Coroner, and the Warden. After being ushered back into the room, astonished, they stare at you like they're staring at a ghost! But, you're not a ghost...you're a risen miracle!

The Warden asks the Coroner, "You did perform a thorough inspection of the body, didn't you? Did you not pronounce this man dead?" "Well...yes, Sir...of course I did! I can assure you, Warden, this guy was deader than a Mackerel!" he replies. The Warden ponders the situation for a long moment then responds, "Well, I suppose I have no choice but to free this man from this prison." They all gasp, then he explains: "This man was found guilty and suffered the judgment prescribed by the laws of this state for his crime—death! He was executed and pronounced dead, yet through some sort of inexplicable miracle, he is now alive. Therefore, he must be set free! We cannot execute him twice for his crimes. Gather his belongings and let him go!"

Amazingly, that is exactly what happened to you and me by virtue of our having received Jesus and His death for our sins. When He died, we died. Then, just as God's miraculous power raised Him from the dead, He has raised us from the dead (spiritually) to walk in newness of life (eternal life) and now we are forever free! In Christ, you are a risen miracle! (Go back and read Romans 6:3-11 again.) We were raised spiritually by the same power that God used to raise Jesus from the dead! (Ephesians 1:19, 20)

You can't kill a dead man twice. Not only is it impossible, but to re-judge someone for the same crime would constitute "Double Jeopardy." This is a legal term that refers to a person being tried again for the same offense after either having paid for that offense, or having been acquitted (declared innocent). In our country it is prohibited by the Fifth Amendment to the U.S. Constitution, which states: "...nor shall any person be subject for the same offense [sic] to be twice put in jeopardy of life or limb..."This clause in the Fifth Amendment protects against: [1] a second prosecution for the same offense after a defendant has been acquitted; [2] a second prosecution for the same offense after they have been convicted; and [3] multiple punishments for the same offense.

Granted, God is not bound by this earthly law. However, God, in His absolute righteous justice, would never allow us to suffer spiritual "Double Jeopardy." In our case, we were found guilty, punished, and like article [3], He is not going to impose multiple punishments for the same offenses. Praise God! Jesus has removed the death clothes of sin that held us bound, and has forever loosed us! (John 11:1-45)

We have been acquitted (declared innocent—justified) and, in Jesus, paid for our crimes against God! When we receive Jesus, the last "Lamb of God," our name is written in His Book of Life. Despite what some might believe, I do not believe God erases our names from His book of eternal life. Our names are written in the "Lamb's Book of Life" (Revelation 21:27) with the indelible Blood of Jesus Christ. Following is another song the Lord inspired in my heart about the blood of Christ.

"The Blood Won't Wash Away"

Crimson red it trickled down from the nails that held him bound;
From his flesh and to the ground, the blood ran.
From his wounded side it flowed for the debt of sin I owed,
It changed a life when it changed the soul of this man.

It washed away my sin, cleansed and made me whole within,
Washed away the pain, years I spent in vain, let me start again.
Washed away the doubt, but left a stain that won't wash out;
Washed it all away but the blood won't wash away.

Some are dyed in the wool it's said;
I've been dyed in the blood instead,
The old man died when the blood was shed, I'm a new man.
I was stained indelibly when his red blood covered me,
I became a man set free when the blood ran.

It washed away my sin, cleansed and made me whole within,
Washed away the pain, years I spent in vain, let me start again.
Washed away the doubt, but left a stain that won't wash out;
Washed it all away but the blood won't wash away.

Born to Overcome!

Some would say: "What about Revelation 3:5? Doesn't that verse say that unless we "overcome" it is possible for God to blot our names from the Book of Life?" Consider this: First, if this is referring to saved, born again Saints, then our salvation is preserved by our faithfulness and our works.

Secondly, if this is true, then why would God, who is omniscient (all-knowing), write our names in the Lamb's Book when He knew in eternity past that He would eventually have to erase them? That doesn't make sense, does it?

Thirdly, If God can erase our names, can He re-write them in the book again? According to Hebrews 6:4-6, it is impossible to renew those who have fallen away unto repentance. Therefore, if you get erased, you are history! It's odd, but I know Christians who believe that believers can lose their salvation, who just happen to be "backslidden" themselves, yet they don't believe that they have lost their salvation. However, they are quite certain that other believers who have fallen into the same sin have lost theirs. If a proud look is an abomination to God, then to what degree does one have to sin to get erased??? Funny how that works...

Shortly before His crucifixion, Jesus spoke these words to His disciples in the Gospel of John:

> These things I have spoken to you, that in Me you may have peace. In the world you will have tribulation; but be of good cheer, I have overcome the world. (John 16:33)

Who is our overcomer? Jesus! Jesus knew as He shared these encouraging words with his fearful, wavering disciples, that they would soon be scattered. As they witnessed their worst nightmare—His gruesome death on the cross—their faith would be shaken and temporarily shattered. Indeed, after His crucifixion, Peter, "Mr. Water-walker" himself, denied ever knowing Him (Matthew 26:69-75) just as Jesus told Peter he would (John 16:36, 37). Peter had promised Jesus that he would lay down his life for Him, but fear can certainly squelch our faith when we are in the heat of the threat of death.

If God blots names from the book of life because we falter and fail as Saints, then surely, Peter's name was erased, and we will never meet him in heaven. Surely, his sin of denying Jesus before men would have caused Jesus to deny him before his Father in heaven. (Matthew 10:32, 33) It would have been impossible to renew Peter again unto repentance (Hebrews 6:4-6), considering he had surely fallen away from his association with Jesus. But, thank God, He is faithful even when our faith is weak. (2 Timothy 2:13)

Think of all the Old Testament saints who failed in their faith. Take Abraham, for example. He is regarded in the Bible as, "The Founding Father of the Faith," yet he lied and failed in his faith frequently. Knowing God's promise and plan for his life, Abraham was willing to give his wife, Sarah, over to Abimelech, the King of Gerar, claiming that she was his sister, because he feared that the King would kill him on account of his wife. And yet, God blessed him anyway! (Genesis 20:1-15)

Likewise, David, referred to in the Bible as, "A man after God's Heart," (Acts 13:22) failed God horrendously numerous times. As it turns out, this heroic giant-killer, musician, poet and "forerunner of the Messiah" would become the King of Israel, but he would also be known as an unfaithful husband, a murderer, and a sorry father. Do you really believe that Abraham and David will be MIA (Missing In Action) when we get to heaven? I don't think so.

Did God not know ahead of time when He chose these imperfect men as part of His plan to bring salvation to mankind that they would sin as they did after He chose and anointed them for His purposes? If He is truly omniscient, of course He did! Yet, He chose them, knowing that they would fail as human beings. These were saints who never experienced the promise of the Spirit (Galatians 3:14) like you and me. They may have experienced the *influence* of the Holy Spirit *on* their lives, but they never experienced the *indwelling* Holy Spirit *in* their lives.

With this in mind, we are forced to ask ourselves, "Is there another human being in the history of mankind, beside Jesus, who could qualify to know or serve God based on their ability to live a sinless life?" Other than Jesus, there are *no* candidates. That's right, not one. God sees our lives from beginning to end before He chooses us for His purposes. He knows that we will sin and fail, yet He also knows His son, has paid *in advance* for all of our sins and failures. Otherwise, no one could serve Him and no one could remain saved. Think about it...

Must true Christians endure, remain faithful, and overcome until Jesus comes, in order to remain saved and avoid having their names erased from the Lamb's Book of Life? I believe true believers were *born to win!* How does the Bible say that we become overcomers? We find the answer in these verses:

> For whatever is <u>born of God</u> overcomes the world. And this is the victory that has overcome the world— even <u>our faith</u>. Who is he who overcomes the world, but <u>he who believes that Jesus is the Son of God</u>?
> (1 John 5:4, 5)

We are overcomers because *we have been born of God.* We overcome by *believing that Jesus is the Son of God.* Faith in Jesus is our victory! I don't know about you, but I don't intend to place my faith in anyone else but Jesus while I'm here! Who else could we go to? Jesus has the words of eternal life! (John 6:68)

Are we saved by our works or by our ability to faithfully endure to the end? No. Can we keep ourselves saved by our works or our ability? Some believe we must, but what does God say?

...being confident of this very thing, that <u>He who has begun a good work in you will complete it until the day of Jesus Christ</u>; (Philippians 1:6)

Now may the God of peace Himself sanctify you completely; and may your whole spirit, soul, and body be preserved blameless at the coming of our Lord Jesus Christ. <u>He who calls you is faithful, who also will do it.</u> (1 Thessalonians 5:23, 24)

Who do these verses say has begun His good work in us? God has. Who will complete it until Jesus comes? God will. Who will sanctify us completely, and preserve us blameless, spirit, soul and body at the coming of our Lord Jesus? The God of peace Himself will! He alone is the beginning, the middle, and the end of our salvation! Even when we lose our grip on Him, He does not lose His grip on us! Thank God!

Fallen from Grace?

I've heard well-meaning Saints refer to a backslidden believer as someone who has "fallen from grace" because of some sin that they have fallen into. In fact, I had a fellow believer come to me one time and tell me, "Pete, I have sinned grievously and fallen from God's grace. I hope that somehow, He can forgive me and restore me to the Kingdom someday." Pitiful... Is this really how grace works? Like "Mr. T," God coldly and harshly states to Saints who sin willfully after their salvation: "I pity you, fool! I'm puttin' you in hell, and you only gonna get three meals a day: oatmeal, miss-a-meal and no-meal! Take that, sucka!" Uh...I don't think so. Those who use "fallen from grace" in this manner certainly misunderstand and misapply it.

> You have become estranged from Christ, <u>you who attempt to be justified by law</u>; you have <u>fallen from grace</u>. (Galatians 5:4)

Please notice, it is not those who mess up and sin that have fallen from grace; it is those who are trying to justify themselves by the works of the law! Grace comes through belief in Christ. To believe in our works of righteousness is to "fall from grace." To misinterpret this passage is a grave error. This is a prime example of taking scripture out of context just to prove a doctrinal stance! Satan has used this grievous misapplication of scripture to discourage and defeat many a believer in Christ.

Go East, Young Man!

What has God done with all of the sin that He has forgiven through the blood of Jesus? His Word says that He has removed it far from us. How far?

> "As far as the east is from the west, So far has He removed our transgressions from us." (Psalms 103:12)

Consider this...God knew the earth was round long before man finally figured it out. If you get on the equator and travel northward, eventually you will cross the North Pole. What happens then? You change directions! All of a sudden, you are traveling in the opposite direction...south. As you continue southward, eventually you reach the South Pole. You guessed it! All of a sudden you have changed direction again. Now, you are going north. Is that the way God forgives...we're saved one day, then unsaved the next if we stumble or sin willfully as Saints? But notice what God said, "As far as the east is from the west..." Get on the equator and travel east. You will never reach a point on the equator where you change directions! You will travel eastward forever!

What this verse is saying is that God has removed our sins *from us* forever, past, present, and yes, future! It is never going to sneak up from behind us and bite us again! That would be "Déjà vu all over again!" This is why there is no other way to come to God except through Jesus and His sacrifice on the cross. No other savior or religion in the world offers so great a salvation!

When He was executed for our sins, we were executed for our sins. The debt was paid by His death, and our death in Him becomes our co-payment by faith in what He did. We do not have to pay in eternity because it was eternally paid 2,000 years ago on His cross when both He, *and we*, were crucified for our sins! Hallelujah!

Married but Miserable

Let's suppose you are married to a husband, Mr. Perfect Law. He is completely domineering and authoritarian; constantly demanding absolute perfection from you. He is cold and never "cuts you any slack," ever! You are miserable in the marriage but his death is the only way you could ever be free to marry another. Problem is, Mr. Right is the picture of health, and he's just fine with the marriage. He isn't going anywhere! Alrighty, then...

Meanwhile, you have met your dream man, the love of your life, Mr. Amazing Grace. Instant infatuation! Your heart longs for him, yet you can never have a relationship with him as long as you are attached to Mr. Law. Since Mr. Law isn't about to die anytime soon, the only way to possibly be free to marry Mr. Grace is for you to die. Impossible! Well, this option would be impossible unless, miraculously, you could be raised again from the dead. Then, your miserable marriage to Mr. "Hard-hearted" would be dissolved and you would be free to marry your "Knight in shining armor," Mr. Grace.

Once again, that is exactly what happened to you and me when we accepted Jesus as our Lord and Savior. Look at how the apostle, Paul puts it:

> Or do you not know, brethren (for I speak to those who know the law), that the law has dominion over a man as long as he lives? For the woman who has a husband is bound by the law to her husband as long as he lives. But if the husband dies, she is released from the law of her husband. So then if, while her husband lives, she marries another man, she will be called an adulteress; but if her husband dies, she is free from that law, so that she is no adulteress, though she has married another man. Therefore, my brethren, you also have become dead to the law through the body of Christ, that you may be married to another— to Him who was raised from the dead, that we should bear fruit to God. For when we were in the flesh, the sinful passions which were aroused by the law were at work in our members to bear fruit to death. But now we have been delivered from the law, having died to what we were held by, so that we should serve in the newness of the Spirit and not in the oldness of the letter. (Romans 7:1-6)

The Law is never going to die, and we should be thankful that God is never going to compromise His righteousness revealed by the Law. However, in Jesus, we died to what we could never live up to and were raised again spiritually that we might be free to live with Mr. Grace, the man, Jesus Christ, who fulfilled the righteous requirement of the law for us and in us eternally.

In this analogy, the real problem is not the Law of God; it is perfect and good. It is a reflection of God's perfect righteousness.

The real problem is our sin nature. Look at Paul's words about this:

> I was alive once without the law, but when the commandment came, sin revived and I died. And the commandment, which was to bring life, I found to bring death. For sin, taking occasion by the commandment, deceived me, and by it killed me. Therefore the law is holy, and the commandment holy and just and good. Has then what is good become death to me? Certainly not! But sin, that it might appear sin, was producing death in me through what is good, so that sin through the commandment might become exceedingly sinful. (Romans 7:9-13)

Do you understand what Paul is saying? The law is life, but because we cannot live up to it perfectly, it becomes death to us.

Christ lived the Law perfectly because He, Himself, is the righteousness of God. Because He is the righteousness of God, He is LIFE. When we are in Him, we become dead to what we were hopelessly bound to, and become (by grace) alive in Him and instruments of righteousness for Him. Paul made this statement earlier in Romans:

> And do not present your members as instruments of unrighteousness to sin, but present yourselves to God as being alive from the dead, and your members as instruments of righteousness to God. For sin shall not have dominion over you, for you are not under law but under grace. (Romans 6:13, 14)

The Gospel, "Good News" is Jesus, Himself. Christ *in us* is the good news of eternal life and our only hope of glory! (Colossians 1:27) His life, which is our salvation, is offered freely by faith to "whosoever" will receive Him. Jesus has not called us to Christianity. We are not called to religious rules, rituals or regulations. We are not called to religious morality or even Christian values. None of these things save us or keep us saved. Jesus has called us to Himself. He is the Good News. He is the righteousness of God. He is eternal life. When we have Him, we have everything we need for life and Godliness! (2 Peter 1:3)

Deeper Life?

> Without controversy great is the mystery of godliness: God was manifest in the flesh... (1 Timothy 3:16)

I love these comments from Christian author, Ian Thomas:

> "Beware lest even as a Christian, you fall into Satan's trap! You may have found and come to know God in the Lord Jesus Christ, receiving Him sincerely as your Redeemer, yet if you do not enter into the mystery of godliness and allow God to be in you the origin of His own image, you will seek to be godly by submitting yourself to external rules and regulations and by conforming to behavior patterns imposed upon you by the particular Christian society that you have chosen and in which you hope to be found 'acceptable.' You will in this way perpetuate the pagan habit of practicing religion in the energy of the flesh, and in the very pursuit of righteousness commit idolatry in honoring 'Christianity' more than Christ!" [8]

> "God did not create you to have just an ape-like capacity to imitate God. There would be no mystery in

that, nor would this lift you morally much above the status of a monkey or a parrot! The capacity to imitate is vested in the one who imitates, and does not derive from, nor necessarily share the motives of the person being imitated, who remains passive and impersonal to the act of imitation." [9]

What the author is relating to in these quotes is often referred to as "The Deeper Life" by many of the writers of his generation. This deeper life is more than the practice of "Christianity," it is the "mystery of Godliness," which means that God, Himself, is the source of the life lived out. The revelation of Jesus through us is not found in our ability to imitate God, but in our surrender to His empowerment in us. Only as we rest in His life, are we able to genuinely live the Spirit-filled life.

Early in my Christian experience, I had a pastor tell me: "Listen, Pete, we don't need to be concerned about this so-called 'deeper life' stuff, we just need to be busy for God. That's how you get the deeper life!" Bless his heart. I know he was sincere, but we know by now that sincerity is not the test for what is true, don't we? I thank God, that true Christianity is much, much more than merely being busy for God. Make no mistake about it, I believe that we should be busy for God but Jesus must be both the motive (inspiration) and the motor (power) of our busyness. It is God who works in us, both to will and to do for His good pleasure. (Philippians 2:13)

Though God gives to each of us talents and abilities, He will never settle for our ability. Rather, He insists that we rest in and rely upon the "deeper life" of His Holy Spirit in us. I've learned that the only thing for me to be busy about is asking Him to help my unbelief, and asking Him to manifest Himself in me as I surrender my abilities to His supernatural life! I will guarantee you, if we live out our life in this manner, we will truly begin to love people. That is true holiness. When we begin to love people, we will become driven to serve Him by serving others, and we will be empowered by His miraculous, loving energy. This is true Christianity. (Matthew 25:31-46)

So what does all of this mean? We are free from the law, because we are now indwelt by the Spirit of the law of God—our righteousness and eternal life. It has been engraved upon our hearts and written in our minds as new creations. We are freed from the practice of Christianity, and from every other performance based practice of religion. We are free to be *naturally* who we are in Christ. We are the earthen containers of the divine nature with both feet planted firmly on the ground as His Ambassadors of Grace and life. We don't have to walk on water; we just have to walk on land for Him!

I don't know about you, but I can hardly contain myself, when I realize *who* is contained within me! The more light God gives us, the better the "too good to be true" good news gets, doesn't it? Let the blessed Holy Spirit soak your heart with these truths! Take just a minute, and let these liberating words sink in! In fact, go over these pages again if you haven't been able to fully comprehend them. Our understanding of what the Word of God says is what frees us and empowers us to be more than conquerors in Christ!

> Stand fast therefore in the liberty by which Christ has made us free, and do not be entangled again with a yoke of bondage. (Galatians 5:1)

Along with the late Dr. Martin Luther King Jr., we can gloriously declare: "Free at last, free at last, Thank God almighty, we are free at last!"[10] Stand straight, hold your head high and walk tall in the newness of your eternal life and liberty!

Together Again

Reconciled Forever

Romans 5:8-10

> But God demonstrates His own love toward us, in that while we were still sinners, Christ died for us. Much more then, having now been justified by His blood, we shall be saved from wrath through Him. For if when we were enemies we were reconciled to God through the death of His Son, much more, having been reconciled, we shall be saved by His life.

Having been forever redeemed (paid for) and washed clean (sanctified), we are now free to come into an eternal, personal, intimate relationship with the infinitely unapproachable, omnipotent (all-powerful), invisible God of the universe. Up to this point, we have spent a lot of time laying out what it means to be truly saved, but have you ever wondered *why* God saves us in the first place?

Well, I believe to better understand the answer to this question; we need to understand the reason that he created man in the first place. Why do you suppose God created Adam...and then, a woman named, Eve? I believe God created Adam, not just to be the caretaker of His newly created world, but for a personal relationship with Himself. Then, I think He created Eve so Adam could understand the nature of the relationship for which he was created. After God presented Eve to Adam, he said,

> "This is now bone of my bones, and flesh of my flesh: she shall be called Woman, because she was taken out of Man. Therefore shall a man leave his father and his mother, and shall cleave unto his wife: and they shall be one flesh." (Genesis 2:23, 24)

Firm Family Foundations

In this passage, we see God's blueprint for the family...one man with one woman, for life—Adam and Eve, not Adam and Steve! Pardon me, but when I was growing up, the term, "gay," meant happy and care-free. God created Adam and Eve "male and female" and instructed them to "be fruitful and multiply." (Genesis 1:27, 28) That would have been impossible to accomplish if God had created them male and male, or female and female...would it not???

I never thought I would live to see the day when these statements would be considered "bigoted and politically incorrect" in our country. Nevertheless, (God, have mercy on us) that is where we are today in America. Believe me, I don't hate sinners, and God certainly has not commissioned me to judge sinners. That does not mean, however, that we are to ignore sin and not make judgment calls on what is right or wrong. God doesn't hate sinners, He hates sin. We are all guilty of going our own way in one way or another. Great or small, God calls it all sin. (Isaiah 53:6)

Anyway...in the scripture above, we have a picture of a union so close and so intimate that they were considered to be one flesh. Eventually, that oneness of flesh manifests itself literally with offspring, in whom both parents are seen. Okay, so why does God save us?

First, ultimately, God created man for a relationship with Himself and He saves us for the same reason. The relationship He creates us for and saves us for is a family relationship with Him. This is why the family is extremely important to God, and why it should be important to us.

The modernist, progressive liberals of our day can try to redefine family for us, but God laid the correct foundation for the family in the very beginning. The strength and stability of any superstructure is its foundation. Likewise, the foundation of every individual is their family, and the strength and stability of any society is the God-designed family unit. Balanced, Godly parents are the heart and fiber of any healthy home and the strength of our homes is the only hope for our society. Unfortunately, the strength of the family unit in America has been disintegrating for decades and we are now reaping the ruinous results. Each generation, intentionally or unintentionally, passes their family values and strengths (or lack, thereof) on to the generations that follow them with each generation either preserving the strength of those values, or becoming more and more decadent.

Secondly, believers must understand that God does not save us to serve Him, but to know Him. To know Him and His Son, Jesus is ETERNAL LIFE. (John 17:3) Sin had separated those He had created for Himself from Him, but even before sin reared its ugly head, God had a plan to bring them back into that relationship, like nothing had ever happened to separate them. (Romans 5:11; 2 Corinthians 5:19) That is what reconciliation in the Bible means: to be brought back together like nothing ever happened.

Like me, you have probably experienced times when disagreements or disputes with family members or very close friends tore the relationship apart. There was a time of hurt and resentment that may have left deep scars, but over time perhaps both sides were able to forgive, if not forget. However, it wasn't long before it became apparent that the relationship was never going to be quite the same as it was before the incident occurred. It is heart-breaking to go through this.

I still miss some of the dearest friendships I've ever had and the times we shared together. The absence of their unique personalities has left a void in my life that will never quite be filled again. It makes me sad. Oh, that we could forgive and forget as God does! Satan is a professional thief, murderer and destroyer! He is constantly accusing the brethren and wreaking havoc on earth...oh, I hate that guy! He never takes a coffee break!

Come on in!

God has eternally forgiven us of every sin we have ever committed, and ever will commit, breathed His Spirit of life back into our hearts, and set us free from the power of sin. But, as wonderful as these aspects of our salvation are, they are not all that His saving work in Christ has accomplished. Because those works are finished, He can now reconcile us back to the family relationship with Himself that He created us for in the first place.

The day Jesus died on the cross; the Bible says that the veil in the Jewish Temple in Jerusalem was torn from top to bottom.

> "Then, behold, the veil of the temple was torn in two from top to bottom; and the earth quaked, and the rocks were split," (Matthew 27:51)

What is the significance of this earth-shaking, historical event? Like God and man, the temple was triune in its makeup. Those who brought their sin sacrifices could come into the outer court, but only the Priests could enter into the inner court with the blood of those sacrifices. Then, only the High Priest could enter through the veil into the Holy of Holies where the glorious presence of God hovered over the Ark of the Covenant. No man could truly have an intimate relationship with God under the Old Covenant. Though He inhabited the Temple, God and man were separated by a thick, heavy veil. Man's sinfulness before a Holy God would kill him if he entered without the blood of a spotless lamb to atone for his sins.

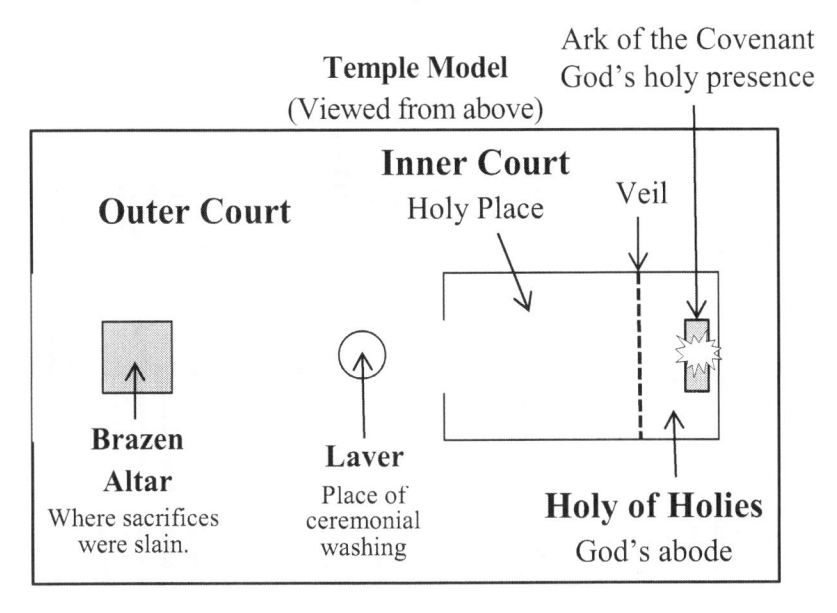

Temple Model
(Viewed from above)

- Ark of the Covenant — God's holy presence
- **Outer Court**
- **Inner Court** — Holy Place
- Veil
- **Brazen Altar** — Where sacrifices were slain.
- **Laver** — Place of ceremonial washing
- **Holy of Holies** — God's abode

OUTER COURT — analogous to our outward man, body

INNER COURT — analogous to our inner- man, soul

HOLY OF HOLIES — analogous to our spirit, the inner-most part of who we are, God's abode.

The tearing of the Temple Veil represented the fact that this awesome, fearsome God had accepted the sacrifice of His only begotten Son, Jesus, the perfect sacrificial lamb. Because we are cleansed of all our sins by that blood, God can declare us holy and clean, a royal priesthood. As a result, we can know Him by a new and living way. (Hebrews 10:14-22)

God has allowed man back into His holy presence where we can go in and out and find pasture.

> "I am the door. If anyone enters by Me, he will be saved, and will go in and out and find pasture."
> (John 10:9)

The barrier that stood between a holy God and sinful men has been taken out of the way. God, Himself, has torn the veil that separated us from top to bottom. Now all who are IN Christ have free access to Him. In fact, as we stated before, God, through His Spirit, actually takes up residence in us.

> "Or do you not know that your body is the temple of the Holy Spirit who is in you, whom you have from God, and you are not your own?"
> (1 Corinthians 6:19)

> "And because you are sons, God has sent forth the Spirit of His Son into your hearts, crying out, "Abba, Father!" (Galatians 4:6)

You and I don't have to go to a church or a temple to find God because *we* are now the temple of God.

> God, who made the world and everything in it, since He is Lord of heaven and earth, does not dwell in temples made with hands. (Acts 17:24)

Our body is now His flesh and blood temple! He has taken up permanent residence in us by making Himself one spirit with us! That changes everything! The only thing that makes a room in a church building a "sanctuary" is the presence of those who are the "temples of the living God!" When we show up, He shows up!

The term, "Reconciled," means we and our Creator are brought back together into an eternal union that will never be broken again. I hate to beat a "Live horse" but, this is because our sin debt, past, present and future has been cleared! We have been paid for by His blood, born again, and God has declared us justified. We now have absolute freedom to walk each and every day with Him on the journey. Look at these verses:

> And not only that, but we also rejoice in God through our Lord Jesus Christ, through whom we have now received the reconciliation. (Romans 5:11)

> Now all things are of God, who has reconciled us to Himself through Jesus Christ... (2 Corinthians 5:18)

> And you, who once were alienated and enemies in your mind by wicked works, yet now He has reconciled... (Colossians 1:21)

Life begins to take on a whole new dynamic when our minds are renewed to the truth found in the scriptures.

Let's talk about the renewing of the mind for a minute. Like we stated before, we all have physical life, but the quality of life we experience definitely depends on our state of mind. How we see ourselves absolutely affects the way we live each day. The Bible says, *"...For as he thinks in his heart, so is he."* (Proverbs 23:7) It is impossible to live consistently contrary to the way we perceive ourselves to be. I hope the Rest Stops we have visited are beginning to change your perception of who you really are.

As I shared earlier, when I was a kid growing up, I struggled from a lack of confidence and self-esteem. Looking back, I would have to say that much of that was due to the words I heard expressed about me over and over again: "You're stupid! You'll never amount to anything!" I even had a teacher in the sixth grade tell me that I was the dumbest student she had ever tried to teach. Bless her heart; I must have really frustrated her! I must admit, I wasn't exactly the brightest bulb in the academic Chandelier.

As a result of all this negative programming, I felt insecure and inferior most of my life. Not that I was never encouraged by anyone, but as I was entering my teens, it seemed like my life was taking the course that everyone predicted it would. I didn't apply myself very well in school, so my school days were frustrating and tension-filled as I struggled to make any grade above an F just to advance to the next grade level.

I tended to keep my mouth shut most of the time because I didn't want to confirm everyone's suspicion that I was dumb. Besides, I didn't think my opinion mattered to anyone anyway. I realized that I had inherited some natural talents with music and art, but I became unmotivated, lazy, and had no confidence to pursue or develop them. I was living down to the way I saw myself in my mind, and when I quit high school, my life began to spiral down the course of meaningless mediocrity.

BUT, God intervened! That is His specialty! He is able to take what appear to be hopeless failures and make them into *"...more than conquerors...!"* (Romans 8:37) Nevertheless, when I first got involved in church after my salvation experience, I still had my self-defeating mindset to overcome.

I remember what a struggle it was when my first Sunday school teacher, Rosco Brewer, asked me to share with our class how I came to know the Lord. It was painfully intimidating because of the way I saw myself, not to mention that there were more than 100 people in our Sunday school class. Hardly making eye contact with anyone, I stammered and stumbled my way through my testimony the way that I had always done with everything else I had ever attempted. Rosco understood the newness of my faith and was kind and encouraging, but I felt humiliated and embarrassed, nonetheless.

When you fail over and over again in your feeble attempts, at anything, failure becomes your expectation and those expectations become your mode of operation. After a while, you just quit trying. Nevertheless, as I began to explore the Bible, God began to gradually renew my mind. As I slowly began to understand and accept who He said that I was, my life began to change. I'm not just talking about my outward journey; I'm talking about the little world between my ears—my self-perception. I'm talking about ideas that develop into strongholds in our mind that prevent us from becoming who and what God says we can become. God is able to help us to overcome these as He equips us with the truth of His Word.

> For the weapons of our warfare are not physical [weapons of flesh and blood], but they are mighty before God for the overthrow and destruction of strongholds, [Inasmuch as we] refute arguments and theories and reasonings and every proud and lofty thing that sets itself up against the [true] knowledge of God; and we lead every thought and purpose away captive into the obedience of Christ (the Messiah, the Anointed One) (2 Corinthians 10:4, 5)
> (Amplified Bible)

Baby step by baby step, I began to venture outside of my self-protection zone. With God's view of me slowly transforming the way I saw myself, I began to come out of my shell and God began to gently stretch me. I began to believe and accept who He said that I was. I was God's son! There is no person on earth more significant than one of God's children! I was not a stepson anymore. I was not a welfare kid anymore. I wasn't stupid anymore, I had the "...mind of Christ" (1 Corinthians 2:16), so there wasn't anything I couldn't learn or understand if I just made myself available to be taught. This is why it is so important for new believers to make the commitment to place themselves in a position where God can give them a steady diet of new information from the Bible. Unfortunately, many who trust Christ as their Savior fail to get into the habit of attending church and Bible study on a regular basis.

Slowly, but surely, I began to believe that it was possible to become whatever God wanted me to become. Of course, in my old self, I felt totally unworthy. That is the way I felt all of my life, but according to God, I wasn't the same person I used to be. I was His newly created, new-born son! I was a brand new person with the potential to become anything, and accomplish anything in life, if I would simply trust Him and follow His leadership.

I remember the night I was saved. I was sitting in that little church in Arkansas because several of my family members kept telling me about Jesus and how I needed to believe in Jesus and accept Him as my Lord and Savior. I thought to myself, "Yeah, but I'm not as bad as some people I know." They kept on and on about me going to church with them that night, but I had been in church a few times, and to tell the truth, I didn't like the whole church experience. I really couldn't get into organ music unless it was by the "Doors" or "Deep Purple." Even though I did believe there was a God, I didn't know anything about Christianity. I thank my mom and several family members on her side for that basic belief in God. I just didn't know anything about Him. I had prayed like this: "Oh, my God! Help me!" most of my life. Haven't we all? But, that is not a real relationship.

I sat through the service as the preacher shared his message, listening, but thinking to myself, "I'll sure be glad when this thing is over. I sure hope my coming tonight will get my family off my back about going to church." Nevertheless, this question kept popping into my mind over and over again, "I wonder what you have to do to be saved?" At the end of the Pastor's message, he read where the Philippian Jailer asked Paul and Silas, *"Sirs, what must I do to be saved?"* (Acts 16:30) When I heard that, I thought to myself, "There really is something more to this Christianity thing than just going to church! This is real, man!"

They started the altar call and I thought, "What should I do? What will everyone think if I go forward?" Basically, that is the struggle we all have within our natural mind when Jesus says, *"Come unto Me and I will give you rest."* (Matthew 11:28) We live with other people's opinions in mind all of our lives...don't we?. Finally, I decided that I was going forward to accept Jesus into my heart, regardless of what anyone thought or did. God's opinion was all that mattered. That would be my very first, "Yes, Lord." It would also be my first step to where I am today. Have you taken that first, life-changing step?

Well, after about, what seemed like, ten verses of the invitation hymn, I finally let go of the pew in front of me. I went forward and knelt down to pray. I had no idea what was going to happen next. I didn't even know what to pray. Soon, the pastor and my uncle George came and prayed with me. More than twenty years later, that same pastor told me that he and my uncle had determined before the service that night that I was going to be saved, even if it took 100 verses of the invitation hymn to get me to the altar. I'm thankful that they were so committed to seeing me come to salvation in Christ and that they prayed ahead of time on my behalf. I sure hope someone loves you that much.

Here I am 38 years later, and it's the same thing every day, will I respond to God with a, "Yes, Lord," or answer Him with something else? There has been a long series of "Yes, Lords" in my life since I decided to follow Jesus. Not that I have always responded the correct way, but I can say this, when we decide to give God any other answer but "yes" to what He asks from us, our faith walk stalls out on the side of the road. Has your life broken down?

My second "Yes, Lord" was when I decided I would give up my right to sleep in on Sunday mornings and start attending church each week. Then, Sunday school, Sunday evening service, Wednesday evening bible study and prayer meeting, then choir, then the bus ministry, next singing in the choir, then singing solo specials, eventually teaching Sunday School, then working in the

Nursing Home ministry...well you get the point. The faith walk is a series of steps where we learn and grow in our willingness to say, "Yes," to the Lord, and as a result, grow in the reality of our faith. Many Christians, for whatever reason, get into the bad habit of saying, "No, Lord, not me, not now, I can't, maybe someday, I'll decide when," anything but, "yes, Lord." Consequently, they miss what God has for them and never realize what could have been.

I believe that when we get to heaven and we *"know as we are known"* (1 Corinthians 13:12), God will allow us to see what His ultimate plan for our life on earth was, contrasted by how we actually chose to live our lives. Not only will it be heart-breaking to see what we missed, but we will realize how going our own way in life short-changed our families and others.

Certainly, God doesn't save us to serve Him. We're not His slaves; we're His sons. We're not just His servants; we're His heirs. He is our Awesome God, but he is also our Abba, Father. The term, "Abba," holds two meanings. It is a term that a young son would use to address his Father in a manner that communicates respect, reliance and submission. It is extremely important for us to trust Him and obey Him on the journey. However, this new reconciled relationship is of such an intimate nature that God allows us to address Him as "Papa." Our American equivalent would be "Daddy." Amazing!

I am so offended when my children call me "Dad!" I hate it when my grandchildren call me, "Papa!" If you are smiling, you know this is not true. It warms my heart when my grandchildren call me "Papa." I love it! Because of my unique relationship with my children, I am proud when they call me, "Dad." I'm not at all offended. I know they respect who I am. God knows our heart. I don't think He is offended when we think of Him as our Daddy. He knows that we respect who He is. We look up to Him. He is God, Almighty!

Learning this changed my life. Of course, our motive for serving Him is love, not obligation, not gratitude, and not duty. All of these human motives fail, ultimately, but love never fails.

We're "Family-tight" with God now, eternally together again, and nothing is ever going to separate us from His love!

> For I am persuaded that neither death nor life, nor angels nor principalities nor powers, nor things present nor things to come, nor height nor depth, nor any other created thing, shall be able to separate us from the love of God which is in Christ Jesus our Lord. (Romans 8:38, 39)

These lines from the old country song, "Together Again,"[11] say it best.

> Together again, my tears have stopped falling;
> The long lonely nights are now at an end.
> The key to my heart, you hold in your hand;
> And nothing else matters 'cause we're together again.

God & Sons, Inc.

Heirs or hired help?

John 1:12, 13

But as many as received Him, to them He gave the right to become the Children of God, to those who believe in His name: who were born, not of blood, nor of the will of the flesh, nor of the will of man, but of God.

The Family Business

Have you ever noticed that people, who work for an employer that is not a part of their family, simply work by the hour? In other words, they merely put in their time. More often than not, they would prefer to start late and quit early; and they are always clock-conscious. I suppose that would describe the way I worked most of my life. I figured, "This isn't my business, so I'll give 'em eight for eight, but after 4:30 PM I get overtime pay." I worked for various contractors in the building trades for nearly thirty years.

One contractor for which I worked many years was headed by the founder, his son, and two grandsons. While the grandsons were on summer break from college, they would come out on the job site and work alongside the hired help. It didn't take long to realize that their motive for work wasn't the same as mine.

They would show up on the job as early as it took, do whatever it took, and stay as long as it took to assure that their father's business prospered. They weren't hired help and they didn't work by the hour. They worked with an "ownership attitude." They were totally committed to the "Family Business" because it belonged to them. When they first started working in the business, they may not have had full control, but they knew that day would eventually come. They didn't have to be motivated to work hard because they were working for themselves. Working in the family business was more than merely their job, it was their inheritance. Today, those two grandsons have full control of that business.

I think too many Christians fail to see that when God saves us, He saves us into His family business, "God & Sons, Inc." Like the two grandsons in the analogy, God's children are not hired help; we are heirs and joint heirs with Jesus to all that God has created for us, now and for eternity. If this is true, then each of us should examine our hearts to see whether we serve Him like we are heirs or hired help.

Are we too clock-conscious during the church service? Would that attitude describe how we tolerate a church service? Are we too reluctant to commit our time to work in the Father's business? Are we too eager to quit before the work is done? Do we take pride in our work for the Lord? As a hired hand, I worked hard and took pride in my work, but I was always working toward break time, lunch time and quitting time. Funny thing is, when I contracted jobs myself, I would work straight through my breaks most of the time.

To be sure, love always involves faithful commitment. That commitment is not always easy, but we serve God because we love

Him and what is His is ours, ultimately. We don't decline the opportunity to serve Him and we don't quit at the first difficulty. God isn't our employer, He's our Father! Let these words soak into your heart:

> For as many as are led by the Spirit of God, (those of us who are born of God) these are sons of God. For you did not receive the spirit of bondage again to fear, but you received the Spirit of adoption by whom we cry out, "Abba, Father." The Spirit Himself bears witness with our spirit that we are children of God, and if children, then heirs—heirs of God and joint heirs with Christ... (Romans 8:14-17)

It is clear that, as God's children, we are very special to Him, and that He intends to bless us abundantly because we are His heirs. Of course, we serve Him, not because we are supposed to, but because we love Him, and want to bless Him. We are family, and as such, members of the family business. We should work in the business with an ownership attitude because we are heirs, not hired help.

What Manner of Love?

> Behold what manner of love the Father has bestowed on us, that we should be called children of God! Therefore the world does not know us, because it did not know Him. Beloved, now we are children of God; and it has not yet been revealed what we shall be, but we know that when He is revealed, we shall be like Him, for we shall see Him as He is. (1 John 3:1-2)

> ...for in Him we live and move and have our being, as also some of your own poets have said, 'For we are also His offspring. (Acts 17:2)

Once again, the truth is just too good to be true, but it is true! We who believe in Jesus and receive Him have actually become God's kids! Incredible! Why would God go this far? Could it be that Adam was created for a family relationship with God? I believe he was and that we are saved for the same reason!

Have you ever wondered why God allowed the first couple, Adam and Eve, to procreate? Why didn't God just create every human being himself, as He had the first two? Consider this; do you think we could begin to understand the way that God loves us, if we didn't have little ones who bore our likeness and our name, to love as our own? Think about the way you love your children and grandchildren. Would you say that your love for them is unconditionally sacrificial? No question. Is there anything that you would not do for their good? Certainly, we would do whatever it takes to protect them and provide for them because of their unique relationship to us.

I loved each and every one of my children and grandchildren before I ever had the opportunity to see them, hold them, or know them personally. If the doctor had come to me just before they were born and said to me, "Mr. Whitebird, I'm afraid that in order for this little one of yours to be born, we'll have to take your life," honestly, I would not have had to think or pray about it. I would have gladly died for all of them <u>before</u> they were even born.

I still love the grandkids who look like the in-laws that way! Now, that's amazing grace! Actually, the quality of love I'm talking about is natural, God-instinctual, parental love. It's the kind of love that never did, and never will depend on my kids or grandkids. Our relationship with our offspring is unique, isn't it? They don't do anything to earn it. It isn't based on their actions, good or bad. It is not even dependent upon their love in return. It is entirely unconditional! We don't love anyone quite like we do our own children. I've always been puzzled by parents who can heartlessly discard their own offspring. It doesn't make any sense to me. That sort of loveless callousness has to come straight from the devil, himself. God would never inspire that!

What manner of love could God bestow upon us that would allow Him to refer to us, and relate to us, as His dearly beloved children? How about...parental love? I'm convinced that the primary reason God allowed us to have children of our own is so we could understand how He loves us. He wanted us to understand the nature of the relationship that He saved for us—a parent-child relationship. We are more than simple servants, we are His beloved children, and He is our heavenly Father.

He loved us enough to lay down His life for us, even before we were born again. (Romans 5:8) Even though some of us who belong to Him might not always reflect or represent Him very well, His love for us never changes. You see, just like our love for our own children, His love never did, and never will, depend on us! Think about the way you love your children and multiply it infinitely; you are still not even beginning to approach the magnitude of the love that God has for the worst of sinners, much less for those of us who have been born of His Spirit and become His offspring. I didn't have my children for what they could do for me or give to me. Likewise, God does not love us and save us to do something for Him or for what we can give to Him. He simply wants us to be His! He wants us for the relationship.

When I married my second wife, she had a son from her first marriage. Travis was approximately 18 months old when we met. I was a step-son who became a step-dad. To my surprise, like my step-dad, I had a hard time accepting my new step-son. Funny how walking in someone else's shoes gives us a bit more understanding and clarity, isn't it? Even as a Christian, I struggled with my inability to love the son I was raising for years. I felt ashamed and prayed about it constantly, but the love was just not there. The truth is my lack of fatherly love for him was due to my selfish male pride and jealousy.

Finally, in answer to my prayers, God began to manifest *His* love for my step-son in my heart. I began to look at him differently. About the time Travis was 12 years old; I adopted him and gave him my last name. Somehow, that seemed to seal my love for him. Like me, he never knew his biological father. Unlike me, he never got the opportunity to meet his dad. I am the only dad that he has ever known. I love my son today as if he were my flesh and blood son. He is the only son I have ever had and, in spite of me, has turned out to be the best son any father could ever hope to have. In my heart, He is not my "step-son" anymore. I am proud that he carries my name. If I could, I would give my life to make him my son genetically, but unfortunately, that is impossible.

However, it is not impossible for the God who adopts us as His children! Not only has God chosen and adopted us; He is able to miraculously make us His eternal children genetically through a spiritual new birth! As God's children, what do you think He most wants from us? Once again, we find the answer in the Bible.

> Then one of them, a lawyer, asked Him a question, testing Him, and saying, "Teacher, which is the great commandment in the law?" Jesus said to him, 'YOU SHALL LOVE THE LORD YOUR GOD WITH ALL YOUR HEART, WITH ALL YOUR SOUL AND, WITH ALL YOUR MIND.' This is the first and great commandment. And the second is like it: 'YOU SHALL LOVE YOUR NEIGHBOR AS YOURSELF.' On these two commandments hang all the Law and the Prophets." (Matthew 22:35-40)

According to these words from Jesus, everything that we base our Christian faith on comes down to keeping these first two commandments. Everything that we consider to be Christianity comes from focusing on only two commandments. The Apostle, Paul agrees:

> Owe no one anything except to love one another, for he who loves another has fulfilled the law. For the commandments, "YOU SHALL NOT COMMIT ADULTERY," "YOU SHALL NOT MURDER," "YOU SHALL NOT STEAL," "YOU SHALL NOT BEAR FALSE WITNESS," "YOU SHALL NOT COVET," and if *there is* any other commandment, are *all* summed up in this saying, namely, "YOU SHALL LOVE YOUR NEIGHBOR AS YOURSELF." Love does no harm to a neighbor; therefore love *is* the fulfillment of the law. (Romans 13:8-10)

Think about it, what God wants from you and me the most is for us to love and trust Him. He knows that when we truly love Him, we will begin to truly love people. When we begin to truly love others, we must become servants, not because we are *supposed to*, but because we *want to* serve them. It becomes our passion! I truly believe that when it is all said and done, everything that we ever did for Jesus that wasn't motivated by love will be "wood, hay, and stubble." Those things will burn up.

> But if anyone builds upon the Foundation (Jesus), whether it be with gold, silver, precious stones, wood, hay, straw, The work of each [one] will become [plainly, openly] known (shown for what it is); for the day [of Christ] will disclose and declare it, because it will be revealed with fire, and the fire will test and critically appraise the character and worth of the work each person has done. If the work which any person has built on this Foundation [any product of

his efforts whatever] survives [this test], he will get his reward. But if any person's work is burned up [under the test], he will suffer the loss [of it all, losing his reward], though he himself will be saved, but only as [one who has passed] through fire. [Job 23:10.] (1Corinthians 3:12-15) (Amplified Bible)

Learning this amazing truth absolutely simplified my Christian walk and completely set me free. I began to realize that all we have to do every day is focus on knowing and loving God better! It became clear that all of the commandments recorded in the Bible come out of keeping the first one...LOVE GOD. Loving God produces LOVING OTHERS. This love for God and others forces us to be active in the Family Business, not passive, spiritually lazy family deadbeats! I suppose most families have members like that.

I always make it a point to tell new believers in Jesus that they only have one commandment to worry about, the first one. Simply get up each day and focus on getting to know God, your new, eternal "daddy" better through His Word and prayer. As you do, you will begin to love Him. Everything else in the Christian life comes from loving God! Certainly, life is complicated because we are complex beings, but our relationship with God is very simple. Love Him, trust Him, listen to Him, follow Him, obey Him, and rest in Him. Our new law is LOVE. Following are the lyrics to another song that came out of this realization in my life.

"All I Ever Really Wanted"

My heart aches at your empty resignation;
You try to please me but don't know me well enough.
It hurts to see you as you struggle with religion, vain tradition
While forgetting what I died for is your love.

All I ever really wanted is a loved one to love me.

Affection, devotion is enough;
'Cause when you love me, you will serve me,
Pour your heart out 'til it's empty
All I ever really wanted is your love.

You're a precious earthen vessel, recreated,
A living letter, gently written from above;
A priceless revelation in a Christless generation,
As I make you a reflection of my love.

All I ever really wanted is a loved one to love me.
Affection, devotion is enough;
'Cause when you love me, you will serve me,
Pour your heart out 'til it's empty
All I ever really wanted is your love.

It's pretty simple, isn't it? Though it may be suppressed by religious doctrine or duty, The Spirit of the law, LOVE, lives in the heart of every true believer. God designed us to be living love revelations to the world...let Him out!

> Beloved, let us love one another, for love is of God; and everyone who loves is born of God and knows God. He who does not love does not know God, for God is love. In this the love of God was manifested toward us, that God has sent His only begotten Son into the world, that we might live through Him. In this is love, not that we loved God, but that He loved us and sent His Son to be the propitiation (substitutionary sacrifice that completely satisfies God) for our sins. Beloved, if God so loved us, we also ought to love one another. (1 John 4:7-11)

Cheap Christianity?

Sometimes, when people hear me teach this, they will come up to me and ask: "Aren't you over-simplifying Christianity and making the Christian life too soft with all of this family love stuff? You make the Gospel sound too easy." Maybe that is what you are thinking as you read this book. If so, let me answer you with a question that I always answer them with: When we love our earthly father and mother, children and grandchildren, how much does our love require of us; 10 percent or 100 percent? Our love for family demands everything from us, doesn't it? We don't even think in percentages when it comes to family, do we? Love is neither easy nor cheap! When we truly love someone, we are willing to deny ourselves and do anything, or sacrifice anything, for their good. I can guarantee that my love for my wife and children has cost me far more than 10 percent over the years. In fact, love costs far more than money; it costs YOU.

I know Christians who feel proud and perfectly satisfied with the fact that they tithe (give 10 percent) to the church; but they refuse to forgive another brother or sister in the Lord who may have offended them in one way or another. They simply cannot sacrifice their right to be apologized to or their right to hold on to the "debt sheet" of those who have hurt or offended them. Which do you suppose our Father considers the greater sacrifice: 10 percent or love that freely forgives whatever is necessary??? Under the New Covenant of life and love, we are not under bondage to tithe.

If Christianity is simply serving an impersonal God that saves us to serve Him as His slaves, and we are not in the family relationship with Him that I have described, then maybe we could get by with giving ten percent, but that is not the relationship. Our love for Him demands everything from us. We should be willing to sacrifice anything for Him. We're family to Him…not hired help. We don't demand overtime pay because we don't work by the hour. We are willing to do more than we're asked to do for the sake of the family business because it is our business. Our motive is pure love! Does this describe the way you serve Him?

Picking up the Check

When we are born, we don't actually love our parents, do we? We need them, especially mama! When we are newly born, we don't even know our parents or what they are like, except that they give us what we need and most of the time, what we want, if we scream loud enough or whine enough. All we have to do is scream and cry, and they come running. As we get older and become more aware of our relationship to them, we begin to develop a love for them. However, this early love is still very immature. It is almost completely based on our need for their protection and provision. In other words, it is an, "I need you, love."

As we grow and mature, even into our teens, if we are honest, we must admit that our love for our parents is still more need-oriented than sacrifice-oriented. Unfortunately, some of us never learn to love anyone any other way. Consequently, when someone says: "I love you," whether they realize it or not, what they really mean is, "I need you." They need us to do something, say something, feel something emotionally or give something they need.

My wife and I have four adult children and now, seven grandchildren. When we all get together to eat out, the bill for our meal can be very expensive! I'll never forget the first time I "picked up the check" for the family; it was well over $100.00, and that did not include the added gratuity! I thought to myself, "I cannot believe that I am paying what used to be a week's wages for one meal!" My goodness, how things have changed! Don't get me wrong, my wife and I enjoy picking up the check for our adult children and grandchildren, because we love them. However, we began to see that their love for us was beginning to mature when they began to say: "Hey, mom and dad, we'll pick up your check." They still need our financial help occasionally, but as they have matured, their love for us has also matured. That is the way love is supposed to work. Peter calls it "Growing in grace." (2 Peter 3:18)

Unlike my heavenly Father, I have been far from perfect as a parent. However, in spite of me, God has blessed me with wonderful children. I could not be more proud of them. Not that they are perfect either, but they have seldom caused me heartache or embarrassment. Like my heavenly Father wants to bless me, I want to bless them!

The same is true with our love for God. When I was first introduced to Jesus, I can't say that I truly loved Him. I needed Him. I needed everything He had to offer me. Even as I learned more about Him and began to develop a love relationship with Him, I had to admit that it was mostly an, "I need you," kind of love. There is nothing wrong with that. That was the stage I was at in my spiritual growth.

One of the sure indicators of this type of love for God is our prayers. Almost always, the majority of our prayers consist of our asking Him to do something for us, or for Him to give us something. True, isn't it? As our heavenly parent, he loves to "pick up the check," because we are His children. However, He knows that when our prayers begin to change to, "What can I do for you, Lord," our love for Him is maturing. It warms His heart.

God loves us unconditionally, but don't you think that when God sees our, "I'll pick up the check for this, Lord," attitude, that it blesses Him and causes Him to want to bless us even more? I used to do things for the Lord because I thought, "If I do this, He'll bless me." However, over time, I have learned to do what I do in the family business because He has *already* blessed me. Of course, I still need Him to do many things for me and in me, and I still ask. But now, I do what I do for Him because I understand my relationship to Him much more clearly, and I love Him more intimately. As His adult spiritual son, I want to please Him and be like Him. I've learned that when we are faithful over the "little things," our Father gives us "bigger things" to do in the family business. (Matthew 25:21)

Just think of all the things I have presented in this book up to this point. They are infinitely beyond earthly value. Nothing on earth compares to them. Many of the wealthiest individuals on Planet Earth are spiritual paupers because these blessings are beyond what their earthly wealth can purchase. They are priceless! The truths I've shared are the "Spiritual blessings in the heavenly places" that God has richly blessed his children with. (Ephesians 1:3)

What Manner of Inheritance?

No one in my earthly family is going to leave me a rich inheritance when they pass on. As far as I know, no one in my family is wealthy. In fact, I don't have much to leave behind to my heirs when I go to be with the Lord. I'm doing the best I can to make sure they don't have to pick up the check for my funeral! I can, however, leave to them a rich spiritual legacy for Jesus Christ through my music and this book. Though I may not possess any earthly wealth, I can leave to them the wealth that I have inherited from my Heavenly Father's Family Business! My hope is that they will pass that rich inheritance and heritage on to my grandchildren. I don't want anyone in my immediate or extended family to miss the inheritance that God promises to His children.

So...just what are the future benefits of being an heir to the Family Business? What kind of inheritance can we anticipate?

> Blessed be the God and Father of our Lord Jesus Christ, who according to His abundant mercy has begotten us again to a living hope through the resurrection of Jesus Christ from the dead, to an inheritance incorruptible and undefiled and that does not fade away, reserved in heaven for you, who are kept by

the power of God through faith for salvation ready to
be revealed in the last time. (1 Peter 1:3-5)

Not only does the newness wear off of everything we could possibly possess or inherit on earth, but we must continue to spend money on those things, just to maintain them, because they are in the constant process of deterioration! Not so with our heavenly inheritance. Like the old TV commercial used to promise—our heavenly inheritance is "guaranteed not to chip, crack, or peel!" Think about this, all that God has created on this earth will be ours someday. Then, it will be replaced by a new earth that is infinitely more glorious.

In my travels around our grand nation, I have witnessed God's magnificent handiwork, but America is just one small sampling of the planet upon which we live. We cannot begin to imagine all that He has created in the universe, but it also is part of our inheritance. The benefits extend even beyond this creation! Things beyond created time and space will be ours!

> But as it is written: "EYE HAS NOT SEEN, NOR EAR HEARD, NOR HAVE ENTERED INTO THE HEART OF MAN THE THINGS WHICH GOD HAS PREPARED FOR THOSE WHO LOVE HIM."
> (1 Corinthians 2:9)

We cannot begin to imagine what awaits us in heaven. Even if, somehow, someone like the apostle, Paul, who was caught up into the third heaven, were able to describe it to us, it would be so beyond what he or we could understand that it would be impossible to comprehend.

> I know a man in Christ who fourteen years ago—whether in the body I do not know, or whether out of the body I do not know, God knows—such a one

was caught up to the third heaven. And I know such a man—whether in the body or out of the body I do not know, God knows—how he was caught up into Paradise and heard inexpressible words, which it is not lawful for a man to utter. (2 Corinthians 12:2-4)

It was just as difficult for the apostle, Paul, to describe in earthly terms what he saw as it was for the apostle, John, to describe what he witnessed in his visions on the Isle of Patmos. God opened up heaven for them both to see. John attempted to describe the things he saw by the things he knew in his day. Yet, it was impossible because not only was what he saw in heaven beyond anything that existed on earth, but much of what He saw taking place on earth was far into the future and far beyond the knowledge and technology of his day.

What if you were able to travel a mere 150 years backward in time...do you think you could explain a computer or television to those folks? Think of all the things we understand and use today that were unimaginable to people just 150 years ago. They had not seen a light bulb yet, much less any of the modern marvels we take for granted every day. My ten-year-old granddaughter has her own computerized smart-phone! Are you kidding me?!

We could speculate about what awaits us in heaven, and I'm sure every person has their own idea about what would make heaven special to them, but none of us can begin to fathom how wonderfully beyond our wildest imagination it is going to be. Most of all, I look forward to seeing my sweet Jesus face-to-face. Then, I'll see my mom, dad, and grandparents. I'll be reunited with all of my family and friends, who have gone there before me. That is going to be far beyond wonderful!

Folks have said to me, "Won't it be wonderful to meet all of the Saints of the Bible and spend eternity talking with them and asking them questions about their experiences with God?" I must say, I look forward to that, as well, but let's go another wild step beyond that.

Since heaven exists in a dimension beyond created time and space, it stands to reason that we will not be limited by time and space. We will be able to see and move from realm to realm effortlessly and instantaneously! If this is true, do you suppose that it might be possible for us to witness, first-hand, all of the events of human history, since Adam, as they are actually taking place?

Like the angels, we will be able to watch as God creates the heavens and the earth and all living creatures and witness the creation of the first man, Adam! I'm not talking about simply watching these events take place on a celestial television screen; I'm talking about literally standing "on location" as they take place...you know, like a roving reporter on television news! We will be able to walk the earth at any point in history in real time and witness and experience all of the Bible stories in person. Can you imagine walking with the dinosaurs, and at no time, being in any kind of danger? Okay, I'm getting carried away by my imagination. The point is this, no matter what you think would make heaven great, it is going to be infinitely more spectacular than you and I can even begin to imagine!

Imagine this, no more gravity and no more struggles with temptation or sin. What a relief it will be to be free from the devil and everything that is influenced or affected by evil. There will be no more pain, sickness or sorrow and no more goodbyes, caused by death. I don't know if you have ever thought about this, but the next time we see our parents and grandparents, we are all going to be about the same age, a glorious age, unlike anything we have ever seen or experienced in our time on earth. I can't wait to see them all in that condition. I can't wait to be in that condition myself! Someone has said: "Growing old isn't for sissies!" I agree, it isn't easy, but we won't ever have to worry about that again when we graduate to the next phase of our eternal life in Jesus Christ.

> Behold, I tell you a mystery: We shall not all sleep, but we shall all be changed—in a moment, in the twinkling of an eye, at the last trumpet. For the trumpet will sound, and the dead will be raised incorruptible, and we shall be changed. For this corruptible must put on incorruption, and this mortal must put on immortality. So when this corruptible has put on incorruption, and this mortal has put on immortality, then shall be brought to pass the saying that is written: "DEATH IS SWALLOWED UP IN VICTORY." "O DEATH, WHERE IS YOUR STING? O HADES, WHERE IS YOUR VICTORY?" (1Corinthians 15:51-55)

I can't imagine living out our life on earth without this eternal hope.

> If in this life only we have hope in Christ, we are of all men the most pitiable. (1 Corinthians 15:19)

I wouldn't trade any of the eternal blessings that await me for any of the fleeting, temporal things of earth. With that in mind, let me share the lyrics to one of my songs that I believe God inspired.

"I Wouldn't Trade Heaven for the World"

Sometimes dreams can disappear like tear drops in the dust,
Hopes fade into harsh reality;
But God's Word holds a promise from a friend I've learned to trust,
About a brighter, better place to be.

Somewhere beyond the blue, where all good dreams come true;
Where loved ones never fade away,

>   Where there is bright eternal day
>   Where the streets are paved with gold,
>   And the gates are laid with pearl,
>   Though my eyes have never seen it,
>   I wouldn't trade heaven for the world.
>
> Now, some chase dreams and pleasure, like feathers in the wind,
>   But, riches like an eagle fly away.
> But, I have stored my treasure where my life will never end,
>   Heaven is where I'm gonna live someday.
>
> Somewhere beyond the blue, where all good dreams come true;
>   Where loved ones never fade away,
>   Where there is bright eternal day
>   Where the streets are paved with gold,
>   And the gates are laid with pearl,
>   Though my eyes have never seen it,
>   I wouldn't trade heaven for the world.

Boy, all of this too good to be true good news makes me want to turn my back on God and jump right back into the dumpster of sin...how about you? Get serious! God forbid! Are you kidding me? Since I have been on the road with my music ministry, I have actually had pastors tell me, "Brother, we preachers have to insert just enough law into our preaching to get people to stay straight and do what they are supposed to do." If that is how we motivate Christians to live faithfully in the Christian life, we don't have much of a Christian experience to offer them! We should be motivated by who we are in Christ, who we are as God's children, and how much we love our heavenly Father.

We are members of the Family Business and heirs with the "first born among many brethren," Jesus Christ. (Romans 8:29) The wealthiest people on earth will be paupers in Heaven, if they even get there. There are a lot of reasons to serve God beyond what we get down here!

Whether we realize it or not, no matter what our status on earth is, those of us who have believed in and received Jesus are extremely wealthy, even though we may not appear to be much more than hired help for the time being. We have much to be thankful for and much to look forward to. We have every reason to give ourselves completely to Him! We're not working for an inheritance; we're working in partnership with a loving Father who has already guaranteed our inheritance in His Son, Jesus Christ!

> ...That [Spirit] (Holy Spirit) is the guarantee of our inheritance [the first fruits, the pledge and foretaste, the down payment on our heritage], in anticipation of its full redemption and our acquiring [complete] possession of it—to the praise of His glory. (Ephesians 1:14 - Amplified Bible)

Can you see why I am still as excited and motivated today as I was when I first began to learn these truths? Let's live and serve in our Father's business, "God & Sons, Inc." like it belongs to us...because it does! And, you thought this Christianity stuff was about religion...

Driving Under the Influence
Rocked & Rolling

John 8:31, 32

"...If you abide in My word, you are My disciples indeed. And you shall know the truth, and the truth shall make you free."

I have purposely spent a lot of time to this point establishing the truth about what God has accomplished on our behalf through His Son, Jesus, and who we are as a result. Our earthly environment may have shaped us for better or for worse, but God sends forth the Spirit of His Son into our hearts to radically free us from ourselves. We are all slaves to our personalities, hangups, and selfish ambitions until Jesus enters into our lives.

One of the first things we receive with our "salvation package" is a new identity based on His truth. When His Word becomes our reference point for absolute truth, we become liberated more and more each day. I believe it is impossible to live out the Christian life without having a firm grip on these truths. Like Believer's Boot

Camp—Basic Training—these fundamentals are absolutely essential to our spiritual journey. Occasionally, when they find themselves struggling, even highly-trained professionals must revisit and reestablish the fundamentals of their profession in order to get back on track again. It is no different with those of us who follow Jesus.

The hard part of Christianity is living it out here on earth. Jesus never promised us that life would be easy after we accept Him. In fact, He promised that we would have difficulty here.

> "...These things I have spoken to you, that in Me you may have peace. In the world you will have tribulation; but be of good cheer, I have overcome the world." (John 16:33)

God doesn't insulate us from the difficulties of life; He escorts us, empowers us, and matures us through them. Therefore, no matter what difficulties we encounter, we can navigate the course of life with confidence because He has overcome the world.

When it comes to living the Christian life, God insists that we "drive under the influence." That might be illegal in the natural world, but when Jesus is our Rock, that's the way we roll! As we journey through life, Jesus is not merely *with us*, He is *within us*. He gave this promise to His worried disciples:

> And I will pray the Father, and He will give you another Helper, that He may abide with you forever— the Spirit of truth, whom the world cannot receive, because it neither sees Him nor knows Him; but you know Him, for He dwells with you and will be in you. (John 14:16, 17)

At the time, Jesus could only dwell *among them* because He was limited by time and space in His physical body. However, after His death, resurrection and ascension, to their advantage, He was able to dwell *in them*. Today He indwells us to influence us, empower us, and transform us, and as a result, to complete His purpose in and through us.

God doesn't take up residence in us to simply give us spiritual gifts to do His work; He moves in to radically rock our little inner-world. Although Jesus accepts us the way we are, He isn't the least bit interested in leaving us as we are; for one thing, He isn't impressed with, nor does He need, our natural abilities. Secondly, He simply loves us too much to settle for the way we are. His intention is to change us from the inside-out, making us stronger and wiser in order that we might live life abundantly. (John 10:10)

It is true that we cannot give what we do not possess. If our life is weighed down with excess baggage to the point that we are not able to live life freely, what do we have to offer to others? However, when Jesus is our life, we can check our excess baggage at the cross. With our baggage gone, we are free to share the life we have in Christ with others more effectively. How can a father give his children Godly character when he doesn't possess it? How can a mother give her daughter the assurance of heaven when she doesn't have it? Whether we realize it or not, for better or worse, we are giving our children and our families what we have every day. Our children observe and, ultimately, emulate our lives as they grow up. He expects us to give everything He gives us back to Him by giving it to others. Jesus taught this principle in Matthew 25:31-46.

War of the Worlds

We all live in two worlds. There is the huge physical outer-world (Terra Firma) where all of our EUV (Earth Utility Vehicle-physical body) activity takes place. Then there is our little inner-world where our "soulical" and spiritual life takes place.

When it comes to traveling, two things are vitally important: the operating condition of the vehicle and the operating condition of the operator. I'm not much of a mechanic, but when my wife and I are traveling on tour, I try to make sure that everything on our van is well maintained and in good working order. When we fly to our destinations, these factors become even more critical.

It gives me great peace of mind, as I drive the roads of America, to know that my belts and hoses, fluids and tires are not going to cause me a breakdown or accident along the way. I just hope and pray that other drivers are able to keep their vehicles well maintained, as well. However, the condition of the operators of those other vehicles is just as important! We never know what kind of unbalanced characters are whizzing around us! I don't know about you, but I'm praying that all of the operators around me are in good operating condition! Sound vehicle plus unsound operator equals potential catastrophe! Drivers cause far more wrecks than vehicles do! Likewise, though the physical condition of our EUV is important, the condition of our inner-life is even more critical. Sound EUV plus immature character equals certain conflict!

The condition of our inner-world determines how successfully we live and interact in the world around us. Therefore, it is vitally important to have our little world in good working order. The majority of the conflicts in our lives occur because we don't understand ourselves, and not understanding ourselves hinders our ability to understand others. Inevitably, that puts us on a collision course with their "little world." No doubt about it, knowing and understanding ourselves begins with knowing God. (Proverbs 9:10) Only then can we begin to truly understand and love others.

God wants to grow us in His grace, which simply means He wants us to be conformed to the image of His Son, Jesus. (Romans 8:29) That is His ultimate purpose for us. This is the first calling for every believer. Likewise, it is the first calling for every minister who is called to communicate the Gospel, to become like Jesus – period.

God does not merely give us a ministry to perform. HE *is* our ministry, and His intention is to perform HIMSELF through us. It is easy to miss this, and many ministers have missed it. When we are willing to allow Him to be our ministry, it is amazing how His heart shows up in our ministry and makes us more effective. The real dynamic of any ministry is not the style or charisma of the minister; it is the resemblance of Jesus in their character. He is the real "anointing" that makes any ministry or minister of the gospel genuine.

Growing in grace sets us free from the pain of the past, as well as, the pride of the present. Jesus sets us on a course that is focused on the future where anything is possible because He indwells us and empowers us with His grace. This is what was missing in the lives of Jesus' disciples before His death and resurrection. They were insecure, contentious and wavering in their faith most of the time, but that would not be the case after Pentecost.

As the disciples prayed and waited, in one accord, in that upper room on the day of Pentecost, (Acts 2:1-4), they were filled with the Holy Spirit. The "other helper" Jesus had promised was now within them. In the same manner, when we come to Jesus, He baptizes us with His Spirit. What is the purpose for this baptism of the Holy Spirit? The answer to that question depends on just *who* you think the Holy Spirit is.

According to the Bible, The Holy Spirit is a person, not a power. He is not an "it." He is not a holy "ghost." Unfortunately, this term in the old King James Bible describes Him this way. More accurately, He is the "Spirit of God." He is the "Spirit of Christ." He is the "Spirit of Truth."

> But you are not in the flesh but in the Spirit, if indeed the Spirit of God dwells in you. Now if anyone does not have the Spirit of Christ, he is not His. (Romans 8:9)

Please notice what Paul says in this verse: first, we are in the "Spirit" (the fact that the translators capitalized this reference means that this is a reference to the Holy Spirit); then in the same breath, Paul refers to Him as the "Spirit of God"; next, He is referred to as the "Spirit of Christ." Obviously, these terms are interchangeable when referring to the Holy Spirit. Amazingly, when we are filled with the Holy Spirit; All three persons of the Godhead: God, the Father, Jesus, the Son, and the Holy Spirit take up permanent residence in us because they are one. The Jesus, who is all the fullness of the Godhead, now indwells us and completes us! (Colossians 2:9, 10) Great! Why?

Some would say that the purpose of the presence of God's Spirit within us is to equip us with what I like to refer to as the "power tools" i.e. Spiritual gifts. We are equipped by God with these tools in order to complete His current agenda on earth—making disciples of all nations (Matt 28:19,20) and building His church (The body of Christ; made up of all true, born again believers). This may be true, but ultimately, the Holy Spirit fills us with the power of God to make us like Him. This is exactly what the apostle prayed for in Ephesians 3:13-21. I love the way the Amplified Bible lays it out for us.

> For this reason [seeing the greatness of this plan by which you are built together in Christ], I bow my knees before the Father of our Lord Jesus Christ, For Whom every family in heaven and on earth is named [that Father from Whom all fatherhood takes its title and derives its name]. May He grant you out of the rich treasury of His glory to be strengthened and reinforced with mighty power in the inner man by the [Holy] Spirit [Himself indwelling your innermost being and personality]. May Christ through your faith [actually] dwell (settle down, abide, make His permanent home) in your hearts! May you be rooted deep in love and founded securely on love, That you may have the power and be strong to ap-

prehend and grasp with all the saints [God's devoted people, the experience of that love] what is the breadth and length and height and depth [of it]; [That you may really come] to know [practically, through experience for yourselves] the love of Christ, which far surpasses mere knowledge [without experience]; that you may be filled [through all your being] unto all the fullness of God [may have the richest measure of the divine Presence, and become a body wholly filled and flooded with God Himself]! Now to Him Who, by (in consequence of) the [action of His] power that is at work within us, is able to [carry out His purpose and] do superabundantly, far over and above all that we [dare] ask or think [infinitely beyond our highest prayers, desires, thoughts, hopes, or dreams]--To Him be glory in the church and in Christ Jesus throughout all generations forever and ever. Amen (so be it).

I believe this is God's primary purpose for us, individually and collectively. Without this, individual believers can never truly become one in heart, mind, purpose and direction. Why would we, as containers of His divine presence, want to settle for less? Paul's prayer for believers is my prayer, as well. He continues in the next chapter,

> His intention was the perfecting and the full equipping of the saints (His consecrated people), [that they should do] the work of ministering toward building up Christ's body (the church), [That it might develop] until we all attain oneness in the faith and in the comprehension of the [full and accurate] knowledge of the Son of God, that [we might arrive] at really mature manhood (the completeness of per-

sonality which is nothing less than the standard height of Christ's own perfection), the measure of the stature of the fullness of the Christ and the completeness found in Him. (Ephesians 4:12, 13)

(Amplified Bible)

Notice that God's intention is that His indwelling Spirit would empower us to bring us to complete maturity in Christ...the result of that being unity and oneness in the faith. Our faith might separate us from the world but it should never divide the body of Christ. Yet, in my travels, ministering in many denominations, I have observed that we are divided by our interpretation of the truth of Scripture on many issues, including what it means to be "Spirit-filled."

What is the purpose of this extraordinary power? Jesus Christ, in the person of the Holy Spirit, taking up permanent residence in us, thoroughly infecting and revolutionizing our personality. That does not mean we lose our uniqueness as individuals. It simply means that His character and personality begins to so color ours that it becomes impossible for Him not to shine through. God doesn't measure our spiritual maturity by how much of the Bible we know, how eloquently we communicate, what great achievements we accomplish in the ministry or what Spiritual gifts we possess and how we use them. He measures our maturity by what we allow Him to accomplish in our character. When this happens, Jesus shines through us.

Shine, Jesus, Shine!

When little 8-year-old Christian and his mom returned home from church, his mom asked him, "Did you enjoy Sunday school today, son? Christian replied: "I loved it! I'm a little confused though." "About what?" mom asked. He answered, "My teacher told us that when we ask Jesus to come into our heart that God comes to live inside of us, too." His mom affirmed, "That is right Christian. God comes to live in our heart when Jesus comes into our heart. Don't you believe that?" With a puzzled look on his face, Christian answered, "Well, yes I do...but...God is so big and I'm so little. If He comes to live inside of me, won't He show through?" Priceless! I love it! Unfortunately, a tremendous amount of confusion and disagreement has developed in the Christian realm about what it means to be "Spirit-filled," but I believe this cute little story illustrates it best.

Spiritual DNA

Often, when I'm in a church, I'll ask the question: "How many of you folks here today were born?" Laughing self-consciously, and a little confused, some will reluctantly raise their hands. Then, I explain: "Life begins with a birth. It is an event in time, not a process of evolution. We don't evolve into a person; we are born as a person. Hopefully, we are born or adopted into a family that loves us and takes care of us. Likewise, no one evolves into a Christian. We must be born again to become a Christian."

When we are born into a family, we are given the family name and are extended all of the benefits of being a family member, including becoming joint heirs. When we are born biologically into a family, we are born with the genetics of our parents. Within our genes are all the natural born qualities and abilities of our parents. We don't ask for them, pray for them, or work for them; they are part of our birth package. Sometimes this inherited DNA is good and unfortunately, in some cases, not so good. Whatever the case may be, the condition for receiving your genetics is simply being born, nothing else. It is the same with our spiritual new birth.

The Spiritual DNA we inherit from Jesus at our new birth is perfect, powerful, and eternal! When we are born again, everything that we need for life and godliness is in our new spiritual genetics. Look at what Peter tells us. (2 Peter 1:3, 4)

> ...His divine power has given to us all things that pertain to life and godliness, through the knowledge of Him who called us by glory and virtue, by which have been given to us exceedingly great and precious promises, that through these you may be partakers of the divine nature, having escaped the corruption that is in the world through lust.

Filled, Equipped and Fruity!

Included in our new spiritual genetics are the Spiritual gifts (power tools), and the fruit of the Spirit (character) of our new heavenly Father. They are imparted to us by His Holy Spirit whom He pours out on us abundantly through Jesus.

There is disagreement within the body of Christ on the difference between the *baptism* of the Holy Spirit and the *filling* of the Holy Spirit. Personally, my understanding is that they are two distinct experiences. We should understand that one is an *outside-in* job, while the other is an *inside-out* job. The "Baptism" happens when God's Holy Spirit is poured *into us* from the outside as a cleansing regeneration. The "Filling" occurs when God's Holy Spirit, now indwelling us, is poured *out from within us* for our transformation and the benefit of others. The first is a matter of us allowing Him to come in. The second is a matter of us allowing Him to come out!

Isn't it true that many of us, who claim to contain Him, continually restrain Him? We who profess to know Him seem to have a great deal of difficulty letting Him out in a manner that reveals Him in our personality. I know many believers who boast in their Spiritual gifts, who exhibit none of the loving traits of Jesus in how they relate to or deal with people. Which, do you suppose, is more important to the Giver of the Spiritual gifts???

Next, there is the issue of exactly when we receive this "baptism" and exactly what it is. First, I believe the baptism of His Spirit takes place when we receive Jesus. At that time, we experience a "washing and a regeneration."

> ...not by works of righteousness which we have done, but according to His mercy He saved us, through the washing of regeneration and renewing of the Holy Spirit, whom He poured out on us abundantly through Jesus Christ our Savior... (Titus3:5, 6)

Undeniably, the context of this passage reveals that this baptism is a cleansing, regenerating, *saving* work of the Holy Spirit that occurs from the outside-in. It is a baptism that is not based on our own works of righteousness, but purely on God's mercy. This is when we receive everything we are ever going to need in order to be who we need to be and what we need to do as God's children and heirs. If we look at the context of this verse, we can see that it is very similar to what Paul said in Ephesians.

> For by grace you have been saved through faith, and that not of yourselves; *it is* the gift of God, not of works, lest anyone should boast. (Ephesians 2:8, 9)

Conversely, the *filling* of His Spirit is an inside-out experience. Not only is it a recurring experience, but it is an ongoing, progressive *sanctifying* work. It is a process through which God's Spirit works His character into our character and out into our daily lives. The apostle, Paul, exhorts us:

> And do not get drunk with wine, for that is debauchery; but ever be filled and stimulated with the [*Holy*] Spirit. (Ephesians 5:18) (Amplified Bible)

If you read all of Ephesians chapter five, you will discover that Paul makes this comment within the context of his instructions on how we should live in holiness and, as Christians, how we should treat one another. Therefore, the "filling" is something that empowers us from the inside-out to conduct ourselves in love, which is the fruit of His Spirit.

> But the fruit of the [*Holy*] Spirit [*the work which His presence within accomplishes*] is love, joy (gladness), peace, patience (an even temper, forbearance), kindness, goodness (benevolence), faithfulness, Gentleness (meekness, humility), self-control (self-restraint, continence). Against such things there is no law [*that can bring a charge*]. (Galatians 5:22, 23) (Amplified Bible)

The Spirit-filled life is not just about the gifts of the Spirit. We must remember that our Family Business is a construction business. We are constructing a spiritual building that our preeminent "Architect" (God), has designed. An architect's job is to design buildings and to advise on their construction. A draftsman draws the blueprints. Blueprints are the technical drawings and specifications for the construction project. They layout the exact measurements and floor plans for the structure.

I spent more than 25 years in commercial construction work. During that time, I learned the construction process. As we go forward, it is important to remember what God's finished building is supposed to look like. Not every worker has the ability to read blueprints; they merely carry out the instructions of the Job Foreman. A

Foreman is a tradesman who supervises a construction crew. During the construction process, the Foreman, building Contractors and Job Superintendent constantly refer back to the blueprints to assure that the project is being built according to specifications.

It might be a good idea to refer back to God's blueprint for the church once again for a reminder of what the building is supposed to look like. (Read Ephesians 3:13-21 and 4:12, 13 on pages 230, 231 and 232) When the construction workers are inaccurate in their measurements, or the quality of their work is sub-standard, the Job Superintendent gets together with the Foremen and they see to it that the proper adjustments and corrections are made.

The Apostles laid the foundation and those of us who have been born into the business since, are gifted with Spiritual "Power Tools" to complete the building project. (1 Corinthians 3:9-11)

Of course, the foundation of this super-structure (the Church) is Jesus Christ; those of us who possess and use God's power tools (the Gifts of the Spirit) are instructed to meticulously carry out our work; using only the finest materials (the Fruit of the Spirit) to the completion of God's building project.

Our Equipment - The Power Tools

> But the manifestation of the Spirit is given to each one <u>for the profit of all</u>: for to one is given the word of wisdom through the Spirit, to another the word of knowledge <u>through the same Spirit</u>, to another faith <u>by the same Spirit</u>, to another gifts of healings by the same Spirit, to another the working of miracles, to another prophecy, to another discerning of spirits, to another different kinds of tongues, to another the interpretation of tongues. But <u>one and the</u>

same Spirit works all these things, distributing to each one individually as He wills.
(1 Corinthians 12:7 11)

The Holy Spirit Himself issues these tools to the workers individually as He sees fit. Paul continues to describe the gifts:

> ...Now you are the body of Christ, and members individually. And God has appointed these in the church: first apostles, second prophets, third teachers, after that miracles, then gifts of healings, helps, administrations, varieties of tongues. (1 Corinthians 12:27, 28)

He instructs us further:

> For as we have many members in one body, but all the members do not have the same function, so we, being many, are one body in Christ, and individually members of one another. Having then gifts differing according to the grace that is given to us, let us use them: if prophecy, let us prophesy in proportion to our faith; or ministry, let us use it in our ministering; he who teaches, in teaching; he who exhorts, in exhortation; he who gives, with liberality; he who leads, with diligence; he who shows mercy, with cheerfulness. (Romans 12:4-8)

According to these passages, as members (tradesmen) of the body of Christ, we are individually gifted with power tools in order to accomplish what Jesus (Architect, Job Superintendent and Foreman) has instructed us to do. He did not leave us here to "have church." He left us here, and supernaturally empowered us, to make disciples of all men. A disciple is a learner/student (apprentice). Our task in not merely to influence them to receive Jesus as their personal Savior; but rather, like spiritual parents, we are to take these newborn "babes in the Lord" and guide (disciple) them to spiritual maturity. It is relatively easy to birth a baby (unless you're the mama!), but it is extremely difficult to raise a baby to maturity. One is a momentary event while the other is a life-long commitment.

Having Babies

My first pastorate was to a congregation of a whopping fifteen people! Considering my lack of credentials, God knew that I needed to begin small. During a message one Sunday morning, I asked my little flock, "Wouldn't it be wonderful if next Sunday God sent 300 lost souls through our church doors to hear the message of the gospel?" With great enthusiasm, they replied, "Yes! Amen! Amen!" Then I asked them, "Wouldn't it be wonderful if all 300 received Jesus as their Savior during the altar call?" Again, they answered with a resounding, "Amen! Amen!" Next, I asked, "Wouldn't it be exciting if they were all baptized, all 300 joined our church, and instantly, we became a congregation of 315?" "Amen! Amen, brother!" they replied back. Finally, I commented, "That would mean that all 17 of us would have to take responsibility as spiritual parents for 300 new babies. Wouldn't that be great?" Dead silence...

It is one thing to have babies; it is entirely another to take responsibility for raising them. It would have been a huge commitment for our small church, and everyone knew it. God grew that little church in His timing, His way. I must say, that was five of the best years of my life. My wife and I loved those folks!

Spiritual Gifts and Spiritual Fruit

Remember this: the difference between the gifts of the Spirit and the fruit of the Spirit are that the gifts are the *power tools for the work of ministry* (spiritual abilities), while the fruits of the Spirit are referring to *the character of the minister* (spiritual qualities). It is one thing for a construction "tradesman" to own power tools. It is another thing for that tradesman to become a skilled, proficient "craftsman." During my years in construction work, I worked alongside many tradesmen who never quite developed into skilled craftsmen.

A tradesman is merely someone who has been trained and equipped with the tools for a trade. A craftsman, on the other hand, is someone who has learned how to practice his trade with a high degree of skill and proficiency. A true craftsman is much more conscientious about the quality of his work than he is about the quantity of his work. Nevertheless, his attention to detail doesn't diminish the quantity of his work because his skill has made him more efficient.

Fortunately, while I was learning my craft in the building trades, I was trained by older "Journeyman" craftsmen who took the time to show me the proper way to apply my tools. What amazed me is that these much older craftsmen were able to do as much, if not more work than us younger, quicker apprentices...and with less effort! Their years of experience had taught them all of the little "tricks of the trade" and how to apply them almost effortlessly. They used to tell me: "Kid, it is not how many licks you make that count, it is how you make your licks count. Pay attention to how you use your tools because that is what will make you a true craftsman who produces the best quality of work." I have never forgotten that principle, and I have applied it to my Christian life, as well. You don't have to run and gun when you know how to gun without running!

Construction or Confusion?

I was in a small town in the Panhandle of Texas to sing and preach in a small Cowboy church. It was led by a zealous, young cowboy preacher. Despite his enthusiasm, it became apparent to me that he was somewhat of a novice in the Word and the ministry. During my musical presentation of the Gospel, I noticed a group of about a half-dozen Hispanics who had come to the church together. At the conclusion of my part of the service, I extended an invitation for attendees to come to the altar for salvation and prayer. The group of Hispanics all stood up and came forward to receive Jesus as their Savior. I was playing the music and the Cowboy preacher received them for prayer.

To my amazement, instead of praying with them to receive Christ, he and a few other "Spirit-filled" altar volunteers, immediately began to speak and pray in tongues, grasped these Hispanic family members, who barely spoke or understood English, by the head and began to command them to be baptized in the Spirit with the evidence of speaking in unknown tongues! It soon became apparent, by the looks on their faces, that the only thing this strange activity produced was fear and confusion in this group of sincere candidates for regeneration. In the end, nobody ever explained to them how to be saved, and nobody ever prayed with them to receive Jesus. They all left that experience totally confused and probably unsaved! I must say, I was as befuddled as they were. I hope that they eventually came to know Jesus as their savior.

After the service, I gently let it be known to this young pastor that, as far as I was concerned, what had happened was a spiritual train wreck. Predictably, He has never invited me back to minister in his church. This is what can happen when a spiritual tradesman is not a skilled, and biblically accurate, spiritual craftsman. Do you see the difference? The proper use of our Spiritual power tools will never cause confusion, distraction or "deconstruction."

The difference between the gifts and the fruit of the Spirit is apparent when you look at 1 Corinthians 13:1-3.

> Though I speak with the tongues of men and of angels (gift), but have not love (fruit), I have become sounding brass or a clanging cymbal. And though I have the gift of prophecy, and understand all mysteries and all knowledge, and though I have all faith, so that I could remove mountains, but have not love, I am nothing. And though I bestow all my goods to feed the poor, and though I give my body to be burned, but have not love, it profits me nothing.

Paul makes it clear that the gifts (power tools) are nothing without the fruit (craftsmanship).

The word for love here is "Agape" in Greek, the original language in which the passage was written. Agape is God's supernatural quality of love. It is the real power of the Spirit. If this is true, then many of us who describe ourselves as "Spirit-filled" need to ask ourselves which spirit we are filled with, the Holy Spirit or the spirit of pride and selfishness. According to Paul, without this quality of spiritual power (love), we are nothing. The point is clear; our ministry is not true ministry without Agape (perfect love). Love is the essence of God.

> Beloved, let us love one another, for love is of God; and everyone who loves is born of God and knows God. He who does not love does not know God, for God is love. (1 John 4:7, 8)

The real power of ministry; is not found in the power tools, it is in the fruit of the Spirit—love! Based upon the context of all the statements Paul makes on this issue, I believe he is trying to point out that Agape is the true evidence of the "Baptism of the Spirit," not any of the gifts, including the tongues of men *or* of angels.

There are two things that we should remember about the Gifts of the Spirit. 1. They are gifts. This means that the Spirit of God gifts us with these unconditionally through no merit of our own. 2. These gifts are given to us, not for us to minister to ourselves, but to minister His life to others.

Tool Time

You've probably seen the television sitcom where the know-it-all lead character, Tim Taylor (Tim Allen), is the host of a do-it-yourself, home-improvement television program called, "Tool Time," a show within a show called, "Home Improvement." [12] Much of the humor in the show revolves around Tim's obsession with power tools. He believes that his tools define his manliness, which he often expresses through his humorous primal caveman grunts, primitive facial expressions and gestures.

In Tim's perfect world, a "Man's man" is in his natural element when he owns and operates a well-rounded assortment of power tools. However, with Tim, more power is always better. He often takes a conventional power tool and adds more power to it! Of course, forgetting crucial steps, ignoring instructions and drawing wrong conclusions along the way, Tim's ill-advised tool modifications and accident-prone efforts usually result in the destruction of his projects and many times, painful injury to himself. Consequently, all of the doctors and nursing staff at the local hospital know him on a first name basis.

Of course, the over-confident Tim sees himself as the real star of the show. He is completely oblivious to the fact that his pudgy, bearded, straight-faced, and more conventional co-host, Al Borland (Richard Karn), is actually more popular with the viewers. Tim always turns a deaf ear to his flannel-shirted sidekick's wise advice about safety regulations and proper protocol. I've laughed many times at Tim's power tool antics. However, when it comes to God's power tools and His building projects, it is not a laughing matter when our obsession with the power tools produces the same result.

Over the years I've learned that when the gifts of the Spirit are used properly in the hands of skilled, spirit-filled craftsmen, it always results in a strong, level foundation, upon which a secure, fully functional, thriving church can rest. When that is not the case, you will always find unrest and division. God's people get hurt, and His building project is delayed, damaged or destroyed. Spiritual leaders and laypeople alike should honestly ask themselves, "Does this describe the results of my ministry?"

That is why it is vital that we are wise concerning what the true nature of being "Spirit-filled" means. James talks about two types of wisdom:

> Who is wise and understanding among you? Let him show by good conduct that his <u>works are done in the meekness of wisdom</u>. But if you have bitter envy and self-seeking in your hearts, do not boast and lie against the truth. <u>This wisdom does not descend from above</u>, but is <u>earthly</u>, <u>sensual</u>, <u>demonic</u>. For where envy and self-seeking exist, confusion and every evil thing are there. But the <u>wisdom that is from above</u> is first <u>pure</u>, then <u>peaceable</u>, <u>gentle</u>, <u>willing to yield</u>, <u>full of mercy and</u> <u>good fruits</u>, <u>without partiality and without hypocrisy</u>. Now <u>the fruit of righteousness</u> is sown in peace by those who make peace. (James 3:13-18)

I suppose we who are in the ministry need to ask ourselves if this is the type of ministry we practice. I have met many so-called "spirit-filled" church leaders who simply don't match up with James' description of the "wisdom that is from above."

A normal dose of genuine spiritual discernment makes it obvious who is genuinely navigating under the influence of the Spirit of Jesus and who is not; I simply believe that when one is operating in the Spirit, they will act like Jesus acts. As a result, they will reflect His heart and character. Through their Spiritual gifts, the church will develop into a solid, well-balanced, fully functional edifice (building of people) for God.

Love & Wisdom

The difference between knowledge and wisdom is this; knowledge is the accumulation of information, while wisdom is the understanding and ability to apply that information effectively in life. From kindergarten to college and post-graduate school, education is about imparting and receiving information. However, wisdom is not a course you can sign up for in school. Wisdom is imparted by God and learned in life.

Ah, the picture is becoming clearer! Perfect love and Godly wisdom are synonymous! There is no difference! Love produces a willingness to look inwardly, and honestly, at one's self. In turn, that self-honesty produces Godly wisdom. Of course, true wisdom begins with God.

> The fear of the LORD is the beginning of wisdom,
> And the knowledge of the Holy One is understanding. (Proverbs 9:10)

Godly wisdom always leads to understanding. These are synonymous, as well. When we apply understanding properly, God begins to free us from our selfishness. We become easier to get along with because we are finally able to get along with ourselves. Therefore, can there be any question that love and wisdom, along with truth and grace, are the true evidences of being Spirit-filled?

When Paul talks about being filled with the Spirit in Ephesians 5:17-21, he is saying that we should be continually living under the influence of the Spirit.

> Therefore do not be unwise, but understand what the will of the Lord is. And do not be drunk with wine, in which is dissipation (useless or profitless activity); but be filled with the Spirit, speaking to one another in psalms and hymns and spiritual songs, singing and making melody in your heart to the Lord, giving thanks always for all things to God the Father in the name of our Lord Jesus Christ, submitting to one another in the fear of God.

Unlike the influence of alcohol which, after having taken control of our faculties, is destructive, operating under the influence of God's Holy Spirit makes us better spiritual operators. Our vision becomes clearer, and we become less of a threat to the safety of the other spiritual operators around us.

Don't Mess with Texas

If you have driven much in Texas, you no doubt have noticed that it is the only state in America where drivers will actually move to the right and drive on the shoulder of a two-lane highway to allow you to pass them. They are graceful yielders! That is just one of the reasons I love Texas. We become graceful yielders when we are willing to allow others to pass us on the journey, instead of blocking their way with our arrogance, insecurity or competitiveness.

When we are trained under the influence of the Spirit, we become more than mere tradesmen, we become skilled craftsmen in the hands of a loving heavenly Father. We are able to help those who are broken down and stranded on the journey to get back on the "good road." We are willing to train others to be skilled spiritual craftsmen and pray that they will become even more effective in the ministry than we are! We prefer and promote them, instead of impeding their progress. In my humble opinion, that is what being filled with the Spirit is really about, what it truly looks like, and what it actually produces in our lives and the life of our churches.

I realize that no matter which side of the "Baptism of the Spirit" and "Spirit-filled" issue I come down on, there are going to be those who vehemently disagree with me. Some are going to be angry with me or simply consider me not "Spirit-filled." Some are going to abandon me because I might not be parroting what they teach. Here's the deal…I simply want to know the truth and live out the real thing. Believe me; I want to preach the "Full Gospel." I want to be like Jesus, and I want to do it the way He did it. Isn't that the whole point of the ministry?

By the way, even if Jesus were to write a book that defined what all of His doctrinal stances are, I'm sure He would get the same response. Oh, wait! He *did* write a book on these doctrinal issues! Sadly, He *has* received the same response. I know, I have probably spent too much time on the subject, but we cannot, as believers, afford to allow our disagreement on these issues to confuse and drive away those whom Jesus wants to deliver and disciple.

Grace = Power

I have always heard *grace* defined as: "God's unmerited favor." That is certainly one aspect of it, but there are instances where this definition doesn't fit. Let's take a look at James 4:6.

> But He gives us more and more grace (power of the Holy Spirit, to meet this evil tendency and all others fully). That is why He says, God sets Himself against the proud and haughty, but gives grace [*continually*]

to the lowly (those who are humble enough to receive it). [*Prov. 3:34.*] (Amplified Bible)

If grace in this verse meant "unmerited favor," He would not withhold it from the proud because it is unmerited. It must be a reference to His power. He resists and refuses to empower the proud and arrogant, but He gladly empowers with his grace those who have a humble heart.

To be sure, God's grace is His unmerited favor, but it is much more than that; it is the power of His life, given to us to empower us to, not just *do* His work, but *be* His life to others. So, in this case, when God "graces" us, He empowers us. Our humility is our willingness to surrender everything to Him and His will for our lives.

If we truly want to rock the world for Jesus, we must be willing to humble ourselves and allow Him to rock our individual little world, as well as, our collective church world. Both Saints and Ain'ts are searching for the real thing. We don't have time to pretend, play games or play church. We must be down-to-earth and real! Aren't you glad Jesus was?

People are dying without Him all around us every day. Plus, I truly believe His return is imminent. Please, don't misunderstand me; I believe that all of the Gifts of the Holy Spirit are operable in the church today. I'm just not convinced yet that all of the activity that I am witnessing in the church is accurate or genuine.

We are living in perilous times and these times demand that we get it right. Let's allow God to make us rock-solid in our spiritual character. In the now famous words of Todd Beamer, heroic passenger on the ill-fated United Airlines, Flight 93 on September, 11, 2001…"Let's Roll!"

Walking Tall

"Speak softly and carry a big stick."

Colossians 2:6, 7

...As you have therefore received Christ Jesus the Lord, so walk in Him, rooted and built up in Him and established in the faith, as you have been taught, abounding in it with thanksgiving.

On September 2, 1901, just twelve days before his predecessor, President William McKinley, was assassinated, Teddy Roosevelt echoed the West African phrase, "Speak softly and carry a big stick," in a political speech at the Minnesota State Fair. That catchy phrase would help to thrust him into the American presidency at the ripe old age of 46. In the 1973 movie "Walking Tall," [13] Joe Don Baker portrays the main character, Buford Pusser, who practices Roosevelt's philosophy literally. The film is based on the true story of the McNairy County Sheriff in Tennessee. Pusser hammers the bad guys and administers his own brand of justice with a four foot Hickory club. Though the bad guys get what they deserve in the movie and justice is served, this is not how we "walk tall" in Christ. In the Christian walk, our "big stick" is the Cross of Christ and we definitely should not pound people with it.

When the Bible refers to walking in life, it is talking about how we live our lives—walking equals living. Our knowledge of who He is and who we are in Him should dictate the way we think and the way we see ourselves based on the Word of God. This knowledge enables us to walk tall, spiritually. The Bible says, *"As a man thinks in his heart, so is he..."* (Proverbs 23:7) Our lives are either empowered or impaired by how we see ourselves.

While we were in our early thirties, my wife and I were part of a young couples Sunday school department that was made up of three or four separate classes. I became the teacher of one the classes. I'll admit that I was very idealistic early in my Christian experience (I still am!) and that made me very enthusiastic in my presentation of the truths I had the great privilege to share as a Sunday school teacher.

One day after class, a member—we'll call him, Mitch—approached me with a pained expression on his face and tears welling up in his eyes. I was somewhat caught off guard because Mitch was a deacon and one of the most respected leaders in our church. Normally, he was the picture of self-confidence. In a broken voice he told me, "Peter, it's obvious that you sincerely believe everything you teach each week. I've been a believer most of my life and over the years, I've attended countless seminars, workshops, revivals, conferences and every other type of meeting you can imagine. I've heard everything you teach a million times and it just doesn't work." Mitch wasn't being sarcastic; he was honesty searching for the real thing and, apparently, had never discovered it.

I was stunned! I could not believe my ears! I didn't know how to respond to him without sounding trite. The last thing he needed to hear from me was some worn out religious cliché. On the outside, Mitch appeared to be very spiritual and knowledgeable about the Bible, and seemed to have all of his spiritual ducks in a row. He was very well educated, successful in business, and lived, at least materially, far better than I could afford to live.

Honestly, because of his speaking skills and smooth self-confidence, I felt that Mitch was much more qualified to teach our class than I was. Yet, on the inside, his little world was tragically empty. The image of his lifeless, almost desperate, face is still fresh in my mind 25 years later. I don't know where Mitch is today, or if he ever came to experience the reality of Christ in his life, but I hope he did.

What the Bible Says & What the Bible Means

Like Mitch, you might be thinking, "Well, all of this sounds great in theory, but how does it actually work?" That is a great question! The good news is God doesn't just tell us what our spiritual life should be like; He instructs us on how to live it. Better yet, He indwells us to empower us to live it! Everything we know about Jesus and this radical life-changing dynamic He brings to our human experience is in His miraculous Word! I've always said that it is not enough to know what the Bible says; we must understand what it means for each of us, personally, and how to walk tall in it.

Far too many Christians "walk small" because they do not know who they are according to God's Word. Consequently, their lives do not look much different than those who have not been born again. Many see themselves as merely "sinners, saved by grace." By nature, we were sinners before Jesus came into our hearts, but after we are born of His Spirit, we become Saints set apart for a supernatural life in Him. Usually, walking small is the result of disappointments, hurts and disillusionment in our heart. These produce feelings of inferiority, insecurity and inadequacy that become strongholds in our thinking.

However, when God's Spirit indwells us, He empowers us to overcome all of these weaknesses. His word says that we are:

FORGIVEN (Colossians 2:13, 14); ACCEPTED (Ephesians 1:6); NEW CREATURES (2 Corinthians 5:17); INDWELT by the Holy Spirit, (1 Corinthians 6:17, 19); supernaturally EMPOWERED (2 Timothy 1:7); SECURE (Hebrews 13:5, 6).

Whom we choose to believe: God or Man, directly affects how we think and determines the quality of our self-esteem and how we live our lives. Jesus makes our heart His home in order to change our little world by first renewing our thinking through the Word.

> And do not be conformed to this world, but be transformed by the renewing of your mind, that you may prove what is that good and acceptable and perfect will of God. (Romans 12:2)

God promises that no matter what difficulties we are faced with in life, the truth of who He says we are, and who He is in us, makes the difference in how we live. No matter what happens, He works all things together for our good, with the purpose of conforming us, from the inside-out, into the image of His Son, Jesus.

> And we know that all things work together for good to those who love God, to those who are the called according to His purpose. For whom He foreknew, He also predestined to be conformed to the image of His Son, that He might be the firstborn among many brethren. (Romans 8:28, 29)

So, how do we live out the reality of this amazing Jesus life? Let's look to Colossians 2:6, 7 for the answer.

First, we live out the life God has given to us the same way we receive it. Observe what Paul says:

> "<u>As you have</u> therefore <u>received Christ Jesus</u> the Lord, <u>so walk in Him</u>." (Colossians 2:6)

Biblical faith begins with the choice to accept, as fact, what the Bible says, instead of what we have trusted as truth in the past. If faith is how we receive the gift of Jesus' life, then certainly faith is how we live out that gift of life each day. How do we receive salvation? When we come to God for salvation, we confess to Him, "I am helpless to save myself. I ask you to do for me what I cannot do. I choose to trust in the sacrifice of your son, Jesus, to save me from my sins" Based upon that confession of faith, we trust that we are saved and born again because the Bible says so.

> But what does it say? "THE WORD IS NEAR YOU, IN YOUR MOUTH AND IN YOUR HEART" (that is, the word of faith which we preach): that if you confess with your mouth the Lord Jesus and believe in your heart that God has raised Him from the dead, you will be saved. For with the heart one believes unto righteousness, and with the mouth confession is made unto salvation. (Romans 10: 8-10)

Our daily walk is no different. We live step by step each day with that same kind of totally reliant faith. We wake up each morning and say to God, "Lord, I know that I cannot live the miraculous life that you have called me to live in my own ability, so I choose to make myself available to your ability. I ask you to do in me and through me what I cannot do for myself. Live your life out in me."

Wheelbarrow Faith

Faith is actually a matter of trust and surrender. God encourages us to trust Him. In order for God to energize and revolutionize our lives, we must surrender to Him. We rest and He does the rest!

For instance, suppose someone were to stretch a cable across the majestic Niagara Falls. A high wire daredevil is preparing to traverse the cable from the Canadian side, half a mile over the falls to the American side while pushing a wheelbarrow. He turns to face the huge crowd that has gathered to watch his monumental feat of courage and asks, "How many here today believe that I can successfully cross these falls on this wire while pushing this wheelbarrow?" The crowd roars with exuberant affirmation, "We believe you can! We believe you can!" Next, the man issues a challenge, "Who, then, will ride in the wheelbarrow?" The crowd falls silent. Only the roar of the powerful, cascading falls can be heard. After a few tense moments, a high-pitched voice rings out, "I believe you can, and I will ride in the wheelbarrow!" As every eye turns to see who this brave soul is, a 10-year-old boy bravely walks forward and jumps into the wheelbarrow. Now that is trust *and* surrender! Absolute surrender is the evidence of genuine faith. Genuine faith always produces absolute surrender. When we are surrendered to Jesus, we will follow Him.

> Trust in the LORD with all your heart, And lean not on your own understanding; In all your ways acknowledge Him, And He shall direct your paths. Do not be wise in your own eyes; Fear the LORD and depart from evil. It will be health to your flesh, And strength to your bones. (Proverbs 3:5-8)

As was illustrated earlier; God's word is our only reliable GPS system, and He is never going to steer us wrong! Who are we going to trust? Surely, you've heard people say this, "If you can't trust yourself, who can you trust?" Or, maybe, "To thine own self be true!" Sounds good...but let me ask you this, have you ever been wrong? Of course, we all have. God, on the other hand, has never been wrong. Have you ever made a mistake? God has never made a mistake. Have you ever failed? We all do. Have you ever broken a promise to yourself or someone else? Of course, we all have, but God has never been wrong, never made a mistake, never failed or broken a single promise. If the human intellect and conscience were trustworthy, our world would not be in the shape it is in today. Based on that reality, who is more trustworthy...us or God? The answer is obvious. True life is lived successfully by acknowledging, trusting in, relying upon and surrendering to God as our strength, life, and source for absolute truth.

Spiritual Roots

Second, we must allow Jesus to be our anchor in life. *"Rooted and built up in Him."* Usually, when we think about our roots, we think about our genetic heritage (our family tree). When we observe how God designed trees and plant life, it becomes easier to understand what this passage means. A tree's *support system* is its roots. Sometimes, there is almost as much of the tree below the surface of the ground as there is above the ground. This serves as the foundation that supports the tree when the howling winds and storms rage against it. The stronger and healthier the roots, and the deeper they run, the more stable and secure the tree.

I have traveled extensively in the western United States. While traveling through the mountains, I have seen trees growing right out of solid rock. Apparently, the tiny seeds of these trees found a crevice or a crack that provided just enough soil and nourishment for that seed to take root and grow in a rock...amazing! Now, that is a foundation that shall not be moved!

> He only is my rock and my salvation; He is my defense; I shall not be moved. (Psalms 62:6)

This brings us to the question; in what is our life rooted? The Bible warns us against laying the foundation of our life in shifting sand.

> "Therefore whoever hears these sayings of Mine, and does them, I will liken him to a wise man who built his house on the rock: and the rain descended, the floods came, and the winds blew and beat on that house; and it did not fall, for it was founded on the rock." But everyone who hears these sayings of Mine, and does not do them, will be like a foolish man who built his house on the sand: and the rain descended, the floods came, and the winds blew and beat on that house; and it fell. And great was its fall." (Matthew 7:24-27)

Notice, those who *hear the words of Jesus*, and *do them* (live by them), are the ones who have a sound foundation for life. Those who hear Jesus' words and live their lives according to them are described as wise. When the storms of life come, as they do for all of us, their lives are secure. Conversely, those who hear His words and live their lives according to the basic principles of the world are foolish. Because their lives are dependent on the things of this world, when those things change, or fail, their lives collapse. Living out the Christian life involves both hearing the truth and living our lives according to the truth.

> You believe that there is one God. You do well. Even the demons believe—and tremble! But do you want to know, O foolish man, that faith without works is dead? (James 2:19, 20)

Acknowledging God's existence and even giving mental assent to His truth doesn't necessarily make a difference in our lives. Even the demons do that much and tremble. Let me give you my paraphrase of this passage: *Without our positive response to God, what we believe about God remains lifeless and powerless!*

Our personal trust and surrender to *who God is* and *what He says* and wants to do in our lives is what makes the difference in our lives. It is how we respond to Him and His truth that changes us and sets us apart from the rest of the world. Many hear, and believe, but few respond with, "Yes, Lord!" Faith, without a response to the truth of God's word on our part, is lifeless and powerless. I believe many true born again believers miss the real experience of Christ because they choose to live their Christianity their way. They have their love, and their roots, planted in Christianity, instead of Christ. Remember? True Christianity is Christ, Himself.

Roots are also the source of *nourishment* for a tree. A tree draws all of the nutrients from the ground that it needs to be healthy and fruitful. Life-giving nutrients come up from the roots through the trunk, out into the limbs and then, into the fruit. Roots are the conduit of life to a tree. Branches are the conduit of life from a tree to others through the fruit produced by that life. When the roots of our lives are planted in God, we can expect a prosperous life that blesses others.

> Blessed is the man who walks not in the counsel of the ungodly, Nor stands in the path of sinners, Nor sits in the seat of the scornful; But his delight is in the law of the LORD, And in His law he meditates day and night. He shall be like a tree Planted by the rivers of water, That brings forth its fruit in its season, Whose leaf also shall not wither; And whatever he does shall prosper. (Psalms 1:1-3)

Jesus taught a lesson on this in the fifteenth chapter of the Gospel of John, when he refers to Himself as the "Vine" and to us as His "branches." He goes on to state: *"...without Me, you can do nothing."* (John 15:5) There are many things we can practice and accomplish in Christianity without Christ, but we cannot truly love with the love of God, without Him. Certainly, we cannot truly be Godly without Him, because as we have pointed out, true Godliness is God in us, living out who He is through us. This is true Christianity. Understanding this not only keeps us humble and reliant on Him; it prevents us from accepting any credit for what He does in our lives.

God is free to bless our lives when we refuse to think and live like the ungodly or travel the path they are on. There comes a time in every Christian's life when we must decide who we are going to identify ourselves with and with whom we will run. When I wanted God to set me free from my alcoholism, I had to choose who was more important to me. Was it going to be my drinking buddies who, quite honestly, didn't have a clue about real life, or my new Christian brothers and sisters whose lives were actually imparting life to mine through their example?

We cannot entertain the counsel of those who don't truly know God or walk on the path they are on and expect God's best in our life. This is where many new believers get detoured and break down on their spiritual journey. They allow themselves to be cheated, *"through philosophy and empty deceit, according to the tradition of men, according to the basic principles of the world, and not according to Christ."* (Colossians 2:8) Paul also puts it this way:

> Do not be deceived: "Evil company corrupts good habits." Awake to righteousness, and do not sin; for some do not have the knowledge of God.
> (1 Corinthians 15:33, 34)

God wants to bless us, but we must make the hard, but correct, choices if we want God's best for our lives. This doesn't mean that we no longer care for our lost friends. In fact, placing Jesus before them actually causes us to care more for them. We simply realize that we can no longer live the lifestyle we were living with them and experience the power of God in our lives.

You can be sure, in many instances, your old friends will not understand your new direction in life. Some will be angered and sometimes accuse you of thinking you are better than them, while others will simply scoff and make fun of what they perceive to be mere religion. However, a true friend will be happy for you and try to understand your life-changing decisions.

Whether we realize it or not, as much as we would like to think of ourselves as individualists, most of us live our lives based on the opinions of others. For example, opinions are the driving force of fad and fashion. As opinions change, and they are constantly changing, on what is considered attractive or what is "in," we tend to change our preferences in order to fit in with the current trend. If that were not true, we would be out of fashion with the rest of the world most of the time.

Pierced

Isn't it amazing what we will do to gain acceptance from our peers? I once saw a handsome young man at a Mall in Modesto, California who had approximately 20 metal studs in his top lip, two in his nose, one in his tongue and one in each of his eyebrows! Like a metallic mustache, he had piercings from one corner of his mouth to the other! Bless his heart; this kid had more chromed metal in his face than the grill on a '53 Hudson Hornet! I'm not kidding!

I thought to myself: "You know? If this guy lives into his seventies, that look is not going to be as cool as he thinks it is now! It just might be out-of-style by then! He probably won't have those things stuck in his face, and the first time he takes a big gulp of cold Sweet Tea without those studs in his lip; he is going to look like a human lawn sprinkler!" Bless his heart!

Honestly, I don't want to be offensive, but this story does illustrate just how far one will go just to conform to the group from whom they are craving attention and acceptance.

I hate to admit it, but in the '70s, I wore powder-blue, bell-bottomed, Nehru suits; flowered, wide-collared shirts; and white, bubble-toed, Patent leather, platform shoes to church. Ahhhhhhhh! Talk about the extremes that one will go to in order to fit in with their peers! We can change clothing styles but once we tat or pierce ourselves, we have pretty much scarred ourselves for life.

I am thankful that we do not have to go to these extremes in order to be accepted by God. We do not have to be pierced in order to "belong" because Jesus was pierced for us. The scars in His hands make us totally acceptable to God, just the way we are...tats, piercings, scars and all. Then, our new heavenly Abba patiently and lovingly fashions us into the person that He designed us to be.

We tend to live up to, or down to, what people in our lives say or think about us. Ultimately, however, God's opinion is the only opinion about us that truly counts. Biblical faith always involves a decision on our part. Therefore, each of us must come to a point in our walk where we decide that God's opinion is going to take precedence over everyone else's opinions. This requires a renewal in our thinking.

In the scripture we discover what God thinks and what He says about us. This makes our personal knowledge and understanding of the Bible extremely important. (Romans 10:17) Biblical faith is not blind faith. It is always based on truth. True faith always has an object upon which it is based. When our mindset is renewed and established by faith in God's Word, we are transformed from the inside-out and set free to abound in the life that God has preordained for us. (Romans 12:1, 2)

We discover true freedom, and our days are truly blessed, when we choose to trust God and what His word says about us, regardless of what our circumstances are, or what anyone else says or thinks. Ask yourself this honest question. "Is Jesus first in my life?" The quality of your life depends upon your answer.

Who do you Love?

Jesus said that in order to be His disciple (student/learner), we must take up a cross and follow Him.

> If anyone comes to Me and does not hate his father and mother, wife and children, brothers and sisters, yes, and his own life also, he cannot be My disciple. And whoever does not bear his cross and come after Me cannot be My disciple. (Luke 14:26, 27)

This means that we must forsake everything, and *everyone*, that our life has been rooted in prior to our relationship with Him. His Lordship in our lives requires that our roots be replanted in Him.

When our old relationships, including those with our beloved family members, are more important to us than our relationship with Jesus, our faith walk is stalled. Initially, those who love us may not understand this seeming departure in loyalty, but ultimately, it is to their advantage. You see, when we make this love sacrifice for Jesus, He is able to send someone (You and me—more like the divine Comforter) back into our relationship with them. Our growth in grace makes us more understanding, loving and giving in that relationship than we ever were before. But…He must come first in our lives.

Until we make this commitment, in one way or another, we unwittingly place the pressure on those we love to do what only Jesus has the ability to do—complete our lives. Ironic, isn't it? When we love our family more than we love Jesus, they are deprived of a more superior love from us. Which manner of love would you rather love them with: your limited, imperfect love or His unlimited, perfect love? He lives within us to empower us to love that way. This is why it is essential for us to give Him the preeminence in our lives. I can guarantee you; the devil will use our love of family against us if they have not made this same commitment to Jesus themselves. He wants to thwart God's plan for our life, and he will use the things dearest to us to accomplish it. They may not realize it, but our loved ones need us to love Jesus more than we do them.

Is God my Co-Pilot?

You've probably seen the bumper sticker: "God is my Co-pilot." That may sound noble, but Christianity is not about allowing God to ride with us as our co-pilot; it's about us riding with Him and allowing Him to direct our life path. We may be making the payments on the vehicle, but He definitely owns it and everything else in our lives, not to mention our next breath. God doesn't need a co-pilot and He isn't the least bit interested in being ours.

Jesus does not come into our lives to *follow us*. He doesn't come into our lives to *accompany us* on our personal journey. Contrary to the popular bumper sticker, God comes into our lives to place us on a unique path that He alone has designed for us, and we are commanded to *follow Him*. He has no desire to serve as the "co-pilot" on our self-designed life path. That doesn't mean that He doesn't care about our dreams and aspirations. In fact, He knew all about us before we were born into this world. I believe that He places some of those inclinations in our hearts before we ever come to know Him. We may not be aware of it, but He is directing our life path long before we become aware of Him.

When we place our faith in Jesus and acknowledge His Lordship in our life; His plan for our life kicks into second, third and fourth gears. As we follow Him and get to know Him more personally, He begins to reveal to us His plan for our life, and He is able to bring it to its completion. That requires us to put our self-designed plans on hold (or maybe to completely abandon them) until we discover His plans for us. Sometimes we discover that He has given to us the desires and passions we have in our heart because He knew ahead of time that they would inspire us to pursue and develop the talents He put within us.

For instance, I have had people ask me what influenced me to become a musician. Of course, because I am a Christian and perform Christian music, they assume that it was someone in Christian music that inspired me to play the guitar, write songs and sing. They are always surprised when I tell them that the Beatles[14] inspired me to pick up a guitar for the first time.

I was twelve years old in 1964 when I first heard, "I Want To Hold Your Hand," their first smash hit on American Rock and Pop music charts. Something inside of me said, "You need an electric guitar! You need to play and sing!" By the time I was 14; I had learned a few guitar chords and was playing in a "Garage Band" with a few of my buddies. It was the last year that I wore a "Burr" haircut, as well! Amazingly, the "Buzz" hairdo is back in style again. Bald is beautiful! See how opinion changes fashion?

Is it possible that God could use a secular influence like the Beatles to guide someone and equip them with the tools and talents they will need in ministry, long before they come to know Him personally years down the road? Absolutely! I suppose He could have used anyone or anything in my life to inspire me to music, but God knew who I was. He knew what would impact me as an impressionable 12-year-old. Before I heard that song and got caught up in "Beatle-mania," I never considered playing the guitar or singing. Many years later, God would take that hidden music ability that He had given me through my inherited genetics and transform it into a ministry tool that would influence many to give their lives to Him.

I believe that I inherited my talents for art and music from the Whitebird (Native American) side of my family. My dad and several other family members in Wisconsin were artists and musicians. Likewise, my mom was lyrically and artistically talented.

Some of her siblings are, as well. Thanks to the Beatles, my genetic and spiritual roots, and ultimately God's plan, my music has opened many doors for me that preaching alone might not have opened.

Simply put, when it comes to following God and His plan for our lives, we must put Jesus first. This is not an option if you want to progress with God. As Luke 14:26, 27 states, compared to our love for, and trust in Jesus, our love for even our own family and closest friends must seem like hate.

I know that these words sound extreme. Indeed, they are radical! Nevertheless, if you want to experience His life, I can assure you, He must have the preeminence in your life. God knows that when we love Him more than everyone else in our lives, then our love for them becomes supercharged with His amazing love and grace!

We simply cannot put anyone or anything before Him if we expect Him to lead us on the journey. Isn't it true that we enjoy spending most of our time with whomever or whatever we love most? Don't we become more familiar with, and better understand, whomever or whatever we spend the majority of our time with? Absolutely! Based on this fact, who and what do you know and understand the most about? How we answer this question may reveal just who or what we love the most and put first in our lives.

This brings us to yet another question. Just who is the cross Jesus tells us to take up for? Us? No. As we pointed out in a previous chapter, those of us who have been born again suffered our spiritual death experience 2,000 years ago in Christ. The discipleship cross is what we sacrifice everything dear to us on: our family; our preferences; our desires; our personal dreams, goals and aspirations...anything that we would prefer before Him. In other words, everything I had my life rooted in before must be uprooted and placed on this cross so my life can be re-rooted in Him. Then, and only then, is my life secured on a rock-solid foundation...a root system that supports me and nourishes me with His abundant life.

The cross is the "big stick" we carry on our new life journey. When we decide that nothing comes before Him, life takes on a whole new dynamic and anything becomes possible. If we are planted in anything other than the solid rock of Jesus, whatever we are rooted in is shifting sand. Inevitably, the storms of life blow and our little world begins to crumble and collapse around us.

Get out of the Boat!

We are "built up" as a result of consistently making the choice to follow Jesus. Responding to Him with "Yes, Lord" allows Him to prove that He is always faithful and more than able to fulfill every promise He makes to us.

Jesus' disciples were in the midst of a storm in the Sea of Galilee when Jesus came walking to them on the water. (Matthew 14:24-33) They were not sure if it was Him or not, so Peter cried out, "Lord, if it is you, command me to come to you on the water." Jesus answered, "Come." Peter didn't wait around to see what the others were going to do! Out he went! Miraculously, Peter was walking on the water! Predictably, however, he became distracted by the wind and the waves around him, and he took his eyes off of Jesus. Doubt and fear began to take over, and he began to sink into the tempestuous waves. Desperately, Peter cried out for Jesus. Immediately, Jesus reached out and pulled him from the deep.

There is a lesson about faith that we can learn from this account in the scriptures. When Jesus calls us, we must not wait to see what those who are in the boat with us are going to do. No doubt, some of the other disciples believed that Peter was going to drown, and they probably advised him to stay in the boat. However, when Jesus bids us, "Come," we cannot be concerned with those who doubt His call; we must step out of the comfort and safety of our present environment and walk by faith.

Many times, when I extend an invitation for folks to come to the altar to receive Jesus as their Savior, or to settle whatever issue the Holy Spirit is dealing with them about, I see their reluctance to step out from the crowd. I know that there are a multitude of reasons for their hesitancy. It could be fear, pride or just plain apathy. I remind them that if Jesus said, "To the first one who comes unto me, I will give a million dollars," there would be a stampede to the altar! I can guarantee you; no one would be concerned about decorum or what anyone else thinks about their decision to follow Jesus. I then remind them that what Jesus offers us is far more valuable than a million bucks!

We never discover what simple faith can accomplish in our lives until we are willing to do what Jesus challenges us to do. He knows that there will be times when our fear and lack of focus will get the best of us, but He is always there to lift us out of the waves when we cry out to Him. Without a faith risk on our part, we never experience the miraculous or learn just how real and faithful Jesus is.

When we are obedient, the Bible changes from religious theory to living reality! It only takes faith the size of a mustard seed (Matthew 17:20) to move the immovable when that little seed of faith is planted in a great big God. Most of the time that seemingly immovable obstruction that blocks our progress on the pathway is, in reality, none other than you and me!

So first, we must trust Jesus in our walk like we trusted Him for our salvation. Secondly, we must root our lives in Him. Third, we must be "established in the faith." If the foundation of our inner-life is rooted, nourished, and built up in Jesus, and we become established in the faith, not only can we endure anything, but we can overcome anything that the devil puts in our path to rob us of God's best for our lives.

Have you ever considered how arrogant, utterly foolhardy and preposterous it is for anyone to believe that their plans for life could possibly be better than what God has planned for their lives? Let me ask those who insist on living life their own way: "How is that working for ya?" Placing our faith in His plan is the only way we overcome the world.

> For whatever is born of God overcomes the world. And this is the victory that has overcome the world—our faith. Who is he who overcomes the world, but he who believes that Jesus is the Son of God?
> (1 John 5:4, 5)

The goal of our faith journey is that we might grow into a perfect (spiritually mature) man. This is defined by how much we become like Christ. Earlier in Ephesians; Paul establishes this truth.

> I, therefore, the prisoner of the Lord, beseech you to walk worthy of the calling with which you were called, with all lowliness and gentleness, with longsuffering, bearing with one another in love, endeavoring to keep the <u>unity of the Spirit</u> in the bond of peace. There is one body and one Spirit, just as you were called in one hope of your calling; one Lord, one faith, one baptism; one God and Father of all, who is above all, and through all, and in you all.
> (Ephesians 4:1-6)

In order to walk in faith consistently, we must be established in "the faith." Look at Paul's words earlier in this chapter:

> ...till we all come to the <u>unity of the faith</u> and of the knowledge of the Son of God, to a perfect man, to the measure of the stature of the fullness of Christ;
> (Ephesians 4:13)

"The Faith" is the collection of biblical truths that have been taught and passed on to us by the founders of the faith in the Bible. Of course, the founders of the faith are the Prophets and the Apostles. These truths are foundational to living and growing in faith. I believe that if the church is going to be effective, it is imperative that we get it right and agree on what the "faith" is. This is critical because it is our only reliable road map for the journey.

The church cannot afford to be divided on scriptural truth. As the body of Christ in the world, today, we are the only representation of God's truth available to those who are trying to discover it. We make that life available to a dying world that has become lost and stranded on the journey, only when we are unified and real. How can we expect the lost to get on board when we who claim to have "the faith" have not come to the unity of the faith? The unity of the Spirit in the bond of peace (love) demands our unity on the truth.

Paul exhorts us: *"Watch, stand fast in the faith, be brave, be strong."* (1 Corinthians 16:13) He reminds us again: *"Examine yourselves as to whether you are in the faith. Test yourselves."* (2 Corinthians 13:5) And finally, late in Paul's life, he shares his ministry testimony:

> I have fought the good fight, I have finished the race, I have kept the faith. Finally, there is laid up for me the crown of righteousness, which the Lord, the righteous Judge, will give to me on that Day, and not to me only but also to all who have loved His appearing. (2 Timothy 4:7, 8)

Despite his human frailties, and foibles, Paul fought the good fight, finished his race and kept the faith. His faith was centered in Jesus Christ, not in religious dogma, denominational decorum or any other man-made tradition that is not faithful to the truth of the Gospel. He battled with the legalism of Judaism, the superstition of

Greek mythology, demonism and just about every other "ism" and "wasm" (sic) that existed in his day.

I don't know about you, but, despite my human frailties and foibles, I want to have the same testimony when my journey transitions to the hereafter. Paul's "good fight" was his struggle for the integrity of the truth contained in "the faith." I want to be established in the faith, and I want the body of Christ to be unified in the faith. Like my honorable predecessor, Paul, I intend to contend for the integrity of the faith. For those of us who are true believers, we cannot afford to lock-step with those who simply parrot what they have been taught without the ability to "rightly divide" the word of truth. (2 Timothy 2:15)

Paul says that we are to be established in the faith, as we were taught. This is where the problem lies. As I stated earlier, when I gave my heart and soul to Jesus, I didn't know what truth was. I had never been taught the Bible. I had never been dyed in the wool by denominational doctrine or tradition. I was not in lock-step with any group of Bible teachers or preachers. When I came to Jesus, I was raw clay in the potter's hands, a diamond in the rough. Spiritually, I was at square one. My mind was a blank slate upon which God could write His timeless truths, and I was eager to learn.

I had no religious or denominational presuppositions or doctrinal biases regarding biblical interpretation. I was forced to ask God to guide me into the truth because I did not know what truth was. It has been, and continues to be, a perilous journey to the truth. The return of Jesus is drawing near. Satan knows his time is short and he is increasing his efforts to spawn error through false teachers. Jesus warned against false teachers. (Matthew 7:15, 16) Likewise, the apostles, Peter and Paul, warned against false teachers. (2 Peter 2:1-3; 2 Timothy 4:3, 4)

When God's Holy Spirit indwells us, He gives us spiritual discernment. If our pure desire is simply to know the truth, He will give us an uneasy or unsure feeling in our heart when we are exposed to errant teaching. Instead of swallowing it whole, He will urge us to chew first, and then to spit out what doesn't fit correctly with the other truths we have learned from the Bible. If the pieces don't fit, we don't force them.

Let me share another illustration that will help us to see this clearer. When we are going to put a Jigsaw Puzzle together, what is the first thing we do? We pour the puzzle pieces out on a table and set the box lid close by where we can see the "big picture" on the front of the lid. As we assemble the pieces of the puzzle, we keep referring to the big picture to assure that we are putting the pieces where they belong. First, we begin by searching for the frame/border pieces. These are the pieces that have a flat edge on them. They are the foundational pieces of the puzzle.

After connecting the border pieces, we have the frame of our picture assembled. Then, we begin to separate the remaining pieces according to color by observing how the colors correlate within the big picture. Piece by piece, we begin to put the puzzle together in sections, while constantly referring to the picture. Sometimes a piece may appear to belong in a certain position, but it just doesn't quite fit correctly. As first glance, it appears to be shaped like the void we are trying to place it in, but it just doesn't fit. Thus, we quit trying to force it and search for a similar piece that fits correctly. This process is repeated until the picture matches the big picture on the box lid.

This is how we rightly divide the truth of scripture. First, there are fundamental foundational truths that are centered in Jesus Christ. All of biblical truth belongs in and are centered in Him. The foundational pieces include His deity and His saving work on the cross. Then, we begin to assemble the truths that are colored similarly; His resurrection pieces; His Spirit of life in us pieces; our reconciliation to God through Him pieces; our adoption and new birth in Him pieces; our family relationship that makes us heirs with Him pieces. When a doctrinal piece just doesn't fit where we are trying to force it, we reconsider where it actually belongs according to the big picture. The key to getting the truth puzzle assembled correctly is our understanding of what the big picture is supposed to look like. I have been sharing God's big picture in the pages of this book. Any doctrine that does not fit the fact that God saves us for a personal, intimate, eternal family relationship with Himself is painting the wrong picture.

Here are some things to ask yourself when you encounter various teaching, preaching and religious practices that claim to be from God:

1. Does what is being taught truly edify (build us up and strengthen us in Christ)? Does it make a Christ-like difference in the way we live life. In order to make a difference in our life, we must be able to understand what they are saying and how to apply it in a practical way to our life.

2. Does what is being taught or demonstrated glorify Jesus? Is it consistent with what Jesus would say and do? We can observe how Jesus conducted Himself with others in the four Gospels. Even if what He was attempting to convey to others was hard to comprehend, He would use parables (down to earth illustrations) to make it clearly understood.

3. Do the teachings and actions of those who are sharing contradict other clear biblical truths? Do their teachings or actions have clear scriptural support? Does their doctrine exclude, or add to, clear biblical teaching? A clear sign of error is when a certain group or denomination claims that they, exclusively, are the "true church."

Many times error occurs when scripture passages are taken out of their natural context. In Paul's day, there were no denominations as we know them today. Denominations were developed within the church over time. However, believers were already beginning to segregate themselves.

In 1 Corinthians chapter 3, Paul called those who follow men, rather than Christ "carnal," (natural, fleshly) and accused them of behaving like mere men, rather than spiritual new creations in Christ. Some followed Paul, while others followed Apollos, and no doubt, many other individual teachers and preachers, unmentioned.

Today we have Lutherans who follow Luther; Methodists who follow Wesley; Calvinists who follow Calvin. Some have the "Full Gospel" while others are assumed to be Gospel deficient. On and on it goes, but Paul would tell each of us that none of these men are anything; we should follow Christ alone. Paul stated that it is not important who gives us the truth but that we get the truth in a way that God can use to bring a genuine, Godly, spiritual increase to our life—individually and collectively. In other words, teaching in a manner that makes us more like Jesus in our character.

Christlikeness is always the measure of accurate, effective teaching. Likewise, Christian maturity is always measured by how much we resemble Jesus in the way we live and relate to others, not how much scripture we know or can teach, not how eloquently we speak, or what Spiritual gifts we have and practice.

Though it is vitally important what sort of seed is planted, it is not important who plants and who waters it. However, we must understand that it is God, alone, who gives the spiritual increase. A farmer can plant and irrigate, but farmers do not grow crops, God does. Preachers and teachers can plant the seeds of truth, but they cannot grow or change anyone, only God does. God, alone, is the life-giver and life-changer! God, alone, is the absolute source of truth. Ultimately, only He gets the credit for it. Someday, He will reveal who was faithful to the truth and reward them accordingly.

In my ministry travels, I have met and made close friends with many believers who disagree with, at least some points, of my theology. Many of them assume that my scriptural views were derived from denominational teachers. This is not the case. As I have stated, I have no Seminary or Bible College training. (This fact, alone, will discredit me in the minds of some Bible Scholars.) Instead, I have read and listened to Bible teachers from every persuasion in my quest for the truth. I must say, I have had to weed through a lot of conflicting theological opinions on my journey to the truth, and God has been faithful to me.

I have had to ask Him to show me what truth is. I see what is theologically popular in some circles and wonder if their teaching and practices have not merely become their particular religious tradition. Whether it is reserved, conservative, religious liturgy or anything-goes, charismatic, Pentecostalism, religious tradition can be something that is taught and practiced as reality whether it is or is not genuine. In both camps, believers can go through the motions and do what they are expected to do in a church service whether it is or is not genuinely from God. Regardless, whether it is dead liturgical religiosity or spiritual sensationalism, Paul warns us not to fall into these errors lest we be cheated of the real thing—Christ's life and ministry manifested in us.

Personally, I can think of very few professing believers that I have become friends with that I do not love and appreciate, even though we may not agree on every point of doctrine. Many of them are fellow ministers of the Gospel. We may be able to experience God's Spirit in any denominational worship setting, but the indispensable element in our ability to walk tall in Christ is the accurate teaching and understanding of the truth of the scriptures.

I have heard many say, "We can agree to disagree on the "minor" points of doctrine, as long as we agree on the "major" points. Although I agree that it is important for believers to "coexist," I cannot imagine Jesus or Paul ever agreeing with this sentiment.

In the past, this oath was used to "swear in" witnesses before they were to give their testimony in court: "Do you swear to tell the truth, the whole truth, and nothing but the truth, so help you, God?" The acceptance and credibility of their testimony depended upon their willingness to tell the truth accurately. Likewise, I believe that it is imperative that Christians agree on the truth, the whole truth, and nothing but the truth, contained in scripture, so help us, God.

The problem is, and has always been, that we all believe we have the correct interpretation on the minor and major points of doctrine. My question is this; if the correct interpretation of the minor points of doctrine is not that important, then why are they taught in the Bible? And besides, just who determines what should be considered important truth, as opposed to what is less important truth?

I believe every piece in the doctrinal puzzle is extremely important. Otherwise, God would not have included them in the scriptural Jigsaw Puzzle. Unfortunately, because of our differing doctrinal positions, many of us have become biased and even paranoid about coming together to reason over the Word of God.

I have had pastors refuse to allow my ministry into their churches because I share my ministry in churches outside of their particular denomination. Recently, a pastor told my wife that when he saw that I was willing to take my ministry into all denominations, he knew that my ministry was not right for his people.

I wonder...would he say the same thing to Jesus or Paul? No doubt, they were willing to go to whosoever was willing to listen to the Gospel, and even to those who were not. I have no doubt that they would do the same today! Surely, their willingness to do so would cause these pastors to refuse their ministry in their churches. Surely, Jesus could not pastor in these churches, based on this reasoning. Neither Jesus, nor Paul, was Baptist, Methodist, Lutheran or members of any other modern denomination that we might be affiliated with today. Surely, if they were alive today, this would prevent them from being baptized into or taking part in the closed communion of some these modern religious groups. Since Jesus was not affiliated with any of our modern denominations, He would, no doubt, be rejected as a candidate to pastor in any of our churches in America today.

Please, do not misunderstand me; I do not compromise the truth. I preach the same Gospel message everywhere I go. I do not change my doctrine for whatever denominational group I may be ministering to. Jesus wouldn't, and neither do I. How could I? It isn't my message; it is God's message. They can take it or leave it. It isn't up to me.

I can see it in my mind…the Church phone rings: "Hello, Pastor. My name is Paul…you know…the guy who wrote most of the New Testament. I am booking dates for Jesus to share His ministry with churches across the country. He shares His teaching in churches of all denominations and I would like to know if you would like for Him to come share with your people?" The pastor answers, "Paul, I appreciate your request, but I'm afraid that, since Jesus goes into denominations other than ours and He is not an Independent, Fundamental, Regular, Freewill, General, King James-Only Baptist, His ministry would not be right for our people. Thanks for calling, though. I'll be praying for you." Click! Bless His heart!

No doubt, Jesus was questioned by His Jewish disciples numerous times for being in places that were forbidden by their Jewish traditions. Quite frequently, He committed "un-Jewish-like" acts, like touching unclean people (lepers, sinners and dead people) and associating with folks such as Samaritans and Tax Collectors. The truth of "the Faith" is the main issue, regardless of our man-made traditions or denominations. If your denomination adheres to and practices traditions that do not make a tangible Christ-like difference in your life or worship experience, those traditions and practices should be reconsidered.

In order to walk tall on this life journey, we must know what the truth is (our foundation), who our true life source is (Jesus, our spiritual food), and how to rightly divide the truth (correctly put the pieces of truth where they fit). 2 Timothy 2:15 reminds us:

> Be diligent to present yourself approved to God, a worker who does not need to be ashamed, rightly dividing the word of truth.

Our commission is not just to win souls to Jesus, but to disciple them in the comprehensive truth of the Gospel. James offers a stern warning to those who desire to be teachers of the Word of God:

> NOT MANY [of you] should become teachers (self-constituted censors and reprovers of others), my brethren, for you know that we [teachers] will be judged by a higher standard and with greater severity [than other people; thus we assume the greater accountability and the more condemnation].
> (James 3:1) (Amplified Bible)

The bottom line is this…we live for Jesus the same way we receive Him, by faith. We uproot ourselves from anything that is not centered in the truth and re-root our lives in Him. His truth, exclusively, is our foundation and source of life. We allow His truth to build us up and mature us. We adhere to, and contend for, the faith and discard dead or errant religious ritual and/or denominational doctrine that is not clearly validated by the scriptures. We follow Christ and abound in Him with thanksgiving!

Whether you are a new, or maybe a not-so-new believer, just remember this: Jesus is the way, the truth, and the life. We who truly follow Him and teach the scriptures may be sincere, but we may also be sincerely wrong in our interpretation of biblical truths. Unfortunately, some are intentionally wrong.

To be honest, none of us who handle the Word of God are always 100 percent accurate in our opinions or our presentation of scriptural truth. Nevertheless, I believe that it is the goal of every Bible teacher who loves and truly follows Jesus to get it right, even if the absolute truth forces us to part with the doctrinal status quo of our denomination.

Just keep Jesus as the ultimate founder and sustainer of your faith. Trust Him as your ultimate guide and teacher. He is big enough, and faithful enough, to make sure that you get it right if your pure desire is to know the absolute truth. In fact, as you rest in, and rely upon Him, He will empower you with His discernment, guide you, and give you the ability to Walk Tall on the journey to the center of His life.

Let me close with the lyrics to a song that the Lord gave me about arriving at our final destination, Home.

"Finally Home"

I awoke today and my eyes beheld a place where I've never been,
Yet, it seems as though I already know this light I'm standing in;
And, I feel young again, as I see old friends
And I know I'm not alone;
I can't believe my eyes as I realize, I'm home.

I'm finally home, finally face to face;
I've fought fight, I've run the race.
I'm finally home, finally know as I'm known,
With my sweet Jesus, I'm finally home.

Then with trembling lips, through tears of joy,
I begin to praise His name;
With what looks like millions robed in white,
Singing, "Worthy is the Lamb."

> And it's more beautiful than I ever dreamed,
> As His brightness fills this place;
> And I finally understand His amazing grace.
> I'm finally home, finally face to face;
> I've fought fight, I've run the race.
> I'm finally home, finally know as I'm known,
> With my sweet Jesus, I'm finally home.

Walk tall, my friend, in the confidence of who God says that you are! His is the only opinion about you that truly matters. Home is closer than you think; life is closer than you think, and heaven is closer than you think. The Jesus who is in you has promised to see you through to the end of your journey…Him!

CONCLUSION

Vaya Con Dios *(Go with God.)*

Thanks for tagging along with me for a few miles on the journey. The basic truths I have shared in this book are what have made, and continue to make, the difference in my life. No telling where my self-designed path would have taken me if God had not intervened in my life.

Our journey is our individual quest for the true source of life. Of course, that life is in one person, Jesus Christ. True life cannot be found in anyone else...not even in our beloved family members. Once we have Him, we have what we have been searching for.

> "And this is the record, that God hath given to us eternal life, and this life is in his Son. He that hath the Son hath life; and he that hath not the Son of God hath not life" (I John 5:11, 12)

Our new birth in Jesus is, indeed, the Spirit of Jesus, Himself, taking up residence in our spirit, imparting His eternal life to us as our salvation and hope for eternity. Once He becomes a reality in us, we simply rest in our new life. His life is true Christianity. True Christianity is not determined by a list of law-oriented rules, regulations or rituals that we must live by in order to remain acceptable to God. Rather, it is the outworking of His life in us, the power of true Godliness. In reality, the journey to the center of life is not a long sojourn to a distant place, but simply one step in our heart to a person—Jesus. Have you taken that step? If you have not, you can take that step right now. All you have to do is ask Him to step into your heart and life. It doesn't have to be in these exact words...in fact, it is better if you use your own words from your own heart. The prayer itself is not what saves you; it is your faith in Jesus that saves you.

> *God,*
> *I confess to you that I am guilty of sin, against you, myself and others. Regardless of what others have done to me, or how they may have failed me, I blame no one but myself, and I take full responsibility for my sins in word and deed. I ask you to forgive my sins through the sacrifice of your Son, Jesus. I receive Him now as my Lord and Savior. I invite you to send the Spirit of Jesus into my heart. Give me a new heart and a new life. Change my desires and help me to live for you.*
> *In Jesus' name I pray, Amen.*

Congratulations on taking the first step into your new eternal, abundant life. You will never walk alone again.

> These things I have written to you who believe in the name of the Son of God, that you may know that you have eternal life, and that you may *continue to* believe in the name of the Son of God. (1 John 5:13)

He will never leave you or forsake you, and nothing can ever separate you from His love.

> Let your character or moral disposition be free from love of money [*including greed, avarice, lust, and craving for earthly possessions*] and be satisfied with your present [*circumstances and with what you have*]; for He [*God*] Himself has said, I will not in any way

fail you nor give you up nor leave you without support. [*I will*] not, [*I will*] not, [*I will*] not in any degree leave you helpless nor forsake nor let [*you*] down (relax My hold on you)! [*Assuredly not!*] [*Josh. 1:5.*] So we take comfort and are encouraged and confidently and boldly say, The Lord is my Helper; I will not be seized with alarm [*I will not fear or dread or be terrified*]. What can man do to me? [*Ps. 27:1;118:6.*] (Hebrews 13:5, 6) (Amplified Bible)

...we are more than conquerors through Him who loved us. For I am persuaded that neither death nor life, nor angels nor principalities nor powers, nor things present nor things to come, nor height nor depth, nor any other created thing, shall be able to separate us from the love of God which is in Christ Jesus our Lord. (Romans 8:37-39)

I pray that, from this point on, this book will serve as your constant road companion as you journey with your new eternal life and friend, Jesus. If the trials of life cause you to forget just how wonderful He is, and who you are in Him, just consult your operator's manual, The Bible, and revisit the "Rest Areas" you have visited in this book. Better yet, as you become more confident in these truths, perhaps you can share them with someone else who needs directions on their journey.

Finally, I would like to encourage both, my Arkansas and Wisconsin family members to search your hearts. Make sure that you have genuinely accepted Jesus as your Lord and Savior. (I am not talking about religion or merely going to church.) Not merely so you can go to heaven when you die, but, so you can be abundantly blessed now. I cannot imagine standing before Jesus someday and hearing Him tell any of my loved ones the worst seven words any of us could ever hear Jesus tell us, "I never knew you. Depart from me..." (Matthew 7:22, 23)

Genuine life in Christ is the most valuable possession that a person could ever possess or leave to the ones they love. This book is my attempt to leave a legacy for Christ to the ones I so dearly love. If anyone else is blessed by it, Praise God! Farewell pilgrim! Go with God and be abundantly blessed on your journey to the center of His amazing life!

Bibliography

1. (CBS) June 2005, from the transcript of the *60 Minutes* interview with correspondent Steve Kroft: Gillette Stadium in Foxboro, Massachusetts.

2. *GQ* (*Gentlemen's Quarterly*) a monthly men's magazine focusing on fashion, style and culture for men. Conde Nast Publications

3. John Davidson Rockefeller: (1839–1937) Chairman of Standard Oil Company, investor, and philanthropist.

4. Watchman Nee, "The Normal Christian Life."
Tyndale House Publishers, Inc.

5. Major, Ian Thomas, "The Saving Life of Christ"
Copyright © 1961 by Zondervan

6. Bob George, "Classic Christianity"
Copyright © 1989 by Harvest House Publishers

7. The Twilight Zone. Rod Serling's original series ran on CBS from 1959-1964. The series was revived on CBS from 1985-1989.

8. Major, Ian Thomas, "The Saving Life of Christ"
Copyright © 1961 by Zondervan

9. Major, Ian Thomas, "The Mystery of Godliness"
Copyright © 1964 by Zondervan

10. Dr. Martin Luther King Jr. "I have a Dream" speech, delivered 28 August 1963, at the Lincoln Memorial, Washington D.C.

11. Classic Country Music Hit written by Country Music Hall of Fame inductee (1996), Buck Owens. "Together Again" was released as a single on Capitol Records in 1964.

12. An American television sitcom starring Tim Allen that aired on ABC from September 17, 1991 to May 25, 1999.

13. Movie depicting the life of Sheriff Buford Pusser, a former professional wrestler-turned-lawman in McNairy County, Tennessee. Bing Crosby Productions. Released February 22, 1973 by Cinerama.

14. The popular, most commercially successful and critically acclaimed Rock and Roll Band in music history. The Beatles: John Lennon, Paul McCartney, George Harrison and Richard "Ringo Starr" Starkey, were a band from England that was given credit for initiating the "British invasion" of the American Rock and Pop Music Charts in the 1960s and '70s.

A PERSONAL NOTE

The goal of this book is to impact your life in a revolutionary way through the truth of the Bible. If you have been encouraged and your life has been changed, I would love to hear from you. I share these truths from coast to coast along with my music ministry. If you would like more information about Whitebird Ministries and how to book a concert, revival or conference based on these truths, please contact me.

Email: peterlewiswhitebird@gmail.com

Phone: 785-267-2573

Website: www.peterlewiswhitebird.com

We would love to share our music and teaching ministry with your church or other special group.

May God bless you on your journey. May you be blessed beyond what you ever dreamed was possible. With God, anything is possible. (Mark 9:23)

Made in the USA
Charleston, SC
17 June 2015